First World War
and Army of Occupation
War Diary
France, Belgium and Germany

48 DIVISION
Divisional Troops
241 South Midland Brigade Royal Field Artillery
1 March 1915 - 31 October 1917

WO95/2749/4

The Naval & Military Press Ltd
www.nmarchive.com
Published in association with The National Archives

Published by

The Naval & Military Press Ltd

Unit 10 Ridgewood Industrial Park,

Uckfield, East Sussex,

TN22 5QE England

Tel: +44 (0) 1825 749494

www.naval-military-press.com

www.nmarchive.com

This diary has been reprinted in facsimile from the original. Any imperfections are inevitably reproduced and the quality may fall short of modern type and cartographic standards.

© Crown Copyright
Images reproduced by permission of The National Archives, London, England, 2015.

Contents

Document type	Place/Title	Date From	Date To
Heading	WO95/249/4 48 Division 241 Sth Midland Bde Rfa April 1915-Oct 1917		
Heading	48th Division 2nd Sth Mid'd Bde R.F.A. Became:- 241st S.M. Bde Rfa Mar 1915-Oct 1917		
Heading	South Midland Sun 2nd S.M Bde R.F.A. Vol I 1-31.315		
Heading	War Diary Of 2nd South Midland Field Arty Bde From 1.3.15 To 31.3.15 Vol 8		
War Diary	Ingatestone	01/03/1915	30/03/1915
War Diary	Havre	31/03/1915	31/03/1915
Heading	South Midland Divn 2nd S.M. Bde R.F.A. Vol II 1-30.4.15		
Heading	War Diary Of 2nd South Midland Field Arty Brigade From 1.4.15 To 30.4.15 Vol IX		
War Diary	Hazebrouck	01/04/1915	01/04/1915
War Diary	Caestre	02/04/1915	04/04/1915
War Diary	Armentieres	04/04/1915	09/04/1915
War Diary	Noote Boom	10/04/1915	12/04/1915
War Diary	1/2 Mile S Of Oultersteen	13/04/1915	15/04/1915
War Diary	Tilleul De La Petite Munque	16/04/1915	30/04/1915
Heading	War Diary Of 2nd South Midland F.A Brigade 48th Division From 1.5.15 To 31.5.15 Vol III		
War Diary	Petit Point T.23b.3.6.5	01/05/1915	31/05/1915
Miscellaneous	Appendix I		
Heading	48th Division 2nd S.M. Bde R.F.A. Vol IV 1-30.6.15		
Heading	War Diary Of 2nd South Midland Field Artillery Brigade From 1.6.15 30.6.15 Vol XI		
War Diary	Petit Pont	01/06/1915	22/06/1915
War Diary	Lacreche	23/06/1915	24/06/1915
War Diary	Outtersteene Sheet 36a 1/40000	25/06/1915	25/06/1915
War Diary	Vieux Berquin	26/06/1915	28/06/1915
War Diary	Ecque	28/06/1915	29/06/1915
War Diary	Lemont Evenic	30/06/1915	30/06/1915
Heading	48th Division 2nd S.M. Bde R.F.A. Vol V 1-31-7-15		
Heading	War Diary of 2 S.M.F.A. Brigade 48th Division From 1.7.15 To 31.7.15 Vol XII		
War Diary	Le Mont	01/07/1915	01/07/1915
War Diary	Evenic	02/07/1915	02/07/1915
War Diary	D.19.b05.	03/07/1915	14/07/1915
War Diary	Au. Chel	15/07/1915	20/07/1915
War Diary	Thievres	21/07/1915	21/07/1915
War Diary	Authie	22/07/1915	31/07/1915
Heading	48th Division War Diary Of 2nd South Mid Field Arty Bde. From 1.8.15 To 31.8.15 Vol VI		
War Diary	Authie	01/08/1915	31/08/1915
Miscellaneous	Casualties For Month Of August 1915	30/07/1915	30/07/1915
Heading	War Diary Of 2nd S.M.F.A. Bde From 1-9-15 To 30-9-15 Volume VII		
War Diary	Authie	01/09/1915	04/09/1915
War Diary	Bayencourt	15/09/1915	30/09/1915

Miscellaneous	Unit 2nd S.M.D.A. Brigade Daily Orders Part II	00/09/1915	00/09/1915
Miscellaneous	Daily Orders Part II No. 2	00/09/1915	00/09/1915
Miscellaneous	Daily Orders Part II No. 3	00/09/1915	00/09/1915
Heading	War Diary Of 2nd S.M. Fd Arty Brigade From 1st Oct 1915 To 31st Oct 1915 Volume VIII		
War Diary	Bayencourt	01/10/1915	31/10/1915
Miscellaneous	Unit 2nd S.M.F.A. Brigade Daily Orders Part II. No. 1	00/10/1915	00/10/1915
Miscellaneous	Unit 2nd S.M.F.A. Brigade Daily Orders Part II. No. 2		
Miscellaneous	Daily Orders. Part II. No. 3		
Miscellaneous	Daily Orders Part II No.4		
Miscellaneous	Daily Orders Part II No.5	30/10/1915	30/10/1915
Miscellaneous	H.Q. 241 Bde R.F.A.	30/09/1916	30/09/1916
Miscellaneous	L.O.C. R.A. 48 (South Midland) Div	30/09/1916	30/09/1916
Heading	48th Division 1/2nd S.M. Bde R.F.A. Nov 1915 Vol IX		
Heading	War Diary Of 2nd S.M.F.A. Bde From 1.11.15 To 30.11.15 (Volume XVI)		
War Diary	Bayencourt	01/11/1915	30/11/1915
Miscellaneous	Daily Orders Part II No 1	00/11/1917	00/11/1917
Miscellaneous	Daily Orders Part II No 2	08/11/1915	08/11/1915
Miscellaneous	Daily Orders Part II No. 3	00/11/1915	00/11/1915
Miscellaneous	Daily Orders Part II No. 4	00/11/1915	00/11/1915
Miscellaneous	Daily Orders Part II No. 5	00/11/1915	00/11/1915
Miscellaneous	Daily Orders Part II No. 6	00/11/1915	00/11/1915
Miscellaneous	Daily Orders Part II No. 7		
Miscellaneous	Daily Orders Part II No. 8		
Miscellaneous	Daily Orders Part II No. 9		
Miscellaneous	Daily Orders Part II No 10	31/07/1916	31/07/1916
Miscellaneous	Daily Orders Part II No 11	24/11/1915	24/11/1915
Miscellaneous	Daily Orders Part II No 12	24/11/1915	24/11/1915
Miscellaneous	Daily Orders Part II No 13	27/11/1915	27/11/1915
Miscellaneous	Daily Orders Part II No 14	27/11/1915	27/11/1915
Heading	48th Div 1/2nd Sth. Mid. Bde R.F.A. Dec Vol X		
War Diary	Bayencourt	01/12/1915	31/12/1915
Miscellaneous	Daily Orders Part II	25/11/1915	25/11/1915
Miscellaneous	2nd S.M.F.A. Bde Daily Orders Part II	25/12/1915	25/12/1915
Miscellaneous	For Information Of The A.G.'s Office At The Base	11/12/1915	11/12/1915
Miscellaneous	Field Return		
Miscellaneous	For Information Of The A.G.'s Office At The Base	11/12/1915	11/12/1915
Miscellaneous	Field Return		
Miscellaneous	For Information Of The A.G.'s Office At The Base	04/12/1915	04/12/1915
Miscellaneous	Field Return		
Miscellaneous	For Information Of The A.G's Office At The Base	04/12/1915	04/12/1915
Heading	1/2nd S.M. Bde R.F.A. Jan Vol XI		
War Diary	Bayencourt	01/01/1916	31/01/1916
Miscellaneous	Daily Orders Part II	01/01/1916	01/01/1916
Heading	War Diary Of 2nd S.M.F.A. Bde From 1/2/16 To 29/2/16 (Volume XII)		
Heading	1/2 S.M. Bde R.F.A. Vol XIII		
War Diary	Bayencourt	01/02/1916	29/02/1916
War Diary	Sailly	01/03/1916	10/03/1916
War Diary	Bayencourt	11/03/1916	31/03/1916
Miscellaneous	Report Of Action Of 2nd S.H.F.A Bde And 1st Batt :3rd S.H.F.A. Bde In Support Of 143rd Inf		
Miscellaneous	For Information Of The A.G.'s Office At The Base	04/03/1916	04/03/1916
Miscellaneous	For Information Of The A.G.'s Office At The Base	11/03/1916	11/03/1916
Miscellaneous	For Information Of The A.G.'s Office At The Base	18/03/1916	18/03/1916

Miscellaneous	For Information Of The A.G.'s Office At The Base	25/03/1916	25/03/1916
Miscellaneous		31/03/1916	31/03/1916
Heading	War Diary Of 2nd S.M.F.A. Bde (Volume XIV) From 1.4.16 To 30.4.16		
War Diary	Bayencourt	01/04/1916	30/04/1916
Miscellaneous			
Heading	War Diary Of 241 (S.M) Bde. R.F.A. (Volume 15) From 1/5/16 To 31/5/16		
War Diary	Bayencourt	01/05/1916	11/05/1916
War Diary	Couin	12/05/1916	31/05/1916
Miscellaneous	May 6th/1916	06/05/1916	06/05/1916
Heading	War Diary Of 241st (S.M.) Bde. R.F.A. (Volume XX) From 1/6/16 To 30/6/16		
War Diary	Couin	01/06/1916	30/06/1916
Miscellaneous	16-6-1916	16/06/1916	16/06/1916
Heading	War Diary Headquarters 241st Brigade R.F.A. (48th Division) July 1916		
War Diary		01/07/1916	14/07/1916
War Diary	Courcelles	15/07/1916	31/07/1916
Miscellaneous	Appendices		
Miscellaneous	July 7th/1916	07/07/1916	07/07/1916
Heading	48th Divisional Artillery 241st (South Midland) Brigade Royal Field Artillery August 1916		
War Diary	In The Field	01/08/1916	31/08/1916
Heading	48th. Divisional Artillery 241st. Brigade R.F.A. September 1916		
War Diary	In The Field	01/09/1916	30/09/1916
Heading	War Diary Of 241st. (S.M.) Bde R.F.A. From 1-10-16 To 31-10-16 Volume 20		
War Diary	In The Field	01/10/1916	31/10/1916
Heading	War Diary Of 241st (S.M.) Bde. R.F.A. (Volume 21) From 1/11/16 To 30/11/16		
War Diary	In The Field	01/11/1916	30/11/1916
Heading	War Diary Of 241st (S.M.) Bde R.F.A. From 1/12/16 To 31/12/16 Vol 22		
War Diary	In The Field	01/12/1916	28/02/1917
Heading	War Diary Of 241st (S.M.) Bde RFA From 1/1/17 To 31/1/17 Vol 23		
War Diary		05/02/1917	17/02/1917
War Diary	In The Field	18/02/1917	26/02/1917
Heading	War Diary Of 241st (S.M.) Bde R.F.A. (Volume XXVIII) 1-2-17 28-2-17		
War Diary		14/01/1917	31/01/1917
War Diary	In The Field	09/03/1917	15/03/1917
Heading	War Diary Of 241st (S.M.) Bde R.F.A. Volume XXIX From 1/3/17 To 31/3/17		
War Diary	In The Field	01/03/1917	31/03/1917
Heading	War Diary Of 241st (S.M.) Bde R.F.A. 1-4-17 30-4-17 Volume XXX		
War Diary		01/04/1917	30/04/1917
Heading	War Diary Of 241st. (S.M.) Bde. R.F.A. (Volume XXXI) From 1/5/17 To 31/5/17		
War Diary		01/05/1917	31/05/1917
Heading	War Diary Of 241st (S.M) Bde. R.F.A. (Volume XXXII) From 1/6/17 To 30/6/17		
War Diary	In The Field	01/06/1917	30/06/1917

Heading	War Diary Of 241st (S.M.) Bde. R.F.A. Volume XXXIX From 1/10/17 To 31/10/17		
War Diary	In The Field	01/10/1917	31/10/1917

WO95/2694/4

48 DIVISION

241 STH MIDLAND BDE RFA

APRIL 1915 - OCT 1917

48TH DIVISION

BEF

2ND STH MID'D BDE RFA
BECAME:-
241ST S.M. BDE RFA.
MAR 1915 - ~~MAR 1919~~ OCT 1917

To ITALY

48TH DIVISION

121/5256

Saul Mattausltein

2nd C.M. Bde R.F.A.

Vol I – 31.3.15

2nd C.m Bde R.F.A. Mar 14

CONFIDENTIAL.

WAR DIARY
of
2nd South Midland Field Arty. Bde.

from 1.3.15   To   31.3.15

Vol 8

Army Form C. 2118.

Vol 9.

WAR DIARY
or
INTELLIGENCE SUMMARY.
(Erase heading not required.)

Instructions regarding War Diaries and Intelligence Summaries are contained in F. S. Regs., Part II. and the Staff Manual respectively. Title pages will be prepared in manuscript.

Hour, Date, Place	Summary of Events and Information	Remarks and references to Appendices
INGATESTONE		
1.3.15.	Training. Phg	
2.3.15.	Training. Phg	
3.3.15.	Training.	
	2/Lt F. HADSHEAD joined on 1st Appointment. Phg.	
4.3.15	Training. Phg	
5.3.15	Training.	
	1st & 2nd Battalion conferred with Infantry Musson Phg	
6.3.15	Training. Phg	

Army Form C. 2118.

WAR DIARY
or
INTELLIGENCE SUMMARY.
(Erase heading not required.)

Hour, Date, Place	Summary of Events and Information	Remarks and references to Appendices
INGATESTONE.		
7.3.15 10AM	Church Parade. Rhq.	
	Capt. A.F PENNY left for SALISBURY for Course in "Cooperation of Artillery with Aeroplanes". Rhq	
8.3.15	Training.	
	20 men joined from 2/2 SMFA Register Rhq	
	Musketry Course Commenced. 120 men Completed Course Rhq.	
9.3.15	Musketry 197 men Completed Course. Rhq.	
	Lieuts. DIXEY & WOODS Returned from France Rhq.	
10.3.15	Musketry 200 men Completed Course	
	517 men Total Who Completed Course	
	2/Lt N.J.A FOSTER. Granted 6 days Sick leave Rhq.	
11.3.15	Training. Rhq.	

Army Form C. 2118.

WAR DIARY
or
INTELLIGENCE SUMMARY.
(Erase heading not required.)

Instructions regarding War Diaries and Intelligence Summaries are contained in F.S. Regs., Part II. and the Staff Manual respectively. Title pages will be prepared in manuscript.

Hour, Date, Place		Summary of Events and Information	Remarks and references to Appendices
INGATESTONE			
12.3.15		Training. Officers Charger received & posted to 1st Wore Battery. Mkg	
13.3.15		Training. Capt. A F PENNY returned on Completion of Course at SALISBURY. Mkg	
14.3.15	10 PM	Church Parade. Mkg	
15.3.15		Training. 2/Lt B.T. ADSHEAD returned on Completion of Course at WOOLWICH. 2/Lt P.M.D WYNTER transferred to 2/2 SM FA Brigade. Mkg.	
16.3.15		Training. 2/Lt HUGHES arrived on Transfer from 2/2 SM FA Brigade. Mkg	
17.3.15		Training. Inspection of Horses by I/O Remounts. 36 horses the transferred to 2/2 SM FA Mpfst. 30 " " " " Cont. 5 Veterinary hospital Leamington. 16 " " Dpo & 1 Feeding. Eng	

Forms/C. 2118/10

Army Form C. 2118.

WAR DIARY
or
INTELLIGENCE SUMMARY.
(Erase heading not required.)

Instructions regarding War Diaries and Intelligence Summaries are contained in F.S. Regs., Part II. and the Staff Manual respectively. Title pages will be prepared in manuscript.

Hour, Date, Place	Summary of Events and Information	Remarks and references to Appendices
INGATESTONE.		
18.3.15	Training. Nly.	
19.3.15	Training. Nly.	
20.3.15	Training. Nly.	
21.3.15 10 AM	Church parade. 12 Ptoons & 53 HD horses received from CHELMSFORD. Nly. 2 horses destroyed. Nly.	
22.3.15	Training. 1 horse died. 26 to Sent to VET. HOSP. LEAMINGTON. 10 " to CHELMSFORD 7th S.R. 1 " received from CHELMSFORD Rhq.	
23.3.15	Training. 21 horses received from CHELMSFORD Nly.	

Army Form C. 2118.

WAR DIARY
or
INTELLIGENCE SUMMARY.
(Erase heading not required.)

Instructions regarding War Diaries and Intelligence Summaries are contained in F.S. Regs., Part II. and the Staff Manual respectively. Title pages will be prepared in manuscript.

Hour, Date, Place	Summary of Events and Information	Remarks and references to Appendices
INGATESTONE		
24.3.15	Training. Draft of 36 men arrived from 2/2 S.M. F.A. Dragust Rhq	
25.3.15	Training. Rhq.	
26.3.15	Training. Rhq.	
27.3.15	Training. Rhq.	
5 pm	Orders received & entrain to proceed Newcas on 29.- 30th Rhq	
28.3.15 10 AM	Church Parade. Rhq	
	Lt. SPEAR arrived to take over Surplus Stores etc.	
29.3.15 9 pm	Preparing for departure.	
11 pm	½ A.M. Col. entrained & left. Second ½ A.M. Col. entrained & left Rhq.	

Army Form C. 2118.

WAR DIARY
or
INTELLIGENCE SUMMARY.
(Erase heading not required.)

Instructions regarding War Diaries and Intelligence Summaries are contained in F.S. Regs., Part II. and the Staff Manual respectively. Title pages will be prepared in manuscript.

Hour, Date, Place	Summary of Events and Information	Remarks and references to Appendices
INGATESTONE.		
30.3.15. 1 AM	No 3 Train with ½ 1st Battery left BRENTWOOD.	
3 AM	No 4 Train with second half of 1st Battery left BRENTWOOD.	
5 AM	No 5 Train with ½ 2nd Battery left BRENTWOOD.	
7 AM	No 6 Train " Second half of 2nd Battery left BRENTWOOD.	
9 AM	No 7 Train " ½ 3rd Battery left BRENTWOOD.	
11 AM.	No 8 Train - Second half 3rd Battery & H.Q left Brentwood.	
	The Train arrived SOUTHAMPTON & the Brigade was embarked on the following Ships. CITY of DUNKIRK. "Munich". "Archimedes".	

Army Form C. 2118.

WAR DIARY
or
INTELLIGENCE SUMMARY.
(Erase heading not required.)

Instructions regarding War Diaries and Intelligence Summaries are contained in F.S. Regs., Part II. and the Staff Manual respectively. Title pages will be prepared in manuscript.

Hour, Date, Place	Summary of Events and Information	Remarks and references to Appendices
HAVRE 31.3.15.	The vessels arrived in the morning & the Brigade disembarked 9 were entrained in four trains which left that evening. from pl. 3 & 6 NG The Interpreter (WM WATERS) Joined the Headquarters	J.E. Bickford Lt/Col Cdg 2. S.M. FA Brigade

121/5256.

South Midlaud Divn

2nd S.M. Bde. R.F.A.

Vol II. 1 — 30.4.15

CONFIDENTIAL.

WAR DIARY
of
2nd South Midland Field Arty. Brigade.

from 1.4.15.   to   30.4.15.

VOL. IX ?

Vol II

Army Form C. 2118.

Vol 9

WAR DIARY
or
INTELLIGENCE SUMMARY.
(Erase heading not required.)

Instructions regarding War Diaries and Intelligence Summaries are contained in F. S. Regs., Part II. and the Staff Manual respectively. Title pages will be prepared in manuscript.

Hour, Date, Place	Summary of Events and Information	Remarks and references to Appendices
HAZEBROUCK 1.4.15	The train arrived 4.20 pm, 5.15 pm, 10 pm & [illegible]. Reached Billeting & proceeded to march to CAESTRE & went into billets. Mg.	
CAESTRE 2.4.15	A.M. Col. arrived HAZEBROUCK at 3AM & marched to CAESTRE arriving about 7.30AM. Mg.	
3.4.15	Units collected stores etc & in billets. Mg.	
4.4.15 7.45pm	The Brigade marched to L'EPINETTE when they were attached to regular Brigades as follows:—	
	H.Q. to 38th Bde in ARMENTIERES	
	1st Bty " 2 " at L'ARMÉE HOUPLINES	
	2 " " 12 " " L'ARMÉE	
	3 " " 24 " " ASYLUM. ARMENTIÈRES	

WAR DIARY
or
INTELLIGENCE SUMMARY.
(Erase heading not required.)

Army Form C. 2118.

Instructions regarding War Diaries and Intelligence Summaries are contained in F.S. Regs., Part II. and the Staff Manual respectively. Title pages will be prepared in manuscript.

Hour, Date, Place	Summary of Events and Information	Remarks and references to Appendices
ARMENTIÈRES		
4.4.15.	The batteries came into action in the evening at the above mentioned places.	May
5.4.15.	The Am. Col. protures on RUE DE LYS 1 Mile S.W. of ERQUINGHEM.	May
	The batteries were allowed 3 rds. per gun per diem to be fired. The batteries spent the day improving their gun pits & pulling up cover. 1st & 3rd Batteries registering.	May
6.4.15.	B/From Thorn recceived instruction on various points. 1st & 3rd Batteries registering.	May
7.4.15.	Instruction. All batteries registering.	May
8.4.15.	Instruction. All batteries registered.	May

Army Form C. 2118.

WAR DIARY
or
INTELLIGENCE SUMMARY.
(Erase heading not required.)

Instructions regarding War Diaries and Intelligence
Summaries are contained in F.S. Regs., Part II.
and the Staff Manual respectively. Title pages
will be prepared in manuscript.

Hour, Date, Place	Summary of Events and Information	Remarks and references to Appendices
ARMENTIERES 9.4.15	The battalion were both drawn at Ruth. 9 Reinforcements with him 69 1¾ miles S.W. of ERQUINGHEM. The whole Brigade marches to NOOTE BOOM billet 10 miles 4 hour not killed.	neg.
NOOTE BOOM 10.4.15	Instruction. 1st Battery moved to another billet ½ mile away	neg.
11.4.15	The remainder of the Brigade moved to billets in another area to South of OULTERSTEEN	neg.
12.4.15	Instruction.	"neg."

Army Form C. 2118.

WAR DIARY
or
INTELLIGENCE SUMMARY.
(Erase heading not required.)

Hour, Date, Place	Summary of Events and Information	Remarks and references to Appendices
13nd S.H OULTERSTEEN		
13.4.15	Training	
14.4.15	Training	Reference Map. BELGIUM & FRANCE Sheet 28 SW B Severn 1/20000
15.4.15	OC Brigade & OC's batteries inspected battery positions FRANCE. N.E. of PETIT POINT (B Seven Sheet 28 SW. BELGIUM & FRANCE. previous to taking over from 32nd Brigade R.F.A.)	
TILLEUL de la Petite Munque		
16.4.15 9.p.m.	The 1st & 3rd Batteries took up their positions 1st Battery relieving 134th Battery in T.17 d 4.3. 3rd Battery relieving Left Section 135th Battery & making 2 new emplacements in T.17 b. 6.3	
17.4.15 4 A.M.	The 2nd Battery relieves the 27th Battery in T.17 b. 4.6. PTO	

Army Form C. 2118.

WAR DIARY
or
INTELLIGENCE SUMMARY.
(Erase heading not required.)

Instructions regarding War Diaries and Intelligence Summaries are contained in F.S. Regs., Part II. and the Staff Manual respectively. Title pages will be prepared in manuscript.

Hour, Date, Place	Summary of Events and Information	Remarks and references to Appendices
TILLEUL de la petite MUNQUE. 17.4.15.	The following 3 men were allotted to the Brigade. from LA PETITE DOUVE fm to junction of Roads in U.15.B.2.8. The day was spent in adapting existing cover & making gun pit emplacements. 1st Battery started registering at 1.45 pm. 2nd Battery fired on LA PETITE DOUVE FARM in Washington at 5.30 pm. 3 Rounds per gun per diem in Am Allowance.	Ref map. BELGIUM & FRANCE Sheet 28 sw 1/20000 NG
18.4.15. 4 to 5.30pm	The Battery registered their various 3 men. The German shelled ruined Chateau in U.14.C.1.15 with shrapnel (just in front of 1st Battery O.S.).	NG
19.4.15.	Registering carried out by batteries.	NG
20.4.15.	Registration of 3 men carried out by batteries.	NG

Army Form C. 2118.

WAR DIARY
or
INTELLIGENCE SUMMARY.
(Erase heading not required.)

Instructions regarding War Diaries and Intelligence Summaries are contained in F.S. Regs., Part II. and the Staff Manual respectively. Title pages will be prepared in manuscript.

Hour, Date, Place	Summary of Events and Information	Remarks and references to Appendices
TILLEUL de la PETITE MUNQUE.		
21.4.15	Registration of Guns carried out by batteries	Nhg
22.4.15	do do do	Nhg
23.4.15	" " "	Nhg
24.4.15	" " "	Nhg
25.4.15	" " "	Nhg
26.4.15	" " "	Nhg
27.4.15	" " "	Nhg
28.4.15	" " "	Nhg
29.4.15	" " "	Nhg
30.4.15	Registration Completed.	Nhg

CONFIDENTIAL.

WAR DIARY

of

2nd SOUTH MIDLAND F.A BRIGADE

48th Division

from 1.5.15   To. 31.5.15

VOL III

Army Form C. 2118.

WAR DIARY
or
INTELLIGENCE SUMMARY.
(Erase heading not required.)

Instructions regarding War Diaries and Intelligence Summaries are contained in F. S. Regs., Part II. and the Staff Manual respectively. Title pages will be prepared in manuscript.

Place	Date	Hour	Summary of Events and Information	Remarks and references to Appendices
PETIT POINT T.25.6.5.	1/5/15	3 pm	The batteries fired a few rounds to verify the correctr. Weather fine.	Reg Reference Map BELGIUM and FRANCE Sheet 28 S.W. 1/20000
	2/5/15		Nothing to report. Weather fine.	Reg.
	3/5/15		do do do Weather fine.	Reg.
	4/5/15		Ranges slightly during the evening.	
	5/5/15		Too much all day for observation. Too musty after 10.30 am for observation. Weather fine. Batteries fired 12 rds from 1st Worc Battery in conjunction with 5th Warwick How Battery at farm U.9.C.3.9. in Retaliation. Enemy leaving shells on Trenches & working parties at U.13.C. N.E.	Reg.
		2.35 pm		
		5 pm	Same How. battery fired on La PETITE DOUVE Farm U.8.a.9.6. Same time 8 rds from each 2nd & 3rd Worc Battery was fired at the farm in Retaliation for Sniping from there.	Reg.
	6.5.15		Nothing to report. Weather fine.	Reg.
	7.5.15		Nothing to report do do	Reg.
	8.5.15		Nothing to report do do	Reg.

Army Form C. 2118.

WAR DIARY
or
INTELLIGENCE SUMMARY.
(Erase heading not required.)

Instructions regarding War Diaries and Intelligence Summaries are contained in F. S. Regs., Part II. and the Staff Manual respectively. Title pages will be prepared in manuscript.

Place	Date	Hour	Summary of Events and Information	Remarks and references to Appendices
			Reference map BELGIUM and FRANCE Sheet 28 SW 1/20,000	
PETIT	9.5.15	4.30 AM	A demonstration was made against two areas. Area A. U.28.a.3.9. to U.28.a.7.2.	App. I
PONT			- Area B. U.15.a.6.8. to U.6.d.7.7.	
		7 pm	700 fus rounds rifle allotted to this brigade.	R&q.
T28634	10.5.15		Nothing to report -	R&q.
	11.5.15		Nothing to report -	R&q.
	12.5.15		Nothing to report -	R&q.
	13.5.15		Nothing to report. Weather. Rained all day.	R&q.
	14.5.15	6 AM	Retaliation on the PETITE DOUVE trenches. U.2.a & b. N. 3rd Batn. fired 122 rds. in conjunction with 5th War. Hrs. Battn. Rained during the night 13/14.	R&q.
	15.5.15		Nothing to report. Weather fine.	R&q.
	16.5.15	11 AM	A demonstration was made against a point U.15.a.3.7. by 1st Battery & 5 (How) derrick B.F.	R&q.
			Weather fine.	R&q.
	17.5.15		Nothing to report. Weather fine. Rained in the evening.	R&q.
	18.5.15		Nothing to report. Rained during the day.	R&q.
	19.5.15		Nothing to report. Rained during night 18/19 & during the morning.	R&q.
	20.5.15		Nothing to report. Fine weather.	R&q.

Army Form C. 2118.

WAR DIARY
or
INTELLIGENCE SUMMARY.
(Erase heading not required.)

Place	Date	Hour	Summary of Events and Information	Remarks and references to Appendices
			Ref. Map. BELGIUM and FRANCE Sheet 28 SW. 20000	
PETIT	21.5.18		Nothing to report. Weather fine.	neg.
PONT	22.5.18		Nothing to report. Weather fine.	neg.
T.23.b.6.5.5.	23.5.18		Nothing to report. do do	neg.
	24.5.18		Nothing to report. do do	neg.
	25.5.18		Nothing to report. " "	neg.
	26.5.18		Nothing to report. do do	neg.
	27.5.18		Nothing to report. " "	neg.
	28.5.18		" " " "	neg.
	29.5.18		" " " "	neg.
	30.5.18		" " " "	neg.
	31.5.18		" " " "	neg.

J.C. Bullock 2nd Lt
(A/ 2° S.M.7 A Bde.

Appendix I.

9.15.

Time	Battery	Am'n on Cal'd out	Target
4.30 AM to 5.30 AM	1st / 2nd	24200 / 24200	To Cut wire in front of Enemy's Trenches in Area B
6 AM to 6.30 AM			5" How. & Mountain Battery Shelled Enemys Trenches in areas A & B
7 AM to 7.30 AM			Infantry & machine gun fire on Trenches in areas A & B.
8 AM to 10 AM			Infantry Mortar & rifle grenade supported by Art. fire.
	2nd	8	Commenced about 100x to rt. flank of area B & gradually brought in to the area
10.30 AM	2nd	4	In Area B
11.30 AM to 12.30 pm	1st / 2nd / 3rd	12 / 12 / 12	on Enemys front trenches from U15a 7.8 to U8a 9.7.
1 pm to 2 pm			Machine gun fire
2.30 pm to 3 pm			5" Howitzers fired at La POTTERIES & F'me BELLHEEM. U10a SE & U3d 5.8
3.30 pm to 5.30 pm			Infantry Mortar & rifle grenade fire.
6 pm to 7 pm	1 / 2 / 3	24 / 24 / 24	on Enemys Reserve Trenches from U5a 7.8 to U8a 9.7. Infantry also opened with Rifle fire

R.H. Galloway Capt. & Adjt.
R.F.A.

121/5839

48th Division

2nd S.M. Bde: R.F.A.

Vol IV 1 — 30.6.15

CONFIDENTIAL

WAR DIARY

of

2nd South MIDLAND FIELD
ARTILLERY BRIGADE.

from 1.6.15   30.6.15

VOL. XI

Army Form C. 2118.

Vol XI

WAR DIARY
or
INTELLIGENCE SUMMARY.
(Erase heading not required.)

Instructions regarding War Diaries and Intelligence Summaries are contained in F. S. Regs., Part II and the Staff Manual respectively. Title pages will be prepared in manuscript.

Place	Date	Hour	Summary of Events and Information	Remarks and references to Appendices
PETIT	1.6.15		Nothing to Report. Weather fine. Wind N.E.	Pkg.
PONT	2.6.15		Nothing to Report. do do. 1 horse destroyed	Pkg.
	3.6.15		Nothing to Report. do Wind N.W.	Pkg. BAILLEUL Pkg
	4.6.15		1st Battery fired on Wennelghe in Conjunction with 4 Gun Mountain Artillery in the Trenches. B" Martin 3" R.L. Evacuated to Rest Hospital. N.C.O. wounded slightly at July. Pte No 2976 G. W. Ryan Evacuated to hospital on 10/5/15.	
	5.6.15		Weather fine. Wind W.	Pkg.
			No horse evacuated	
	5.6.15		Nothing to report. Wind W. Weather fine. One Officer and 2 wounded. Slightly at shell.	Pkg.
	6.6.15		Nothing to report " " "	Pkg.
	7.6.15		Nothing to report; Wind N.W. Weather fine.	Pkg.
	8.6.15		do do do do do	Pkg.
	9.6.15		do do do do do	Pkg.
	10.6.15		do do Wind N.E. Weather fine. clear day. Enemy during night	Pkg.
	11.6.15		do do Wind N.E. Weather fine	Pkg.
	12.6.15		do do Wind N.E. Weather fine	Pkg.
	13.6.15		do do Wind N.E. do	Pkg.
	14.6.15		do do Wind N.E. do	Pkg.

WAR DIARY
or
INTELLIGENCE SUMMARY.

(Erase heading not required.)

Army Form C. 2118.

Place	Date	Hour	Summary of Events and Information	Remarks and references to Appendices
	15.6.15		Nothing to report. Wind N.E. Weather fine.	Nil
	16.6.15		Nothing to report. Wind N.N.E do	Nil
	17.6.15		Nothing to report. Wind N.E. do	Nil
	18.6.15		Nothing to report. Wind N.N.E. do	Nil
	19.6.15		Nothing to report. do do	Nil
	20.6.15		Nothing to report. do do	Nil
	21.6.15	10 pm	2nd Battery relieved in position by B battery 64th Brigade & marched to billets at LA CRECHE	Nil
			A.S.d. Sht 36 N.W.	
	22.6.15	10 pm	3rd Battery relieved in position by E Battery 64th Brigade & marched to billets at LA CRECHE	Nil
			HQ. left for LA CRECHE. Command taken over by Section	Nil
LA CRECHE	23.6.15	10 pm	1st Battery Position taken over by D Battery 64th Brigade. 1st Battery	Nil
		11.30 pm	marched to LA CRECHE	
	24.6.15		The Brigade allotted to Group A. Consisting of 145th Inf Brigade - 1st Berks on N.E - 1st Febs	
			Ambulance & the 4 Coy Div. Sup. Train	
			The Group marched to BAILLEUL area	
		8.30 pm	The Brigade marched independently & were billeted in the vicinity of OULTERSTEEN.	Nil
			arriving 10 pm	

Army Form C. 2118.

WAR DIARY
or
INTELLIGENCE SUMMARY.
(Erase heading not required.)

Instructions regarding War Diaries and Intelligence Summaries are contained in F. S. Regs., Part II. and the Staff Manual respectively. Title pages will be prepared in manuscript.

Place	Date	Hour	Summary of Events and Information	Remarks and references to Appendices
OUTTERSTEEN	25.6.15		Ref. Map. Sheet 36a. 1/40000	
OUTTERSTEEN	26.6.15	9.15am	The Group marched to VIEUX BERQUIN. E.E.24.A.	
			The Brigade Marched independently to above place and was billeted in E.11.C. E.11.a. Roly	
			E.11.C. (Section Wet).	
VIEUX BERQUIN.	26.6.15	4.30pm	The whole Group Marched as such now of March. 1.45 Inf. Bde. – 2 S.M. F.A. Sn.	
			– 1st Fd. Coy RE. 1st Fd Ambulance – 2a 4 Coy Sup. Train –	
			to ROBECQ in P.23. from there the various units went to their billeting areas.	
			1st Battery & Am. Col. to BAS RIEUX V.18. 2nd & 3rd Batteries V.17a SW.	
			HQ to GONNEHEM V.17d NE arriving between 3 AM & 4 AM 27.6.15.	Reby
VIEUX BERQUIN	27.6.15	6pm	1st Battery & A.C. moved to a field in D.21.NW. Map Sheet 36.b. 1/40000 Batteries	Reby
			& bivouaced there.	
do.	28.6.15	1pm.	HQ. 2nd & 3rd Batteries move & bivouac in D.16.a. Sheet 36.b. 1/40000	Reby
ECQUE	29.6.15	–	The Brigade moved into from the grounds of the house LE MONT EVÈNIE –	Reby
			some of the afternoon between 2 pm & 6 pm.	
LE MONT EVÈNIE	30.6.15		Nothing to report.	Reby

J.C. Bullock Lt/Col
Cdg 2 S.M. F.A Bde.

12/
6292

an
96

48th Division

2nd S.M. Bde R.F.A.

Vet V

1-31-7-15

CONFIDENTIAL.

WAR DIARY.

of

2 SMFA BRIGADE

48th Division

from 1.7.15   To 31.7.15

Vol XII:

Army Form C. 2118.

WAR DIARY
or
INTELLIGENCE SUMMARY.
(Erase heading not required.)

Instructions regarding War Diaries and Intelligence Summaries are contained in F.S. Regs., Part II. and the Staff Manual respectively. Title pages will be prepared in manuscript.

Place	Date	Hour	Summary of Events and Information	Remarks and references to Appendices
			Reference. Map Sheet 36 B. 1/40000	
LE MONT	1.7.15		Training	Nil.
EVENIC	2.7.15		Training	Nil.
D.19.b.0.5.	3.7.15		do	Nil.
	4.7.15		do	Nil.
	5.7.15		do	Nil.
	6.7.15		do	Nil.
	6.7.15		do	Nil.
	7.7.15		do	Nil.
	8.7.15		do	Nil.
	9.7.15		do	Nil.
	10.7.15		do	Nil.
	11.7.15	Noon	Closed forces. Francs Canons out reconnaissance & position to cover advance 2nd Army. G.31.a.9.c. & G.25.a.9.c.	Nil.
	12.7.15	3 pm	Right Section under Lt PERRINS. Marched to take up position. E. of LES BREBIS. L.35.c. NE.	Nil.
	13.7.15	12:30 PM	Been received by 1st Battery at LOSE NE to return to D.19.b.0.5	Nil.
		5 AM	Rt Section 12th Battery arrived back at D.19.b.0.5.	Nil.
	14.7.15		Training. Released with	Nil.
		2 pm	Received order for the brigade to proceed into Billets at AUCHEL. C.28.	Nil.

WAR DIARY
or
INTELLIGENCE SUMMARY.
(Erase heading not required.)

Army Form C. 2118.

Place	Date	Hour	Summary of Events and Information	Remarks and references to Appendices
AUCHEL	15/7/15	11 AM	The Brigade moved into Billets at AUCHEL.	
"			Officers Kit 10 lb. Equipment in the waggons for the Brigade. At Rest on 15th. The Division comes under VII Corps.	Ref.
"	16/7/15		Training.	Ref.
"	17/7/15		Training.	Ref.
"	18/7/15	10 AM	CHURCH PARADE.	Ref.
"	19/7/15		#0 ? 1st Wircal Battery entrained at BERGUETTE. Train leaving at 6.57 pm.	
			2nd Battery " do do 9.31 pm.	Ref.
"	20/7/15		3" " " " 1.31 AM.	
			Am Col " " " 8.11 AM.	
			The whole Brigade detrained at DOULLENS & marched to THIEVRES when they bivouaced.	May.
*THIEVRES	21/7/15		The Brigade moved to AUCHIE during the afternoon. 18 pr. Equipment Guns & Carriages	Ref.
*AUTHIE	22/7/15		arrived during the day & were taken into use. Training on 15 pr. do do	Ref.
"	23/7/15		do do	Ref.

* Not Map Sheet B set B Sheet 12 AMIENS. 1: 80,000

WAR DIARY
or
INTELLIGENCE SUMMARY.

Army Form C. 2118.

Place	Date	Hour	Summary of Events and Information	Remarks and references to Appendices
AUTHIE			Ref. Maps Set 13 Sheet 12 AMIENS 1: 80000	
	24/7/15		Training Battalions in Encampment	P.h.q
	25/7/15		3rd Battalion received orders to prepare a position immediately SOUTH of HERUTENNE.	P.h.q
	26/7/15		3rd Battalion preparing position. Training remainder.	P.h.q
	27/7/15		do. 1st Battalion reliever down Etripper position (just North of)	P.h.q
	28/7/15		1st & 3rd Battalion preparing position. 2nd Bn Training. 6 men Reinforcements joined	P.h.q
	29/7/15		do. do. Lt B + B ALLEN joined T.	P.h.q
	30/7/15		Ben parties to Am. BT. 3rd & 3rd Battn preparing position. 2nd Bn Training.	P.h.q
		11 pm	1st Section 3rd Battn went into action.	P.h.q
	31/7/15		1st & 3rd Battn preparing position. 2nd Bn Training	P.h.q

J.C. Bullock Lt Col.
(cdg) 2/5 M.F.A. Bde.

48th **Division**

A/Arty

121/6692

CONFIDENTIAL

WAR DIARY
of
2nd SOUTH MID. FIELD ARTY. Bde.

From 1.8.15   To 31.8.15

Vol XIII - VI

WAR DIARY
or
INTELLIGENCE SUMMARY.

(Erase heading not required.)

Army Form C. 2118.

VOL XIII

Place	Date	Hour	Summary of Events and Information	Remarks and references to Appendices
			All map references to French map, 1: 75,000, of 18 Juillet 1915.	
AUTHIE	1.8.15	4 pm	1st Battery occupies position N. of SAILLY au BOIS.	Ren.
		11.15 pm	The remaining Section of 3rd Battery went into action just S. of HEBUTERNE	Rhe.
	2.8.15		1st Battery and under the French Commanded 1st Tactical operation 9 + 3rd Battalion	W.S.6.
			attached to 3rd S.M.F.A. Bde. 1st Battery attacked 3.S.M.F.A.M. for ammunition purposes	W.S.6.
	3.8.15		1st & 3rd Battalion reported 9 am. 2nd Battalion Training	W.S.6.
	4.8.15		do do do	
	5.8.15		do do do	W.S.6.
	6.8.15		2nd D.A.C. ammn. wrote 2nd section for Training	
			1st & 3rd Batteries Registration of Zones. 2nd Bty Training area	W.S.6.
	7.8.15		obtaining men from Ammunition Columns of D.A.C.	W.S.6.
			1st + 3rd Batteries Registration of Zones. 2nd Bty Training	
	8.8.15		1st + 3rd Batteries Registration of Zones. 2nd Bty Training	
		9.30 am	Rear Section of 3rd Battery withdrawn from action to bivouac at Bertincourt	W.R.
			wagon line COIGNEUX	
	9.8.15		1st Battery registration of Zones. 2nd Battery Training. 3rd Battery LtAPiches 3rd + 13th ambulances from action	Dby.
		6.30 pm	at COIGNEUX.	

Army Form C. 2118

WAR DIARY
or
INTELLIGENCE SUMMARY.
(Erase heading not required.)

Instructions regarding War Diaries and Intelligence Summaries are contained in F. S. Regs., Part II. and the Staff Manual respectively. Title pages will be prepared in manuscript.

Place	Date	Hour	Summary of Events and Information	Remarks and references to Appendices
AUTHIES	10.8.15		1st Battn. Registration of Zone. 2nd & 3rd Batteries Training.	W.S.G.
	11.8.15		do	Mej.
	12.8.15		"	Mej.
	13.8.15		do	W.S.G.
	14.8.15		do	W.S.G.
	14.8.15	4pm	2nd Battery went into action 3rd Battery Training	do
	15.8.15		1st & 2nd Battery Registration of Zone S.E of COLINCAMPS	W.S.G.
			21st Dy'm Passing wireless to A Report 2/Lt Hopkins to 3rd Battery Training.	W.S.G.
	16.8.15		" " 2/Lt Hopkins to 1st Bty.	W.S.G.
	17.8.15		do	W.S.G.
	18.8.15		do	W.S.G.
	19.8.15		do	W.S.G.
	20.8.15		1st & 2nd Batteries Registration of Zone 3rd Bty Training. Practice server 15 rounds with howitzer	W.S.G.
	21.8.15		1st & 2nd Batteries Registration of Zone. 3rd Bty Training. Practice server 15 rounds with howitzer	W.S.G.

WAR DIARY
or
INTELLIGENCE SUMMARY
(Erase heading not required.)

Army Form C. 2118

Place	Date	Hour	Summary of Events and Information	Remarks and references to Appendices
AUTHIE	22-5-15		1st & 2nd Batteries Reconnaissance of Zone. 3rd Bty Training	WPC
	23-5-15		1st & 2nd " " " " " " Attachments to Divnl Army. C.O away	WPC
	24-5-15		1st & 2nd Batteries Registration of Zone. 3rd Bty Training	
		9.30pm	2nd Bty withdrew from action at COLINCAMPS & went into waggon lines at AUTHIE.	WPC
	25.5.15		1st Bty. registration of Zone. 2 & 3rd Batteries Training	WPC
	26.5.15		1 " " " " "	WPC
	27.5.15		1 " " " " "	WPC
	28.5.15		1 " " " " "	WPC
		9.0pm	2nd & 3rd Batteries move into gun pits batteries into action	WPC
	29.5.15		North of SAILLY AU BOIS. 1st, 2nd & 3rd Batteries registration of Zone	WPC
	30-5-15	9.30pm	action of 2nd Battery moves into action by CHATEAU DE LA HAIE	WPC WPC
	30-5-15		North of SAILLY AU BOIS. 1st, 2nd & 3rd Batteries Registration of Zone	WPC

J C Bullock
Lieut. Colonel.
2nd South Midland R.A.

Casualties for month of August 1915

2nd SOUTH MIDLAND FIELD ARTILLERY BRIGADE — SEP. 1915

Regt'l No.	Rank & Name	Corps	Nature of casualty, or name of unit from or to which transferred	Date of being struck off or coming on the ration strength	Remarks
1027	Bdr Griffin S.	3rd Battery	To Hospital	30-7-15	
2054	Driver Bould J.	"	From —	1-8-15	
3023	" Dolphin	"	— do —	— do —	
1443	" Welch W (A.S.C.)	Attached 3rd Bty	— do —	— do —	
799	Gunner Maulin W.	2nd Battery	— do —	— do —	
	2nd Lt. Foster N. J. A.	1st Battery	To Hospital	3-8-15	
1024	Corpl Noond A.	2nd "	From Hospital	3-8-15	
2115	Sptr Jones A. E.	Headquarters	do	do	
2232	Gunner Merrick W.	3rd Battery	do	do	
2090	Driver Walkins S.	2nd "	do	do	
2275	Bdr Woodyatt W.	do	To Hospital	1-8-15	
1042	— Styler S.	3rd Bty	do	2-8-15	
756	Corpl Duggins A.	do	do	3-8-15	
2982	Dr Lee E.	do	do	do	
929	Corpl Franklin H.	do	do	do	
1027	Bdr Griffin S.	do	From Hospital	4-8-15	
	2/Lieut Foster N. J. A.	1st Battery	do	5-8-15	
2018	Dr Saunders J.	2nd Battery	do	do	
1910	Pte Chatterton A. (R.A.M.C.)	Attached Amm Col	do	do	
2949	Gr Duffett S. A.	Am Col	To Hospital	do	
2050	Driver Knowles G.	2nd Bty	From Hospital	31-7-15	
756	Corpl Duggins A.	3rd Bty	do	6-8-15	
2624	Gr Lee H.	Am Col	Posted to 1st Bty	6-8-15	
2011	Bdr Hudspeth T. W.	Headquarters	Confirmed in permanent rank	6.6.15	Auth — W.O. Letter 9/Genl.No 14274 (a.5)
924	A/Bdr Elcock W.	— do —	— do —		24-5-15
2311	A/S.M. Ison B. S.	— do —	promoted 2nd Lt.	12-6-15	

2nd SOUTH MIDLAND FIELD ARTILLERY BRIGADE — 2 SEP. 1915

Casualties for month of August

Regtl No	Rank & Name	Corps	Nature of casualty, or name of unit from or to which transferred	Date of being struck off or coming on the ration return	Remarks
466	Sgt Parker A.	3rd Bty			
504	D[o] Paget W.	Am Col			
519	Sgt Boulton G.	2nd Bty			
725	" Kettle H.	Am Col	Signed		
746	Corpl Rayers A.	1st Bty	A.F. W.3126		
747	Sgt Darke A.	do	re engaging for	2-8-15	
764	" Gittens L.	Am Col	4 years or		
765	" Jordan J.	do	duration of		
773	a/Bdr Bird W.	do	war		
830	Dr Caldwell T.	do			
827	" Cantrell J.W.	do			
834	Gr Taylor H.	do			
835	Corpl Green W.	2nd Bty			
	Major Taylor G.H.	do			
35735	B.Q.M.Sgt Sunderland A.J.	3rd Bty	Granted leave	1-8-15 to 8-8-15	
13	F.Q.M.Sgt Jeynes W.	Am Col			
758	Cpl Sealy H.	3rd Bty			
475	Armt S.S. Smith F.A.	Headquarters	Granted	7-8-15 to 14-8-15	
333	Far Sgt Sheward A.	2nd Bty	leave		

2nd SOUTH MIDLAND FIELD ARTILLERY BRIGADE — 2 SEP. 1915

Casualties for month of August 1915

Regd No	Rank & Name	Corps	Nature of casualty, or name of unit from or to which transferred	Date of being struck off or coming on the ration return	Remarks
	Capt Galloway R.L.	Headquarters	To Hospital	7-8-15	
	Surg Major Oldham A.C.	do	Granted Leave	8-8-15	
85	S.Sgt Far Thomas A.W.	1st Battery	"	6	
206	Cpl Evans W.	Am Col	"	15-8-15	
	Capt Galloway R.L.	Headquarters	From Hospital	9-8-15	
2509	Dr Hale W.E.	1st Battery	To Hospital	7-8-15	
2730	" Risburn W.H.	do	do	7-8-15	
2078	Gnr Walker H.	do	Evacuated	7-8-15	
2338	" Bradley E.	do	Transfd to England	17-7-15	
2129	Spr Smith F.	do	To Hospital	8-8-15	
980	Dr Williams D.	do	do	10-8-15	
2129	Spr Smith F.	do	From Hospital	11-8-15	
2406	Dr Cook W.	do	To Hospital	8-8-15	
2730	" Risburn W.H.	do	From Hospital	12-8-15	
1090	" Twining E.	do	do	14-8-15	
2406	" Cook W.	do	do	14-8-15	
2691	" Price A.	2nd Battery	Transfd to England	23-7-15	
3267	" Neale A.	3rd Battery	To Hospital	9-8-15	
2982	" Lee E.	do	From Hospital	11-8-15	
929	Corpl Franklin H.	do	do	12-8-15	
1042	Bombr Stifler S.	do	do	13-8-15	
2949	Gunner Duffett S.A.	Am Col	Evacuated	5-8-15	
2582	Driver Jones F.W.	do	Transferd to 2d Bde	13-8-15	
891	Corpl Sheppard W.	do	— 6 Hd Qrs Bde	13-8-15	
752	Sgt Aston H.	3rd Battery	Signed A.F.W.3126 Re Engaging for 14 yrs or duration of War	11-8-15	
758	Cpl Sealey H.	do			
756	" Duggins A.	do			

Casualties for month of August 1915

Regt No	Rank & Name	Corps	Nature of Casualty, or name of unit from or to which transferred	Date of being struck off or coming on the ration return	Remarks
	Vet Capt Green R.L.	Headquarters			
105	Sgt Tolley E.F.	2nd Battery			
50	" Goodyear W.	do	Granted leave	14-8-15 to 21-8-15	
115	S.Sgt Far. Rose L.W.	3rd Battery			
102	S.Sgt Sad. Rea W.J.	1st Battery			
696	Sgt Hoyle J.M.	do			
33	BQMSgt Summers A.	Am Col			

Casualties for Month of August 1915

2nd SOUTH MIDLAND FIELD ARTILLERY BRIGADE — 2 SEP 1915

Regtl No	Rank & Name			Corps	Nature of Casualty or name of unit from or to which transferred	Date of being struck off or coming on the ration return	Remarks
	Capt	Galloway	R.L.	Headquarters	Granted leave	15-8-15 to 22-8-15	
2021	D.	Howles	S.S.	Am Col	From Hospital	18-8-15	
2509	D.	Hale	W.	1st Battery	do	18-8-15	
980	Gr	Williams	W.H.	1st Battery	do	do	
176	Cpl	Blakemore	J.	Am Col	To Hospital	do	
2275	Bdr	Woodyatte		2nd Battery	From Hospital	16-8-15	
2267	D.	Neale	A.M.	3rd Battery	Evacuated	16-8-15	
467	Sgt	Griffin	J.	do	Sent to Base Time Exp	18-8-15	
3078	D.	Lewis	G.	1st Battery	To Hospital	19-8-15	
2762	Gr	Stanton	P.W.	do	do	19-8-15	
2070	D.	Cook	E.C.	3rd Battery	Transferred to England	4-8-15	
2094	"	Oliver	J.R.	2nd Battery	To Hospital	20-8-15	
2973	"	Slade	H.	Am Col	do	20-8-15	
658	Bomb	Johnson	A.H.	do	Promoted Cpl Vice Cpl Shephard	13-8-15	
2812	Bdr	Davis	J.T.	do	Promoted Bdr	13-8-15	
2593	Gunner	Hall	R.	do	Apptd Act Bomb	13-8-15	
35/435	BQMSgt	Sunderland	S.J.	3rd Battery	Apptd Act Sgt Major	13-6-15	
	Capt	Penny	A.F.	Headquarters 1st Battery			
	"	Smith-Farrington	M.C.	Am Col			
220	Sgt	Willets	A.M.	1st Battery	Granted leave	21-8-15 to 28-8-15	
2276	"	Arnold	H.	2nd Battery			
983	"	Lisseter	G.	3rd Battery			
2148	Bdr	Harris	S.	3rd Battery			
370	SgtSad	Silletoe	H.	Am Col			
2488	Gr	Gwillam	J.W.	do			
963	Cpl	Cameron	H.J.R.	Headquarters	Granted leave	22-8-15 to 29-8-15	

[Stamp: 2nd SOUTH MIDLAND FIELD ARTILLERY BRIGADE — 2 SEP 1915]

Casualties for month of August 15

Regt'l No	Rank & Name	Corps	Nature of casualty or name of unit from or to which transferred	Date of being struck off or coming on the ration return	Remarks
	Capt Green R.L.	A.V.C. attached to Headquarters	Posted to 68th Welsh Div England	21-8-15	
	Lieut Hearn C.G.	A.V.C.	Attached to Headqrs	23-8-15	
	2/Lieut Thacker W.J.	3/2nd South Mid F.A. Bde	Attached to 2nd Bty	22-8-15	
3078	Driver Lewis G.	1st Battery	From Hospital	22-8-15	
2762	Gunner Stanton S.	do	Evacuated	23-8-15	
470	Bdr Dominick P.	3rd Battery	Sent to Base for Discharge	24-8-15	
2929	Driver Tongue C.	1st Battery	Transferred to Am Col	26-8-15	
2875	Gunner Weavers E	Am Col	Transferred to 1st Battery	26-8-15	
963	Corpl Cameron H.J.R.	Headquarters	Returned from leave	23-8-15	
	Capt Smith-Carrington M.C.H.	Am Col		do	
	Capt Smith-Carrington M.C.H.	do			
963	Corpl Cameron H.J.R.	Headquarters			
559	Bdr Winwood W.	1st Battery	Granted leave to 4-9-15	28-8-15	
494	" Cox W.	do			
710	Sgt Tarpey B.J.	2nd Battery			
1148	A/SS. Morgan J.	do			
554	Sgt Hayward F.	Am Col			
1088	Driver Lee O	3rd Battery	Granted leave 29-8-15 to 5-9-15		

Signed: J.V. Bullock
Lieut. Colonel,
Comdg. 2nd South Midland F.A. Bde.

48th Division

CONFIDENTIAL

121/7050

WAR DIARY

of

2nd S.M. F.A. Bde.

from 1-9-15 to 30-9-15

volume VII ~~VIII~~

Army Form C. 2118

WAR DIARY
or
INTELLIGENCE SUMMARY
(Erase heading not required.)

Instructions regarding War Diaries and Intelligence Summaries are contained in F. S. Regs., Part II. and the Staff Manual respectively. Title Pages will be prepared in manuscript.

Place	Date	Hour	Summary of Events and Information	Remarks and references to Appendices
AUTHIE	1/9/15		1st 2nd & 3rd Batteries Registration of Zones	WFG
	2/9/15		- do -	WFG
	3/9/15		- do -	WFG
	4/9/15		- do -	WFG
		3 p.m.	H.Q. moved to BAYENCOURT. Remaining guns of 2nd & 3rd Batteries took up position with their batteries at LA HAIE & SAILLY AU BOIS respectively	WFG
BAYENCOURT	5/9/15		1st 2nd & 3rd Batteries registration of Zone. H.Q. in direct dug out in sunken road	WFG
	6/9/15		1st 2nd & 3rd Btys. team registration of Zone	WFG
	7/9/15		- do -	WFG
	6.30 p.m.		1 gun of 1st Bat. Bty. engages enemy's transports on a road to encampment of Bastions. Registration of Zones.	WFG
	8/9/15		1st 2nd & 3rd Btys - do -	WFG
	9/9/15		- do -	WFG
	10/9/15		- do -	WFG
	11/9/15	8.0 pm	Co-operation of Trench Mortars 1 Bty 2 MS M.F.A. B.00 with 1st Bty 3rd MS M.F.A Bde	WFG
	12/9/15		Registration of Zone	WFG
	13/9/15		- do -	WFG
	14/9/15		- do -	WFG

Army Form C. 2118

WAR DIARY
or
INTELLIGENCE SUMMARY
(Erase heading not required.)

Instructions regarding War Diaries and Intelligence Summaries are contained in F. S. Regs., Part II. and the Staff Manual respectively. Title Pages will be prepared in manuscript.

Place	Date	Hour	Summary of Events and Information	Remarks and references to Appendices
BAYENCOURT	15-9-15		1st, 2nd, 3rd & 3rd Batteries Registration of Zone	WSG
"	16-9-15		do	WSG
"	17-9-15		do	WSG
"	18-9-15		do	WSG
"	19-9-15		do	WSG
"	20-9-15		do	WSG
"	21-9-15		do — 6" howrs ammunition supply	WSG
"	22-9-15		do —	WSG
"	23-9-15		do —	WSG
"	24-9-15	10 pm	1st Bty deliveries 1 section as to position registration	WSG
"	25-9-15		1st, 2nd & 3rd Btys registration in HEBUTERNE for own shrapnel howrs round of GOMMECOURT	WSG
"	26-9-15		do	WSG
"	27-9-15		No firing observed	WSG
"	28-9-15		"	WSG
"	29-9-15		"	WSG
"	30-9-15		"	WSG

J. E. Bullock
Lieut. Colonel
Comdg. 2nd South Midland F. A. Bde.

Army Form O. 1810.
All Arms.

Each issue of orders will be numbered consecutively throughout the year. A fresh series will be commenced with the first issue in each year.

Unit **2nd S. M. I. A Brigade**

DAILY ORDERS. Part II.

No. **1**

Station _____

Date **September 1915**

Sub. No. of Order.	Subject.	Regimental No., Rank and Name.	Sqdn., Batty. or Co.	Particulars of Casualties, &c., and date.
		Lieut Thacker	2nd	Attached D.A.C. 4.9.15
		176 Cpl Blakemore J	A.C.	Transferred to Eylau 26.8.15
		2162 Gr Stanton Coy A	1st	" " "
		2285 S.S. Walker W	"	Evacuated 5.9.15
		728 Th Cpl Buck J	2nd	To be Th Sgt. 7.9.15
		892 Th Cotterell A	"	" " Th Cpl "
		2914 Sdlr Cpl Jones A	"	" " Sdlr Sgt "
		2854 Sdlr Wilcox G. F.	"	" " Sdlr Cpl "
		758 Cpl Sealey	3rd	" " Sgt "
		2046 Bdr Crow R.	"	" " Cpl "
		1054 A/Bdr Heath G	"	" " Bdr "
		2246 " Davis A.	"	" " Bdr "
		2194 " Daniels S	"	" " Pd a/Bdr "
		997 " Saunders W	"	" " " "
		2195 " Harris J.	"	" " " "
		2243 Gr Hicks A	"	" " " "
		Lieut Thacker	2nd	From D.A.C. 8.9.15
		Lieut Hobson A. O. W.	3rd	Leave 9.9.15 to 16.9.15
		681. Rider	1st	Died 9.9.15
		728 Th Sgt Buck J	2nd	⎫
		1812 A/Bdr Finch J	1st	⎬ Leave 9.9.15 to
		2249 Sgt Clarke	3rd	⎪ 16.9.15
		466 D. Sollors (ASC)	A.C.	⎭
		3052 Gr Boucher W.E.		Joined An Col from
		2512 Gr Widdus W		Base Details 11.9.15
		2793 D. Slade W.	A.C.	From Hosp 11.9.15
		2821 Spr Young W.	"	Do "
		2051 Bdr Nicklin	1st	" "
		2634 G. Mackie	"	" "
		35435 Q/S M Sunderland S.J.	2nd	To be 2/Lt RFA 6.9.15
		2634 G. Mackie W.	1st	From Hosp 13.9.15
		1078 G. Davis H.J	"	To Hosp "
		1096 G. Powell L.J	"	To Hosp "
		814 L. D	2nd	Destroyed 14.9.15
		874 D. Avery W.	1st	To Hosp 14.9.15

Officer Commanding or Adjutant.

Army Form O. 1810.
All Arms.

Each issue of orders will be numbered consecutively throughout the year. A fresh series will be commenced with the first issue in each year.

Unit _____

DAILY ORDERS. Part II.

No. 2

Station _____

Date Sept. 1915

Sub. No. of Order.	Subject.	Regimental No., Rank and Name.	Sqdn., Batty. or Co.	Particulars of Casualties, &c., and date.
		2569 Gr. James S	2do	Evacuated 14. 9. 15
		6 L.D. Horses		Joined 15. 9. 15
		2624 Gr. Lee W.	1st	To Hosp 16. 9. 15
		2212 Gr. Eudden	ab	To 1st Bty 16. 9. 15
		3062 Gr. Davis G.	ab	From Base Details "
		2182 Bdr Davis J.G.	"	To Hosp "
		752 Sgt Aston W	3rd }	1 mth leave on } 17. 9. 15
		746 Cpl Rayers A	1st }	syning W.326 }
		834 Rider	2w	Evacuated "
		2008 D. Robinson G.A	"	To Hosp "
		1078 Gr. Davis H.J.	1st	From " "
		220 Sgt Willetts A.M	"	To Hosp. "
		752 Sgt Aston W.	3rd }	Retd from leave } 17. 9. 15
		746 Cpl Rayers A	1st }	'Port closes' }
		2881 Dptr Young H	ab	From Hosp "
		2493 Gr. Holt W.W.	1st	To Hosp 18. 9. 15
		752 Sgt Aston W.	3rd	Leave 1mth 19. 9. 15
		746 Cpl Rayers A	1st	To Hosp 20. 9. 15
		2802 Gr. Turner W.J	"	To Hosp. "
		2624 Gr. Lee W	"	From Cas Cl Stn "
		220 Sgt Willets A.M	"	" Hosp. "
		1 Rider	2do	Evacuated. "
		Lieut Limpenny R.		Attached from 166th Bde 21. 9. 15
		2 L.D. Horses	3rd	Evacuated. 20. 9. 15
		2182 Bdr Davis J.G.	ab	From Hosp 21. 9. 15
		1096 Gr. Powell S.	bt	" " 22. 9. 15
		2723 Gr. Payne W.J.	ab	To Hosp "
		2237 D. Cooke R.	3rd	From Reinforcements "
		830 D. Caldwell	ab	1 mths leave or } 23. 9. 15
		747 Sgt Davis A	1st	re-engagement
		2237 D. Cooke R	3rd	To Hosp "
		2129 Dptr Smith J.	1st }	" "
		2571 D. Jones E.W	1st }	
		2051 Bdr Micklin W.S	}	From Hosp "
		874 D. Avery W.	bt }	
		2493 Gr. Holt W.W.	}	
		2802 Gr. Turner W.J	}	
		2723 Gr. Payne W.J.	ab	" "
		2008 D. Robinson G.A	2w	Evacuated "
		554 Gr. Hayman J.	ab	To be Sgt Major (temp) 9. 15

Officer Commanding or Adjutant.

Army Form O. 1810.
All Arms.

Each issue of orders will be numbered consecutively throughout the year. A fresh series will be commenced with the first issue in each year.

Unit _____

DAILY ORDERS. Part II.

No. 3

Station _____

Date Sept 1915

Sub. No. of Order.	Subject.	Regimental No., Rank and Name.	Sqdn., Batty. or Co.	Particulars of Casualties, &c., and date.
		7 Sgt Chatterley	A/6	From Base Detail 25.9.15
		1061 a/Bdr Mainman	A/6	"
		2571 Dr Jones E.W.	1st	To Hosp. "
		2119 Dr Edwards J	2nd	" "
		Lieut Tunbridge	A/6	Attached D/6. "
		1 H.D.	A/6	To M.V. Hospital "
		1 R.	2nd	Evacuated "
		1 Officers charger	H.Q.	"
		2944 Gr Taylor J.R.	2nd	Special leave 30.9.15 – 7.10.15
		4 Riders & 1 L.D.		Joined 28.9.15
		466 Sgt Parker A	3rd	To be B.Q.M.S.
		2249 Cpl Clarke E.	"	" " Sergt.
		2144 Bdr Harris S	"	" " Cpl. } 7.9.15
		1023 a/Bdr Coomber J	"	" " a/Bdr
		1043 a/Bdr Shyler G.	"	" " Bdr
	2414	2571 Dr Jones E.W.	1st	Evacuated 26.9.15
		2324 Gr Burgess P.J.	"	To Hosp 28.9.15
		812 a/Bdr Finch J	"	" 29.9.15
		2386 Gr Crump W.J	"	
		1 Rider	A/6	Destroyed "
		938 S.S. Cpl Davis	3rd	Leave 1.10.15 – 8.10.15
		3046 Gr Munn S.E.	1st	To Hosp 28.9.15
		499 S.S. Cpl Steward W	A/6	To Base for discharge 1.10.15
		466 B.Q.M.S. Parker A	3rd	1 mths leave on } "
		834 Gr Taylor H.	2nd	re-engagement
		3046 Gr Munn S.E.	1st	Evacuated 30.9.15
		2324 Gr Burgess P.J.		
		864 Cpl Hivons B.	A/6	To be Sergt
		1087 Bdr Edwards J	"	" " Cpl.
		126 Bdr Hardiman J	"	" " Cpl. } 7.9.15
		407 a/Bdr Preece J	"	" " Bdr
		2783 Gr Summers J.E	"	" " a/Bdr

Officer Commanding or Adjutant.

48th Division

CONFIDENTIAL

WAR DIARY

121/7368

of

2nd S. M. Fd Arty Brigade.

From 1st Oct. 1915. to 31st Oct. 1915.

Volume ~~III~~ VIII

Army Form C. 2118

WAR DIARY
or
INTELLIGENCE SUMMARY
(Erase heading not required.)

Instructions regarding War Diaries and Intelligence Summaries are contained in F. S. Regs., Part II. and the Staff Manual respectively. Title Pages will be prepared in manuscript.

Place	Date	Hour	Summary of Events and Information	Remarks and references to Appendices
BAYENCOURT	1-10-15	—	No firing in accordance with Div. Arty. orders.	W.R.C.
	2-10-15	—	" " " " " returned to 166th Bde. after fortnight's attachment.	W.R.C.
	3-10-15	—	No firing. But 3rd Bty fires under special permission at a working party.	W.R.C.
	4-10-15	—	Units improving reserve positions. No firing.	W.R.C.
	5-10-15		" " "	W.R.C.
	6-10-15		" " "	W.R.C.
	7-10-15		" " "	W.R.C.
	8-10-15		Commenced retaliation	W.R.C.
	9-10-15		" "	W.R.C.
	10-10-15		" "	W.R.C.
	11-10-15		" "	W.R.C.
	12-10-15	4 pm	Bombardment commenced retaliation. Enemy retaliates later.	W.R.C.
	13-10-15		" " " "	W.R.C.
	14-10-15		" " " "	W.R.C.
	15-10-15		" " " "	W.R.C.
	16-10-15		" " " "	W.R.C.
	17-10-15		Capt & Adjt R.N. Galloway left to command battery in 84th Bde. Capt J.C. Piercy assumes duties as Adjutant.	W.R.C.
	18-10-15			W.R.C.
	19-10-15			W.R.C.

Army Form C. 2118

WAR DIARY
or
INTELLIGENCE SUMMARY
(Erase heading not required.)

Instructions regarding War Diaries and Intelligence Summaries are contained in F. S. Regs., Part II. and the Staff Manual respectively. Title Pages will be prepared in manuscript.

Place	Date	Hour	Summary of Events and Information	Remarks and references to Appendices
BAYENCOURT	20.10.15	—	Occasional retaliation on our positions.	W.B.
"	21.10.15		Became more active on positions. Retaliation from battery in reserve.	W.B.
"	22.10.15		Firing otherwise little activity. Work constantly	W.B.
"	23.10.15		" " " " "	W.B.
"	24.10.15		" " " " "	W.B.
"	25.10.15		" " " " "	W.B.
"	26.10.15		" " " " "	W.B.
"	27.10.15		" " " " " ass.b.	
"	28.10.15		" " " " "	W.B.
"	29.10.15		Weather very bad.	W.B.
"	30.10.15		Retaliation. Work on positions. Weather very bad	W.B.
"	31.10.15		" " " " "	W.B.

J. C. Bullock
Lieut. Colonel.

Army Form O. 1810.
All Arms.

Each issue of orders will be numbered consecutively throughout the year. A fresh series will be commenced with the first issue in each year.

Unit 2w S. M. F. A. Brigade

DAILY ORDERS. Part II.

No. 1

Station _____

Date October 1915

Sub. No. of Order.	Subject.	Regimental No., Rank and Name.	Sqdn., Batty. or Co.	Particulars of Casualties, &c., and date.
		757 G. Davison R	2w	To Base 10.10.15
		Lieut Limpenny R		Rejoined Unit 2.10.15
		979 G. Small E. W.	1st	To Hosp "
		1812 B. Furch J	"	Evacuated "
		2286 G. Crump W		
		979 G. Small E. W.		
		2 L.D. joined.		4.10.15
		2051 Bdr Micklem W.D.	"	To Hosp. 5.10.15
		1096 G. Powell L.		
	735	Sgt Kettle W.	a.b.	To Hosp while on leave 1.10.15
		2846 D. Wall J	2w	To Hosp 4.10.15
		2119 D. Edwards J	"	From " "
		2259 D. Dicks J	3w	To Hosp "
		2999 G. Shambrook W.		
		3079 G. Leppard W.J.	1st	From Reinforcements 7.10.15
		3041 G. Stanton J.A.		
		764 Whr Sgt Gittens S.	a.b.	1 months leave 8.10.15
		835 Cpl Green W	2w	
		Lieut Hearne A.V.C.		Leave "
		1078 G. Davis W.J.	1st	To Hosp "
		3077 D. Nobbs D.W.	a.b.	" "
		2434 G. Davis W.	"	" " 10.10.15
		2 L.D. Died.		"
		2767 G. Stanton W.W.	1st	" "
		2051 Bdr Micklem W.D.	"	From Hosp "
		1078 G. Davis W.J.		
		1061 B. Merriman W	a.b.	To 1st Bty "
		2267 D. Neale A	2w	From Reinforcements 12.10.15
		3071 G. Freeman W		
		34885 B.S.M. Sinclair B.	a.b.	To be A/S.M. 6.9.15
		2970 D. Browney F.J.	1st	From Reinforcements 12.10.15
		3035 D. Ruff W		
		2237 D. Cooke R.	2w	To Eylau 28.9.15
		2271 D. Yoxall W	"	To Hosp 14.10.15
		2999 G. Shambrook W	"	From " "
		2434 G. Davies W	a.b.	" " 13.10.15
		765 Whr Sgt Jordan J	3w	1 months leave 15.10.15
		756 Cpl Dyzus a W		
		12 drivers joined		"

Officer Commanding or Adjutant.

Army Form O. 1810.
All Arms.

Each issue of orders will be numbered consecutively throughout the year. A fresh series will be commenced with the first issue in each year.

Unit 2nd S. M. F. A. Bde

DAILY ORDERS. Part II.

No. 2

Station _____

Date _____

Sub. No. of Order.	Subject.	Regimental No., Rank and Name.	Sqdn., Batty. or Co.	Particulars of Casualties, &c., and date.
		2011 Bdr Hudspith T. W.	2d.	
		71/t Fiske N. J. A.		
		2312 Gr Allen G.	1st.	
		2219 Dr Dawber L.		
		967 Cpl Trawler S.	2d.	Leave 21-10-15
		892 In Cpl Cottrell A		to
		1024 Cpl Noons A.		
		323 Cpl Pulley G.	3d.	28. 10. 15
		3016 Gr Harper A. E.		
		730 Sgt Hirkle W.	ab.	
		334 Cpl Potts A.		
		541 Bdr Hudson W.	2d.	
		854 Gr Brittain N.	1st.	
		2682 Gr Price E. S.		
		874 Dr Avery W.		
		2914 S/Sgt Jones A.	2d.	Leave 14-10-15
		906 Cpl Powell G.		to
		2708 Dr Painter A.	3d.	21. 10. 15
		2648 Dr Muckewright A.		
		2857 Dr Wright L.	ab.	
		1008 Gr Stokes B.		
		Major J.C. Dallay	1st.	
		Lt Tunbridge W.J.	ab.	From D.A.C. 15. 10. 15
		1025 S/Sgt Sdn Rea W.J.	1st.	To Hosp "
		3075 Gr Preston S.J.		
		Capt Galloway R.L.	2d.	To 34th Div. "
		2009 A/T A/Bdr Collinson E.a	1st.	Reverts to Gr. vice Mauxman return
		2009 Gr Collinson E. a	"	To be A/Bdr vice Finch
		2767 Gr Stanton W. W.	"	From Hosp. 15. 10. 15
		Capt Dicey J.B.	3d.	To be Capt. 6. 10. 15
		2129 2Pte Smith J.	1st.	Muster Dr 12. 10. 15
		2014 Dr Ruff J.	"	Appt Dr
		950 Gr Jastings L.	2d.	To Hosp. 17. 10. 15
		752 Gr Aston H.	3d.	From leave "
		746 Cpl Rayers A.	1st.	
		102 S.Sgt Sdr Rea W.J.	"	From Hosp "
		2454 Dr Fisher H.	"	To Hosp "
		2064 Gr Newman P.	3d.	" 18. 10. 15
		2467 Gr Knott W.	2d.	" 3. 10. 15
		2129 2Pte Smith J.	1st.	From " 24. 9. 15

Officer Commanding or Adjutant.

Army Form O. 1810.
All Arms.

Each issue of orders will be numbered consecutively throughout the year. A fresh series will be commenced with the first issue in each year.

Unit_____

DAILY ORDERS. Part II.

No. 3

Station_____

Date_____

Sub. No. of Order.	Subject.	Regimental No., Rank and Name.	Sqdn., Batty. or Co.	Particulars of Casualties, &c., and date.
		1096 Gr Powell L	1st	From Hosp. 18.10.15
		950 G. Patingo b	2w	" "
		3077 Dr Hobbs J.A	A.6	" "
		2334 S.S. Taylor S.	1st	From reinforcements 19.10.15
		2652 G. Morgan J		
		314 Dr Barrett A		
		3179 " Boyrow W.		
		3451 " Warner E		
		3291 " Hopkins N.W.	A6	— Do — "
		3219 " Smith W.G		
		3253 " Smith A		
		8249 " Shuker G.		
		3108 Dr Wilcox L	3w	— Do — "
		2046 Cpl Crow J	"	Do Hosp 20.10.15
		3075 Dr Preston S.J	1st	From Hosp
		3244 Gr Crowther N.		
		372 " Horner A.E		
		3328 " Michael A.E		
		3231 " Michael S.J		
		3148 " Nosbatt F.J		
		3476 " Pagett H.W.		From
		3224 " Redding J.		Reinforcements
		3167 " Shaw G.G		
		3155 " Taylor J.W.		22.10.15
		1088 " Cross		
		3484 " Woodings J.J		
		2078 " Walker W.		
		3057 " Ireson J		
		3073 " Wainwright		
		2974 Gr Squires A.	2w	Do Hosp 20.10.15
		519 Sgt Boulton G.		
		758 Sgt Sealey	3w	On the leave 21.10.15
		2023 G. Wardman	A6	Do Hosp "
		2239 Dr Bryson A	2d	" "
		2775 Dr Vaux J.	2w	" 22.10.15
		2209 Bv Bennett G	3w	" "
		2064 Gr Newman D	"	From Hosp
		2930 Gr Farley B		
		2875 " Weavers S	1st	Musketry Dr 18.10.15
		2628 " Miles G		
		3075 " Preston S.J		

M52947. W 5901—020 4,750,000 10/14 M. & H. Ltd. Forms O. 1810

Officer Commanding or Adjutant.

Army Form O. 1810.
All Arms.

Each issue of orders will be numbered consecutively throughout the year. A fresh series will be commenced with the first issue in each year.

Unit _____

DAILY ORDERS. Part II.

No. 7

Station _____

Date _____

Sub. No. of Order.	Subject.	Regimental No., Rank and Name.	Sqdn., Batty. or Co.	Particulars of Casualties, &c., and date.
		874 Dr. Avery W.	1st	Moislains Gre. 18. 10. 15
		2729 Dr. Raybourne W.G.		
		2893 Gr. Gane	A Co.	To Hosp. 23. 10. 15
		2066 Cpl Crow	3w.	From Hosp "
		2846 Dr. Wall J.	2w.	"
		857 Gr. Harrison J.J.	"	To Hosp "
		2454 Sh. Fisher N.	1st	From Hosp "
		D. Hearne A.V.S.		" Leave "
		2259 Dr. Dicks J.	3w.	Evacuated "
		2018 Dr. Saunders J.	2w.	To Hosp 25. 10. 15
		2195 Br. Harris F.	3w.	"
		2229 Dr. Blizzard A.	H.Q.	From Hosp 26. 10. 15
		6 L.D. joined.		
		2/S Woods W.A.	2w.	
		" Turpin J.K.	A Co.	
		2216 A/B. Bampfylde S.	H.Q.	
		900 Sgt. Wm Woods G.	1st	
		894 Dr. Griffiths G.		
		2854 Sd. Cpl Wilcox F.	2w.	Leave
		2671 Gr. Owen H.R.		28. 10. 15
		2026 Cpl Crow J.	3w.	to
		2207 Sdr Davis M.		4. 11. 15.
		631 Sgt. Whitmore J.	A Co.	
		126 Cpl Hardiman J.E.		
		997 A/B. Saunders	3rd	To Hosp 27. 10. 15
		2053 Dr. Long V.		
		3062 Gr. Davis G.	A Co.	" "
		2300 Dr. Morris F.S.		
		13 B.Q.M.S. Jeynes		
		2209 B. Bennett	3rd	From Hosp 29. 10. 15
		2893 Gr. Gane		
		2246 Br. Davis A		
		1027 A/B. Griffin S		
		2068 Gr. Field E.	3w.	To Hosp 30. 10. 15
		2253 Gr. Powell G.		
		3004 " Vale J.F.		
		2975 " Spencer F.		
		2247 Dr. Clayton N.		
		13 B.Q.M.S. Jeynes W.	A Co.	From Hosp "

Officer Commanding or Adjutant.

Army Form O. 1810.
All Arms.

Each issue of orders will be numbered consecutively throughout the year. A fresh series will be commenced with the first issue in each year.

Unit _____

DAILY ORDERS. Part II.

No. 5

Station _____

Date _____

Sub. No. of Order.	Subject.	Regimental No., Rank and Name.	Sqdn., Batty. or Co.	Particulars of Casualties, &c., and date.
		2306 Dr Woodward H.	3w.	From Hosp 30. 10. 15
		2092 Gr Maiden W.	H.Q.	Do 3rd 18Ly "
		2306 Dr Woodward H.	3rd	" H.Q. "
		2789 Gr Smith F.	2w.	Do Hosp "
		2051 Br Nicklin W.H.		
		2933 Gr Betts A.	1st	"
		2389 " Clarke A.		
		2084 Bdr Stanton W.		
		2341 Gr Buckley A.E.	2w.	" "
		2059 " Tyler J.		
		2905 Sd Cockell	3w.	" "
		2235 Gr Canadine L.		
		2856 Dr Jaynes W.	A6	" "
		2271 D Yowell	3w.	From Hosp "
		2242 Dr Wedgbury A	3w.	Leave 31. 10. 15
		1504 Cpl Peace W.F.	1st	Leave 7. 11. 15
		2023 Gr Nadiman J.	A6.	From Hosp. 30. 10. 15
		997 2/B. Saunders H.	3rd	" " 31. 10. 15
		2111 Bdr Rimmer W.		
		878 Gr Gwilliam a	2nd	Do Hosp "
		881 " Hart F.V.		
		2909 " Wright Jas.		

Officer Commanding or Adjutant.

H.Q. 241 Bde R.F.A.

Passed to you for information
& retention please.

[signature]
30/9/16
MAJOR,
BRIGADE MAJOR, 48th DIVL. ARTILLERY.

B.M. B + C/241
Passed for your
information
4/10/16
[signature]
Captain, R.F.A.
a/Adjutant 241 South Midland F.A. Bde.

A.
B.
C.

G.O.C. R.A.
48th (South Midland) D'n

I should like to place on record my great appreciation of the excellent work carried out by the 241st (South Midland) Bde. R.F.A. during the period that it has been under my command. On all occasions whether by day or night that the brigade has been called upon to shoot, the batteries have replied with an immediate and accurate fire.

The work which has been continuous and arduous has been carried out with a cheerful keenness by all ranks at all times.

I should be very much obliged

if you would kindly convey
my very sincere thanks to
the brigade

W. H. Kay
Brig. Genl R.A.

30th Sept 16   G.O.C. R.A. 49th (WR) Dn

O.C.
241.
Very satisfactory –

H. D. O. Ward

30 . IX . 16

121/7637

48th Division

1/2nd S.M. Bde R.F.A.

Nov 1915

Vol IX

CONFIDENTIAL.

WAR DIARY.

of.

2nd S. M. F. A. Bde.

From 1-11-15.   to 30-11-15.

(Volume XVI).

Army Form C. 2118

WAR DIARY
or
INTELLIGENCE SUMMARY

(Erase heading not required.)

Instructions regarding War Diaries and Intelligence Summaries are contained in F. S. Regs., Part II. and the Staff Manual respectively. Title Pages will be prepared in manuscript.

Place	Date	Hour	Summary of Events and Information	Remarks and references to Appendices
BAYENCOURT	1-11-15		Occasional retaliation.	W.T.6.
	2-11-15		"	W.T.6.
	3-11-15		"	W.T.6.
	4-11-15		Firing was mostly in billets 1st & 3rd Brigs	W.T.6.
	5-11-15		in SAILLY au BOIS. 2nd Bgd. in dug-outs by Chateau de la	W.T.6.
	6-11-15		HAIE. Waggon lines in COIGN'S & Am. Col'n at RUTHIE.	W.T.6.
	7-11-15		H.Q. been moved H.Q. in from] SAILLY au BOIS.	W.T.6.
	8-11-15		Retaliation	W.T.6.
	9-11-15		"	W.T.6.
	10-11-15		"	W.T.6.
	11-11-15		"	W.T.6.
	12-11-15		"	W.T.6.
	13-11-15		Occasional bombardments of enemy front line	W.T.6.
	14-11-15		"	W.T.6.
	15-11-15		"	W.T.6.
	16-11-15		"	W.T.6.
	17-11-15		"	W.T.6.
	18-11-15		"	W.T.6.

Army Form C. 2118.

WAR DIARY
or
INTELLIGENCE SUMMARY
(Erase heading not required.)

Instructions regarding War Diaries and Intelligence Summaries are contained in F. S. Regs., Part II. and the Staff Manual respectively. Title Pages will be prepared in manuscript.

Place	Date	Hour	Summary of Events and Information	Remarks and references to Appendices
BAYENCOURT	19-11-15		Readjusion	W.R.6.
	20-11-15		"	W.R.6.
	21-11-15		"	W.R.6.
	22-11-15		"	W.R.6.
	23-11-15		"	W.R.6.
	24-11-15		"	W.R.6.
	25-11-15		"	
	26-11-15	1-0 am	'C' coy. 6th Gloucesters assisted by howzs from 3rd S.M.H.Bn. got into German trenches one prisoner & Rues several Ruralation	W.R.6.
	27-11-15		"	W.R.6.
	28-11-15		"	Heavy shelling during night. Some retaliation from our troops.	W.R.6.
	29-11-15			W.R.6.
	30-11-15		Aurora was however up.	W.R.6.

30-11-15

Lt. B. Taylor Major
Lieut. Colonel,
Comdg. 2nd South Midland R.A. Bde.

Army Form O. 1810.
All Arms.

Each issue of orders will be numbered consecutively throughout the year. A fresh series will be commenced with the first issue in each year.

Unit _____

DAILY ORDERS. Part II.

No. _1_____

Station _____

Date _Nov 19__

Sub. No. of Order.	Subject.	Regimental No., Rank and Name.	Sqdn., Batty. or Co.	Particulars of Casualties, &c., and date.
		286 R. Fowler J.	2n.	To Hosp. 1.11.15
		2083 R. Rolls A. E.J.	1st	From Hosp
		2389 " Clarke A.	"	
		2031 B. Nicklin W.A.	"	2.11.15
		212 Foster N.J.A.	1st	
		2670 Dr. Barrett J.J.	"	Attached to
		2236 Cpl Barton W.J.	3rd	26th Aust Aircraft
		893 " Naughton J.	2nd	Section 2.11.15
		857 " Dawson J.	2n	From Hosp
		2907 " Wright J.		
		2217 Dr. Reavold J.W.	H.Q.	To Hosp
		2693 Pr. Mills W.	"	
		3073 " Wainwright	a.b.	
		2578 Dr. Jennings J.	Ord	
		212 Perrins L.S.D.	1st	
		808 Pr. Hopp W.	H.Q.	
		955 Pr. Stallard J.W.	1st	
		1017 D. Hodge J.		
		2212 D. Widdes H.		
		762 B. Ruston J.		Granted 4.11.15
		260 " Boswell J.	2nd	to
		1092 D. Godfrey J.		Leave 11.11.15
		2602 Cp Maypole J.J.		
		2996 Cp Green J.		
		2246 B. Davis A.	3rd	
		993 D. Field J.		
		2649 D. Micklewright W.		
		752 Sgt Lane W.		
		971 Cpl Hickman S.		
		1105 Sgt Bootle W.	a.b.	
		912 B. Porter J.S.		
		2062 Cp Davis G.	a.b.	From Hosp 3.11.15
		773 Pr. Bird W.	a.b.	1 mths leave
		3064 D. Pagett W.		
		3585 Cp. Ruff W.		
		3079 " Leppard W.J.	1st	To Hosp 21.10.15
		2831 " Tulson C.		
		360 Sgt Sheldon W.		
		2008 Cp Pullman H.		
		249 J. Ball J.	a.b.	" 3.11.15
		1038 Cpl James A.		
		2138 " Taylor J.		
		2000 R. Briffa		
		3064 Cp Sanders W.J.		
		2221 " Michael J.		

Officer Commanding or Adjutant.

Army Form O. 1810.
All Arms.

Each issue of orders will be numbered consecutively throughout the year. A fresh series will be commenced with the first issue in each year.

Unit _____

DAILY ORDERS. Part II.

No. 2

Station _____

Date 8 Oct. 1915

Sub. No. of Order.	Subject.	Regimental No., Rank and Name.	Sqdn., Batty. or Co.	Particulars of Casualties, &c., and date.
		2252 S.S. Neal A.J.		
		2252 Pt. Bayne W.E.		
		2106 „ Cooker W.		
		2247 „ Edwards J.	1st	To Hosp 2.11.15
		2075 „ Foster E.J.		
		2264 „ Sharp E.		
		2129 „ Smith D.		
		980 „ Williams W.		
		854 Sgt Brittain W.		
		872 „ Rumsey W.		
		869 Cpl Nixon C.J.		
		865 „ McCann C.		Engrs
		811 B. Bennett J.		Army Horse 10/10/15
		887 „ Newsom H.E.		Sp 366
		782 B. Buston J.		
		828 „ Crawler A.		
		54 R.S.M. Hayward W.W.		
		66 „ Heath P.		
		567 Sgt Parker O.J.		21/9/15
		2999 Cr. Shanewick J.		
		2740 „ Reynolds J.	3rd	To Hosp 3.11.15
		2246 B. Davis A.		
		2168 „ Dell E.	„	From Hosp
		224) Dr. Claydon W.		
		2424 G. Wooderidge E.		
		2793 S. Foote W.		
		2118 G. Walker W.	A.b	To Hosp 4.11.15
		2260 Pt. Hughes E.		
		B. Toms. Jaynes		
		2945 G. Maynard J.	2nd	„ „
		2058 B. Stanton W.	„	From Hosp „
		152 S.S.Sgt Rea W.J.		
		906 B. Harwood J.		
		1090 N. Bright A.C.E.		
		2005 „ Cookson J.G.		
		2441 „ Edwards J.		
		2496 „ Haines D.		
		2511 „ Hessell B.	1st	To Hosp „
		1095 „ Langley B.		
		2053 „ Pawley S.D.		
		2035 „ Powers A.		
		2031 „ Rowe E.W.		
		2178 „ Smith J.A.		
		1106 „ Toms (A.J.C.)		
		2866 S. McDonagh J.	A.b	„ „ 5.11.15
		2111 B. Rimmer W.	2nd	From Hosp „

Officer Commanding or Adjutant.

Army Form O. 1810.
All Arms.

Each issue of orders will be numbered consecutively throughout the year. A fresh series will be commenced with the first issue in each year.

Unit _____

DAILY ORDERS. Part II.

No. 3

Station _____
Date 8 Oct. 1915.

Sub. No. of Order.	Subject.	Regimental No., Rank and Name.	Sqdn., Batty. or Co.	Particulars of Casualties, &c., and date.
		2883 S.S. Neale A.J.		
		2447 D. Edwards J.	1st	From Hosp. 5.11.15.
		2764 " Shaw E.		
		2129 " Smith J.		
		1027 B. Piffer S.	3rd	"
		2255 G. Carradine L.		
		957 Sgt. Jissell F.		
		1054 B. Heath J.	3rw.	To Hosp. "
		2124 D. Styler J.		
		2248 G. Boroston.		
		2454 " Clarke W.	2w.	" "
		1030 " Brook J.		
		2699 D. Powell J.	3w.	" "
		1664 " Brewer C.A.		
		2603 G. Mills W.	"	From Hosp. "
		2217 D. Burrows J.V.		
		1089 D. Kings J.	3rd.	Class II Prof. Pay "
		2053 L. Powell F.		
		3004 " Yale J.F.	"	From Hosp. 6.11.15
		2905 Sdlr. Cockrell W.		
		2414 B. Combes J.		
		510 " Preston W.		To Hosp. "
		2866 G. Weaver J.		
		2919 " Taylor W.		
		2341 G. Buckley	2w.	From Hosp. "
		102 S.S.Sdlr. Rea W.G.		
		956 B. Harward J.W.		
		2352 D. Bayes W.J.		
		2406 " Cooke W.	1st	" "
		2447 " Edwards J.		
		2496 " Harris J.		
		305 " Preston S.J.		
		M1056 " Jaces O. (A.S.C.)		
		360 Sgt. Sheldon W.		
		5793 D. Slade W.		
		2135 " Taylor V.		
		3054 " Tomkins W.A.	A.b.	" "
		3000 " Briggs W.		
		2560 " Hughes E.		
		2078 G. Walker W.		
		2296 D. Jones S.		
		3234 D. Styler W.	3w.	" "
		2700 " Reynolds R.		
		2856 " Jephers W.	A.b.	" "
		2036 " McDonough J.		

Officer Commanding or Adjutant.

Army Form O. 1810.
All Arms.

Each issue of orders will be numbered consecutively throughout the year. A fresh series will be commenced with the first issue in each year.

Unit _____

DAILY ORDERS. Part II.

No. 4

Station _____

Date 7 Nov 1915

Sub. No. of Order.	Subject.	Regimental No., Rank and Name.	Sqdn., Batty. or Co.	Particulars of Casualties, &c., and date.
		1095 D. Langley R.	1st	From Hosp 7.11.15
		2935 " Powell A.		
		2571 " Smith W.P.		
		2031 " Rowe E. C.		
		1076 " Bright A. C. E.		8.11.15
		2511 " Hassell B.		
		2913 " Hawley I. C.		
		2115 2Cpl Jones A. B.	21. a.	9.11.15
		2970 Pte Preston W.		
		1050 " Heath P.		
		2606 L. Weaver D.	3rd	
		2819 " Taylor C.J.		
		2023 D. Long I.		
		2928 " Wiggin A.		To Hosp
		2018 " Saunders D.		
		1080 Q. Brooks I.	2nd	From Hosp
		2006 Pte Sullivan H.	A.b.	10.11.15
		2369 Gr. Ball I.		
		2019 Gr. Tyler I.	2nd	
		2908 Gr. Jones G.		
		2948 " Duffill A.		
		3070 " Payell H. W.		
		2857 D. Wright G.	A.b.	To Hosp
		3249 " Fulcher G.		
		3141 " Barrett A.		
		3243 " Smith A.		
		2414 Pte Coombes D.	3rd	From Hosp
		980 G. Williams W.	1st	
		950 D. Postings C.		
		2267 " Neale A.		
		1073 " Postings M.		
		2956 G. Paxton		
		2558 D. Williams R. B.		
		2050 " Knowles		
		2090 " Watkins S.		
		2968 G. Allan.		
		2094 F. Oliver I. R.	2nd	To Hosp 9.11.15
		2883 " Whitehouse E.		
		347 B. Allen W.		
		2024 F. Partridge R.		
		2119 " Edwards I.		
		2283 " Twembenn G.		
		2173 " Jones A. W.		
		333 I. Sgt. Stewart		
		2555 D. Niles A.		
		2275 B. Woodyatt W.		

Officer Commanding or Adjutant.

Army Form O. 1810.
All Arms.

Each issue of orders will be numbered consecutively throughout the year. A fresh series will be commenced with the first issue in each year.

Unit _____

DAILY ORDERS. Part II.

No. 5

Station _____

Date Nov 19/15

Sub. No. of Order.	Subject.	Regimental No., Rank and Name.	Sqdn., Batty. or Co.	Particulars of Casualties, &c., and date.
		952 Dr Beard G.		
		2672 " Oliver E.W.		
		862 " McCann C.	2nd	To Hosp. 9.11.15
		2163 " Rickards		
		2065 " Rimmer C.J		
		2611 Gr Lewis A.B		
		2572 Dr Jones E.W.		
		3231 Gr Michael S.J	A.b	From Hosp. 11.11.15
		2405 " Cookson J.J	1st	"
		2926 Gr Burch C.	3rd	To Hosp. 12.11.15
		2939 " Seabright J		
		920 " Clements W.G.	2nd	
		924 Br Edwards W.		
		936 " Harwood G.W.		
		1019 Dr Hayres C.	1st	
		981 Gr Potter S.C.		
		898 B. Gallett J		
		857 G. Hanson J D	2nd	Granted
		382 B. Cooke L.		Leave
		528 Dr Weavers A		
		920 Smith C.H		11.11.15
		2951 G. Vale J	3rd	
		2194 4/13 Daniels S.		/15
		792 Gr Brazier W.		
		1089 " Kings J		18.11.15
		864 L/Cpl Havens B.G		
		2289 Sd.Cpl Burton W.	A.b	
		407 Br Preece J		
		2434 Gr Davies W.		
		1073 Dr Postings M.		
		812 " McCann C.		
		2119 " Edwards J		
		2555 " Wiles A.	2nd	From Hosp. 11.11.15
		2924 " Partridge R.		
		2094 " Oliver J.R		
		2611 Gr Lewis A.B.		
		2090 Dr Watkins S.		
		333 2.Sgt Shewan		
		2908 Gr Allan		
		2575 4/13 Woodyatt W.	2nd	" "
		2650 Dr Knowles		
		2575 G. Jennings J		
		3090 Gr Allcott J.	3rd	Attached 148th 12.11.15
		1033 " Rogers J.		Bde Sup. Col.
		2952 Dr Lee H.		
		2555 G. Canavine L.		
		2528 " Nesbitt W.		

Officer Commanding or Adjutant.

Army Form O. 1810.
All Arms.

Each issue of orders will be numbered consecutively throughout the year. A fresh series will be commenced with the first issue in each year.

Unit _____

DAILY ORDERS. Part II.

No. 6

Station _____
Date Nov 17

Sub. No. of Order.	Subject.	Regimental No., Rank and Name.	Sqdn., Batty. or Co.	Particulars of Casualties, &c., and date.
		2288 Pte Trowbridge P.		
		2171 " Jones A. W.		
		2882 " Whitehouse E.	2nd	From Hosp. 12.11.15
		2163 " Rickards		
		2672 " Oliver E. W.		
		950 " Postings C.		
		1038 Cpl James A.		
		3434 Pte Woodings J. H.		
		2948 Pte Duffett A.	A Co	" "
		3243 Pte Smith A.		
		2645 " Fulcher J.		
		1069 " Brewer A. C.	H.Q.	" "
		3083 S.S. Wiltshire C.	A Co	To be Cpl S.S. 17.10.15
		3/0 Sdl Sgt Sillitoe N	"	To be S.S.Sd. 12.7.15
		2209 Pte Bennett P.	3rd	Reverter to Pte at own request 16.10.15

Officer Commanding or Adjutant.

Regt No	Rank	Corps	Nature Corps	Nature of Casualty or name of unit from or to which transferred	Date	Remarks
2908	Gr	Jones G				
3470	"	Paget H.W.	Am Col	From Hospl	13/11/15	
3140	Dr	Barnett A				
2857	"	Wright C				
2995	Gr	Spencer H				
2926	"	Burch C	3rd Bty	"	"	
2939	"	Seabright W				
2233	-	Beaman H	Am Col	To "	14/11/15	
2671	-	Oliver	2nd Bty	" "	"	
2582	Dr	Jones H.W.	"	From Hospl	"	
848	Gr	Gwilliam				
2334	S.S.	Taylor S				
3048	Gr	Edwards D.J.				
2039	Dr	Hail G	1st "	To Hospl	"	
2652	Gr	Morgan J				
2430	Dr	Risburn W.H.				
347	a/Br	Allen W	2nd "	From Hospl	15/11/15	
952	Dr	Beard G				
2171	"	Jones A.W.	" "	To Hospl	"	
2085	-	Rimmer C	" "	From Hospl	16/11/15	
2267	-	Neale A				
854	Sgt	Brittain H	1st "	To Hospl	"	
2970	Dr	Barnett W	" "	"	17/11/15	
2767	Gr	Stanton W.H.				
2334	S.S.	Taylor S				
2430	Dr	Risburn W.H.	" "	From Hospl	"	
2266	Dr	Heath J		To Hospl	"	
2242	Dr	Wedgbury A	3rd "	To Hospl	"	

8

Regtl No.	Rank	Name	Corps	Nature of Casualty or name of unit from or to which transferred	Date	Remarks
967	Cpl	Tranter S.	2nd Bty	To Hosp.	17/11/15	
3014	Dr	Baldwin H.	Am Col.	"	"	
2999	G.	Shambrook	3rd Bty	From Hosp	18/11/15	
2030	Dr	Hail G.	1st Bty	"	"	
881	G.	Hail H.V.	2nd Bty	"	19/11/15	
2775	"	Squires A.				
2962	a/Bdr	Hughes W.	Hd/Qrs			
2nd	Lieut	Sankey H.B.				
2111	Dr.	Rimmer W.				
863	a/Bdr	Chidgly M.	2nd Bty			
2152	2/sh	Sawond C				
2338	"	Brooke F.				
803	Br.	Vale E.				
2861	S.S	Westwood	3rd Bty	Granted Leave	19/11/15 to 26/11/15	
2402	dr.	Churchill A.				
2nd	Lieut	Williams A.G				
2002	Cpl	Newey W.G.	Am Col.			
658	"	Johnson A.H.				
319	G.	Baynton H.				
2194	"	Kenwick W.				
982	Cpl	Evans A.G.				
1018	Bdr.	Baldwin R.	1st Bty			
1021	"	Siv M.				
985	Dr.	Wigley W.			20/11/15 to 27/11/15	
3004	G.	Vale J.F.	3rd Bty	"		
2230	Br.	Willis A.E.	Am Col.			
2182	–	Davis J.T.	"	To be M Tailor		
3052	G.	Boucher W.G	"	" " Shoemaker		

9

Reg'l No	Rank	Name	Corps	Nature of casualty or name of unit from or to which transferred	Date	Remarks
2360	Gr	Bowley. W.	Am Col.	To. 3rd Bty	19/11/15	
2893	Sdr	Gans A.	3rd Bty	To Am. Col.	"	
2207	Sdr.	Davis H.	" "	To be. Sdr. Cpl	1/11/15	
2255	Br	Canby B	" "	" Bt Rough Rider.	"	
2583	S/at Br	Jay. W.	" "	" Bdr.	"	
757	Bdr	Riley. J	2nd "	To Base for discharge	16/11/15	
347	a/B.	Allen W.	" "	To be Bdr.	14/11/15	vice Riley
293	Gr	Haughton G	" "	" " a/Bdr.	"	vice Allen
2450	Dr	Knowles G.	" "	To be Gunner.	"	vice Haughton.
2940	Dr	Barnett F.J	1st "	Rejoined Bty from Anti Aircraft Section	14/11/15	

Army Form O. 1810.
All Arms.

Each issue of orders will be numbered consecutively throughout the year. A fresh series will be commenced with the first issue in each year.

Unit _____

DAILY ORDERS. Part II.

No. _10_

Station _____

Date _____

Sub. No. of Order.	Subject.	Regimental No., Rank and Name.			Sqdn., Batty. or Co.	Particulars of Casualties, &c., and date.
		893	a/By	Haughton L	2nd Bty	
		2884	Dr	Dawe J	"	
		969	Bpl	Trailer L	"	
		2259	Dr	Dicks J	3rd	
		3356	Dr	Ramlans W	"	
		2195	a/By	Harris H	"	
		5266	Dr	Heath J	"	
		844	Dr	Yeates H	"	
		1088	Dr	Cross A.E.	Am Col	
		5300	Dr	Morris D	"	
		3014	"	Baldwin F	"	
		13	A/Smg	Jaynes W	"	
		891	Cpl	Shepard W	H.Dry	
		963	"	Cameron F.J.R.	"	
		1084	"	Rouse A.W.	1st Bty	
		982	"	Evans O.B.	"	
		746	"	Rayers A	"	
		1020	Br	Bacon G.P.	"	Granted ⎫
		956	"	Harwood H	"	Proficiency Pay ⎬ 31/7/15
		2051	"	Nichols W.H.	"	Class T ⎭
		1034	Sgt	Bramwick R.W.	"	
		1059	a/Br	Wood J.G.R.	"	
		1061	"	Merriman W.	"	(Authority F.I Records)
		2009	Hary Gnr	Collinson E	"	AFO. 1614a. - 9/11/15
		1078	Br	Davies H.J	"	
		2029	"	Greaves J.H	"	
		1076	Dr	Bright A.E.E	"	
		1065	"	Currell J	"	

Officer Commanding or Adjutant.

Army Form O. 1810.
All Arms.

Each issue of orders will be numbered consecutively throughout the year. A fresh series will be commenced with the first issue in each year.

Unit _____

DAILY ORDERS. Part II.

No. 11

Station _____

Date 27/11/15

Sub. No. of Order.	Subject.	Regimental No., Rank and Name.			Sqdn., Batty. or Co.	Particulars of Casualties, &c., and date.
		756	Cpl	Duggins H.		
		323	"	Pulley G.		
		929	"	Hanklin H.		
		2142	"	Harris S.		
		803	Bd	Vale E.		
		1038	"	James a.		
		1072	"	Martin G.		
		1044	"	Taylor G.		
		1024	a/Bdr	Griffin S.		
		997	"	Saunders H.		
		2195	"	Harris H.		
		2710	S/a/Bdr	Preston W.	2nd Bty.	Granted Proficiency Pay Class I 31/7/15
		2064	"	Newman R.		
		2074	Gr	Gray W.		
		2461	"	Foster G.		
		940	"	Grubb W.		
		2064	"	Griffin E.		
		2257	"	Hawksworth B.		
		1057	"	Fox J.		
		992	"	Brazier W.		
		113	Dr	Wharrad H.		
		993	"	Field J.		
		994	"	Peach a.		
		2820	"	Tolley J.W.		
		2744	"	Reynolds R.		
		2053	"	Long V.		
		998	"	Evans J.		
		1089	"	Kings J.		

Officer Commanding or Adjutant.

Army Form O. 1810.
All Arms.

Each issue of orders will be numbered consecutively throughout the year. A fresh series will be commenced with the first issue in each year.

Unit _____

DAILY ORDERS. Part II.

No. 12

Station _____

Date 23/11/15

Sub. No. of Order.	Subject.	Regimental No., Rank and Name.	Sqdn., Batty. or Co.	Particulars of Casualties, &c., and date.
		2018 Dr Ratcliffe D.	H Dr	To Hospital 23/11/15
		Lt — Tunbridge W.S	Ambl	retd to England 23/11/15
		2334 S.S. Taylor S.	1st Bty	Allotment incrsd to 1/- per day 8/11/15
		221 Dr Grainger A.		
		119 Gr George W.	H Dr	
		2nd Lt — Allen B.H.B.		
		1022 a/Br Raby W.A.	1st	
		1091 Gr Twining F.H.	Bty	
		1090 Dr do E.		
		1023 Dr Quinsey H.		
		344 Br Allen W.		
		2911 S.S. Francis A.W.	2nd	
		2164 Gr Jackson E.R.A.	Bty	
		862 Dr McCann C		Granted 26/11/15
		2865 Cpl Wright A.C.		to
		2410 Sa/Br Preston W.	3rd	Leave 3/12/15
		2651 Gr Morris G	Bty	
		2984 Dr Shatlock J.		
		2288 Cpl Bowns G.		
		2907 Br Garbutt D.	Am	
		772 Br Perry J.	Col:	
		2559 a/Br Heaven W.		
		2998 Dr Lewis L.H.		
		2970 Dr Barnett T.J.	1st Bty	from Hospital 27/11/15
		2945 Gr Hart A.W.	do	to do 27/11/15
		710 Sgt Tarby B.J.	2nd do	to do 21/11/15
		2916 Dr Timberley J.B.	2nd do	to do 23/11/15
		2404 Gr Clarke H.	2nd do	from do 22/11/15

Officer Commanding or Adjutant.

Army Form O. 1810.
All Arms.

Each issue of orders will be numbered consecutively throughout the year. A fresh series will be commenced with the first issue in each year.

Unit _____

DAILY ORDERS. Part II.

No. 13

Station _____

Date 27/4/15

Sub. No. of Order.	Subject.	Regimental No., Rank and Name.			Sqdn., Batty. or Co.	Particulars of Casualties, &c., and date.
		2030	Dr	Hall G		
		1095	"	Harris G.H		
		1019	"	Haines C		
		2056	"	Penny A.B		
		2031	"	Rouse E.W	1st Bty	
		2014	"	Ruff F		
		1090	"	Twining E		
		2016	"	Wall P		
		985	"	Wigley W		
		864	Cpl	Nixon C.P		
		2248	Gr	Rogers W		
		906	Cpl	Powell R.G		Granted
		964	"	Tranter S		for
		861	Dr	Boycott J		Proficiency
		1024	Cpl	Newey A.G		Pay
		854	Gr	Harris H.G	2nd Bty	31/7/15
		2041	"	Scott W		
		881	"	Hart L.V.		
		893	a/B	Horton G		
		2052	Gr	Rea A.B		
		962	Dr	Beard L		
		899	"	Crouch W		
		2050	"	Knowles G		
		1032	"	Pardoe C		
		1031	"	Powell J		
		2018	"	Saunders J		
		980	"	Watkins W		
		528	"	Weavers A		

Officer Commanding or Adjutant.

Army Form O. 1810.
All Arms.

Each issue of orders will be numbered consecutively throughout the year. A fresh series will be commenced with the first issue in each year.

Unit _____

DAILY ORDERS. Part II.

No. 14

Station _____

Date 27/11/15

Sub. No. of Order.	Subject.	Regimental No., Rank and Name.			Sqdn., Batty. or Co.	Particulars of Casualties, &c., and date.
		2242	Dr	Wedgley H		Granted for Proficiency Pay Class I 31/7/15
		1043	"	Jennings E		
		2145	"	Lowell L	3rd Bty	
		999	"	Barney E		
		1041	"	Mallen W		
		1000	"	Willis H		
		946	Cpl	Dovey		
		812	Dr	Winch	Joined from (Reinforcements)	26/11/15
		3262	Dr	Freeman		
		2455	"	Butcher		
		3258	"	Fletcher		
		3508	"	Hemming		
		77	Sgt	Chatterly W	Ambl	refused to be engaged 23/11/15
		541	Dr	Harbron W	H2	
		858	Dr	Roberts E	Ambl	
		842	Dr	Reeves C	3rd Bty	Signed AFW. 3126
		863	a/Dr	Chidgey W	2nd Bty	
		3572	Dr	Garbutt	Joined (from Reinforcements) 26/11/15

Officer Commanding or Adjutant.

Obstetric: Roe R.I.A.
Doc
vol X

WAR DIARY
or
INTELLIGENCE SUMMARY

Army Form C. 2118

Place	Date	Hour	Summary of Events and Information	Remarks and references to Appendices
BAYENCOURT	1.12.15		Retaliation and occasional bombardments. Weather very wet and conditions of ground very bad.	
	2.12.15			W.S.C.
	3.12.15		"	W.S.C.
	4.12.15		" Retaliation	W.S.C.
	5.12.15		Unsuccessful enemy retaliations. Most trouble from Minnenwerfer	W.S.C.
	6.12.15		"	W.S.C.
	7.12.15		"	W.S.C.
	8.12.15		"	W.S.C.
	9.12.15		"	W.S.C.
	10.12.15		"	W.S.C.
	11.12.15		"	W.S.C.
	12.12.15		"	W.S.C.
	13.12.15		"	W.S.C.
	14.12.15		"	W.S.C.
	15.12.15		"	W.S.C.
	16.12.15		"	W.S.C.

WAR DIARY
or
INTELLIGENCE SUMMARY
(Erase heading not required.)

Army Form C. 2118

Place	Date	Hour	Summary of Events and Information	Remarks and references to Appendices
BAYENCOURT	17.12.15	12.55pm	Bombardment severe against enemy trenches and wire cutting by 3" mortar Btty. Successful. Uneventful. Retaliation	W.R.C.
	18.12.15		"	W.R.C.
	19.12.15		"	W.R.C.
	20.12.15		weather bad & condition "	W.R.C.
	21.12.15		Trenches and dug-outs very bad. Uneventful Retaliation	W.R.C.
	22.12.15		"	W.R.C.
	23.12.15		"	W.R.C.
	24.12.15	1.35 pm	Bombardment against enemy trenches and wire cutting by 3" mortar Btty. Successful	W.R.C.
	25.12.15		Warned against attempts merely to meet by the Germans to fraternise in Christmas Day	W.R.C.
		5.0pm	Germans shelled BAILLY severely with heavy guns	
		6.0 pm	" in our line "	
	26.12.15		Christmas dinners in our line. Retaliation	W.R.C.
	27.12.15		" " "	W.R.C.
	28.12.15		Uneventful	W.R.C.
	29.12.15		"	W.R.C.

Army Form C. 2118

WAR DIARY
or
INTELLIGENCE SUMMARY

(Erase heading not required.)

Place	Date	Hour	Summary of Events and Information	Remarks and references to Appendices
BAYENCOURT	30.12.15	—	Uneventful. Retaliations guns put out in evening by 3rd Bde.	WRe
	31.12.15		70. wire cutting	WRe

W. Bullock
Lieut. Colonel,
Comdg. 2nd South Midland I.A. Bde.

Army Form O. 1810.
All Arms.

Each issue of orders will be numbered consecutively throughout the year. A fresh series will be commenced with the first issue in each year.

Unit 2nd S.M. F.C. Bn

DAILY ORDERS. Part II.

No. _____

Station _____

Date 25/12/15

Sub. No. of Order.	Subject.	Regimental No., Rank and Name.	Sqdn., Batty. or Co.	Particulars of Casualties, &c., and date.
	Leave	Major G.H. Taylor	2nd	26-12-15 to 3-1-16
		Capt A.L. Penny	1st	26-12-15 to 2.1.16
		1069 Dr Brewer C.C.	Hqrs	— do —
		2973 Gr Jones L	1st By	— do —
		1096 " Powell L	"	— do —
		2967 " Bicknell L	2nd "	— do —
		799 " Maulin W	" "	— do —
		1072 Br Martin G	3rd "	— do —
		2999 Gr Shambrook H	"	— do —
		2862 " Williams W	" "	— do —
		3083 Cpl SS Wiltshire C	A Coy	— do —
		2831 Gr Vasey J	"	— do —
		2365 " Bullock C	"	— do —
		2305 Dr Westwood S.H.	"	— do —
		874 " Avery W	1st By	26-12-15 to 25-1-16
		861 Bdr Bowcott J	2nd "	
		2115 Tpt Jones A.E.	Hqrs	19-12-15 to 26-12-15
		2536 Dr Hogan W	3rd By	22-12-15 to 29-12-15
		932 Gr Hewin J	2nd "	
	To Hospital	924 S/Br Elcock W	Hqrs	16-12-15
		308 Sgt Norby	3rd By	18-12-15
		2015 S/Br Underhill H	1st "	22-12-15
		1034 Br Bramwich A.W.	"	25-12-15
		892 Cpl Little Cotterell A	2nd "	21-12-15
		3071 Gr Freeman	"	22-12-15
		206 Cpl Evans W	A Coy	20-12-15
		3243 Dr Smith A	"	23-12-15
		2078 Gr Walker W	"	22-12-15

Officer Commanding or Adjutant.

Army Form O. 1810.
All Arms.

Each issue of orders will be numbered consecutively throughout the year. A fresh series will be commenced with the first issue in each year.

Unit 2nd SW⟨?⟩ Bde

DAILY ORDERS. Part II.

No. _____

Station _____
Date 25/12/15

Sub. No. of Order.	Subject.	Regimental No., Rank and Name.	Sqdn. Batty or Co.	Particulars of Casualties &c., and date
	Discharge from Hospital	924 a/Bs Elcock W	Hqrs	23-12-15
		2802 Gr Turner	1st Bty	18-12-15
		2671 " Owens WR	2nd "	18-12-15
		2050 Dr Knowles G	2nd "	20-12-15
		2846 " Wall J	2nd "	22-12-15
		835 Cpl Green W	2nd "	23-12-15
		2265 Dr Harris	A Clm	21-12-15
		2119 Dr Edwards J	2nd Bty	23-12-15
		892 Cpl Fitter Cotterill	"	24-12-15
		2605 Gr Lawley G	1st "	23-12-15
		2699 Dr Powell J	2nd "	11-11-15
	Promotion	808 a/Bs Heggs W	Hqrs	Cpl 4-12-15 vice Cpl Cameron transferred to 2nd Wore Bty
		2983 Gr Bebb A.T.T.	1st Bty	Nominated for Commission in 3/2 SW⟨?⟩ Bde & proceeded to England 23/12/15
	Gunnery Course	2/Lt AB Edwards	1st Bty	Artillery School HAVERNAS 20/12/15
		923 Cpl Cameron HJR	2nd "	
		2233 Dr Beaman H	A Clm	to England 9/12/15 } Struck
		2887 " Vaux H	2nd Bty	to Base 30/11/15 } off Strength

Officer Commanding or Adjutant.

Army Form O. 1810.
All Arms.

Each issue of orders will be numbered consecutively throughout the year. A fresh series will be commenced with the first issue in each year.

Unit 2nd S.M.F.A. Bde.

DAILY ORDERS. Part II.

No. _____

Station _____

Date December 18th 1915

Sub. No. of Order.	Subject.	Regimental No., Rank and Name.			Sqdn. Batty or Co.	Particulars of Casualties &c., and date
		1369	Gr.	Burgess T.	Am Col	Re-inforcement joined 12-12-15
		Lt.	Col.	Bullock E.C.	HQ	Leave granted from 26/11/15 to 3-12-15
		842	Dr.	Browning A.R.	1st Bty	" " " 19-12-15 to 18-1-16
		1094	"	Harris G.E.	"	" " " 26-12-15
		1095	"	Langley B.	"	" " "
		2nd	Lieut.	Woodward	2nd	" " "
		2084	A/Bdr	Stanton W.	"	" " "
		893	"	Haughton G.	"	" " "
		920	Dr.	Watkins W.	"	" " "
		2395	Gr.	Clements G.	"	" " "
			Lieut.	Hobson A.C.W.	3rd	" " "
		246	Gr.	Foster G.J.	"	" " "
		483	Sgt.	Lane H.	Am Col	" " "
		2663	A/Bdr	Munslow G.	"	" " "
		2893	Gr.	Gane A.	"	" " "
		1029	"	Wise E.	"	" " "
		2115	S/Sgt	Jones A.E.	HQ	" " "
		2605	Gr.	Lawby G.	1st Bty	To Hospital 14-12-15
		2641	"	Owen H.R.	2nd	" 11-12-15
		2846	Dr.	Wall J.	"	" 14-12-15
		2046	Cpl.	Crow J.	3rd	" 13-12-15
		2425	Gr.	Cooke J.	"	" 14-12-15
		3265	Dr.	Harris F.	Am Col	" 15-12-15
		284	"	Foster	ASC	From 12-12-15
		2048	"	Fuller C.	2nd Bty	" 16-12-15
		998	"	Evans J.	3rd	" 12-12-15
		308	Sgt.	Warby H.	"	" 16-12-15

Officer Commanding or Adjutant.

Army Form O. 1810.
All Arms.

Each issue of orders will be numbered consecutively throughout the year. A fresh series will be commenced with the first issue in each year.

Unit 2nd S.M.F.A. Bde

DAILY ORDERS. Part II.

No. _____

Station

Date December 18th 1915

Imp. Hav. — 3,000

Sub. No. of Order.	Subject.	Regimental No., Rank and Name.			Sqdn. Batty or Co.	Particulars of Casualties &c., and date
		No 3048	Gr	Edwards G.H.	1st Bty	Evacuated to Base 11-12-15
		2652	"	Morgan J		" " "
		2386	"	Crump W.J.		" " "
		3046	"	Munn S.H.	"	Joined from Re-inforcements 14/12/15
		979	"	Smart C.H.		
		445	"	Hewlett W.	D.A Park	Rejoined own Unit 18/12/15
		428	"	Underwood A.E	"	" " " " "
		894	"	Griffiths G	1st Bty	" from Res Am. Park " "
		2628	Dr	Miles E.	"	" " " "
		102	S.S.Sgt	Rea W.G.	"	To 48th Div.l Base (dental treatment) "
		747	Sgt	Darke A.	"	Rejoined from Arty Course " "
		2283	Dr	Turnberrow G	2nd "	Allotment of Pay 6/per day. 13-12-15
		3329	"	Hales	" "	Posted to 2nd Bty 16-12-15
		434	Gr	Fear	D.a.C	Allotment of Pay 6/per day 28-7-15
		2697	"	Preston H.	2nd Bty	Add.l Allot of Pay 4/per day 14-10-15
		2667	"	Hott H.	"	Posted to 2nd Bty 16-12-15
		3099	Dr	Maulin	"	" " " " "
		434	Gr	Fear	attachd to 2nd Bty	Sent to rejoin D.a.C 14-12-15
		435	"	Horler		
		963	Cpl	Cameron H.J.R.	" "	transferred from H.Q. 3-12-15
		2246	Sgt	Arnold H	" "	Returned from Arty Course 18-12-15
			2nd Lieut	Hadshead	" "	" " " " " "
		2974	Gr	Gill P.	3rd "	Re-inforcement " "
		510	"	Amos J	" "	Transfd to Sub Park " "
		511	"	Cresee J.	" "	" " " " " "
		844	Bdr	Yates A.	"	Time expired (discharged) 8-12-15

Officer Commanding or Adjutant.

Army Form O. 1810.
All Arms.

Each issue of orders will be numbered consecutively throughout the year. A fresh series will be commenced with the first issue in each year.

Unit _2nd S.M.F.A. Bde_

DAILY ORDERS. Part II.

No. _____

Station _____

Date _11th December 1915_

Imp. Hav. — 5,000

Sub. No. of Order.	Subject.	Regimental No., Rank and Name.	Sqdn. Batty or Co.	Particulars of Casualties &c., and date
		2nd Lieut. Perrins C.F.B.		Admitted to Highland CCS 3/12/15
		2454 Fitter Fisher H.		Attached to R.F.C. 5/12/15
		1021 Bdr Suer W.		Married at Reg. Office Worcester 25/11/15
		976 Cpl Dovey R.F.C.	1st Worc	Rejoined from Reinforcements 10/12/15
		2113 A/Cpl Brettell G.B.		Reverted to Bdr on a/c Cpl Dovey 26/11/15
		1034 A/Bdr Bramwich A.W.		" " a/Bdr - A/Cpl Brettell 26/11/15
		854 Sgt Brittain H.	Rly	From hosp. to ENGLAND 23/11/15
		1084 Cpl Rouse A.W.		Promoted to Sgt vice Sgt Brittain 6/12/15
		2113 Bdr Brettell G.B.		" vice Cpl Rouse 26/11/15
		1034 a/Bdr Bramwich A.W.		" Bdr vice Brettell 26/11/15
		812 S/a Bdr Finch J.		" a/Bdr - a/Bdr Bramwich 26/11/15
		410 Sgt Tarpey D.J.	2nd Bty	Evacuated 1/12/15
		867 Cpl Tyson C.J.		Promoted Serg. 2/12/15
		3509 Dr Haines		Rec'd from Am. Col. 6/12/15
		983 Sgt Lissiter G.E.		Evacuated 29/11/15
		2619 Gr Law W.H.	3rd Bty	Allot. incr. from 6 to 7/day 8/12/15
		2332 " Merrick W.		Transferred to Am. Col. 11/12/15
		2653 " Maiden B.		do 11/12/15
		2854 " Booth P.	Amm. Column	do to 3rd Bty 11/12/15
		2103 " Berry J.W.		" " "
		2838 B.S.M. Winzar A.J.		Granted Leave from 12/12/15 to 19/12/15
		1068 Sgt Johnson S.J.	1st Bty	"
		1061 a/Bdr Merriman W.		"
		2306 Dr Woodward H.	HQ	"
		2284 Gr Martin H.		"
		2912 SS Rogers J.	2nd Bty	"
		2275 a/Bdr Woodyatt W.		"
		Captain Meacher E.		"

Officer Commanding or Adjutant.

For information of the A.G.'s Office at the Base.

Officers and men who have become casuals, been transferred or joined since last report.

Place_____   Date __11/12/15__

Regtl. Number	Rank	Name	Corps	Nature of casualty, or name of unit from or to which transferred	Date of being struck off or coming on the ration return	Remarks*
Capt &	Adjt	Dixey, J.C.	Hd Qrs.	Leave from 12/12/15 to	19/12/15	
2361	Gr	Bradley W	3rd Worcs Bty	Granted leave from 12/12/15 to	19/12/15	
2478	Dr	Gittins E	" " "			
1024	A/Bdr	Griffin S	" " "			
1084	Cpl	Edwards J	Am Column			
2143	Dr	Jones A H	" "	ditto		
2479	"	Grealey M	" "			
2453	Gr	Edwards J.E.	" "			
842	Dr	Reeves C	3rd Bty	Granted one months leave from 12/15/15 to	11/1/16	
782	Bdr	Burston J	2nd Bty			
102	SSSdl	Rea W.J.	1st Bty	from Hospital	7/12/15	
2429	Gr	Ragbourne W.G.	" "	"	9/12/15	
2641	"	Owen H.R.	2nd "	"	5/12/15	
2648	Dr	Micklewright A	3rd "	"	5/12/15	
1041	"	Malins W	" "	"	6/12/15	
2999	Gr	Chambrook H	" "	"	"	
2000	Dr	Briggs W	Am Col	"	"	
2080	"	Duffield C	" "	"	"	
2604	Gr	Lessimore C	1st Bty	"	9/12/15	
2429	"	Ragbourne W.G.	" "	to Hospital	6/12/15	
2802	"	Turner W.J.	" "	"	9/12/15	
284	Dr	Foster S	2nd "	"	5/12/15	
2119	"	Edwards	" "	"	"	
834	Gr	Taylor H	" "	"	6/12/15	
2015	"	Knowles G	" "	"	"	
2642	Dr	Oliver E.W.	" "	"	8/12/15	
835	Cpl	Green W.J.	" "	"	9/12/15	
2048	Dr	Pullen E	" "	"	"	

* State whether absence is of a permanent or temporary nature, adding, in the case of casuals from wounds or disease, any available information for communication to the relatives.

Army Form B. 213.

FIELD RETURN.

No. of Report _____

(To be furnished by all arms, services, and departments (except A.S.C. units) to the A. G.'s Office at the Base in accordance with Field Service Regulations, Part II.)

Date. _____

RETURN showing numbers RATIONED by, and Transport on charge of, _____ at _____

DETAIL	Personnel			Animals.								Guns, carriages, and limbers and transport vehicles				Horsed		Motor Cars	Tractors	Mechanical			Motor Bicycles	Bicycles	REMARKS
	Officers	Other ranks	Natives	Horses			Mules		Camels	Oxen		Guns, carriages and limbers, showing description	Ammunition wagons and limbers	Machine guns	Aircraft, showing description	4 Wheeled	2 Wheeled			Lorries, showing description	Trucks, showing description	Trailers			
				Riding	Draught	Heavy Draught	Pack	Large	Small																
Effective Strength of Unit																									
Details, *by Arms* attached to unit as in War Establishment:—																									
Total																									
War Establishment																									
Wanting to complete (Detail of Personnel and Horses below)																									
Surplus																									
*Attached (not to include the details shown above)																									
Civilians:— Employed with the Unit Accompanying the Unit																									
TOTAL RATIONED ...																									

* In the case of field ambulances, hospitals or depots, the number of patients are to be included here, the names being shown in A. F. A. 36.

_____ Signature of Commander.

_____ Date of Despatch.

For information of the A.G.'s Office at the Base.

Officers and men who have become casuals, been transferred or joined since last report.

Place _____ Date 11/12/15

Regtl. Number	Rank	Name	Corps	Nature of casualty, or name of unit from or to which transferred	Date of being struck off or coming on the ration return	Remarks*
511	Gr	Crew J	3rd Worc Bty	To Hospital	6/12/15	
2032	Dr	Foster JW	Am Column	" "	4/12/15	
3050	"	Bichton GL	" "	" "	8/12/15	
3052	Gr	Boucher W	" "	Shoemakers Granted 1/- per day working pay from	1/12/15	Authority aag GHQ 3rd Echelon
2929	Dr	Yongue C	" "			
2246	Bdr	Davies A	3rd Bty	Tailors Granted 1/- per day working pay from	1/12/15	aag GHQ 3rd Echelon
2182	"	do JT	Am Column			
874	Dr	Avery W	1st Bty			
433	Sgt	Lane H	Am Column	Re-engagements on AFW 1236		
864	"	Havens B	" "			
844	Bdr	Yates J	3rd Bty	Time Expired	2/12/15	

* State whether absence is of a permanent or temporary nature, adding, in the case of casuals from wounds or disease, any available information for communication to the relatives.

Army Form B. 213.

FIELD RETURN.

No. of Report _____

(To be furnished by all arms, services, and departments (except A.S.C. units) to the A. G.'s Office at the Base in accordance with Field Service Regulations, Part II.)

RETURN showing numbers RATIONED by, and Transport on charge of, _____ at _____ Date _____

DETAIL	Personnel			Animals.							Guns, carriages, and limbers and transport vehicles			Horsed		Motor Cars	Tractors	Mechanical			Motor Bicycles	Bicycles	REMARKS
	Officers	Other ranks	Natives	Horses			Mules		Camels	Oxen	Guns, carriages and limbers, showing description	Ammunition wagons and limbers	Machine guns	Aircraft, showing description	4 Wheeled	2 Wheeled			Lorries, showing description	Trucks, showing description	Trailers			
				Riding	Draught	Heavy Draught	Pack	Large	Small																
Effective Strength of Unit																								
Details, by *Arms* attached to unit as in War Establishment:—																								
Total																								
War Establishment																								
Wanting to complete																								
(Detail of Personnel and Horses below)																								
Surplus																								
*Attached (not to include the details shown above)																								
Civilians:— Employed with the Unit Accompanying the Unit																								
TOTAL RATIONED ...																								

* In the case of field ambulances, hospitals or depots, the number of patients are to be included here, the names being shown in A. F. A. 36.

_____ Signature of Commander.

_____ Date of Despatch.

For information of the A.G.'s Office at the Base.

Officers and men who have become casuals, been transferred or joined since last report.

Place_____   Date _4/12/15_

Regtl. Number	Rank	Name	Corps	Nature of casualty, or name of unit from or to which transferred	Date of being struck off or coming on the ration return	Remarks*
959	Gr	Bodderham J	HQrs			
1060	Sgt	Roberts W				
1034	2/Bdr	Bramwell AW				
1059	a/Bdr	Wood WP				
1094	a/Bdr	Ratcliffe EA	1st Bty			
2213	Gr	Brown AW				
1065	Dr	Burrell J				
2133	Bdr	Oakey N				
2164	Gr	Cullen FCW				
2205	a/Bdr	Hughes W	2nd Bty	Granted	4/12/15	
897	Dr	Crouch W			to	
Major		Thompson SJ			11/12/15	
929	Cpl	Franklin H		Leave		
2975	Gr	Spencer F	3rd Bty			
2859	S/a/Bdr	Webb D				
2229	Dr	Davies H				
2038	"	Wheatly SB				
Capt	—	Smith Carrington MBS				
1038	Cpl	James A				
2483	a/Bdr	Summers HE	Am Col			
2022	S/S	Howles A				
1049	Gr	O'Shea D				
812	2/a/Bdr	Finch J		Posted to 1st Battery	29/11/15	
2009	do	Collison EA	1st Bty	Reverted to L.	28/11/15	(on return of 2/a/Bdr Finch)
874	Gr	Avery W	"	Signos AFW.3126	29/11/15	
	2nd Lieut	Perrins CJD	"	To Hospital	30/11/15	
2464	Gr	Stanton W	"	from "	1/12/15	
	2nd Lieut	A Bonham Edwards	"	Joined from Reinforcements	1/12/15	

* State whether absence is of a permanent or temporary nature, adding, in the case of casuals from wounds or disease, any available information for communication to the relatives.

Army Form B. 213.

FIELD RETURN.

No. of Report._____   Date._____

(To be furnished by all arms, services, and departments (except A.S.C. units) to the A. G.'s Office at the Base in accordance with Field Service Regulations, Part II.)

RETURN showing numbers RATIONED by, and Transport on charge of,_____ at _____

DETAIL	Personnel			Animals.								Guns, carriages, and limbers and transport vehicles										REMARKS
				Horses			Mules		Camels	Oxen	Guns, carriages and limbers, showing description	Ammunition wagons and limbers	Machine Guns	Aircraft, showing description	Horsed		Motor Cars	Tractors	Mechanical			
	Officers	Other ranks	Natives	Riding	Draught	Heavy Draught	Pack	Large	Small							4 Wheeled	2 Wheeled			Lorries, showing description	Trucks, showing description	Trailers	Motor Bicycles	Bicycles	
Effective Strength of Unit																									
Details, by Arms attached to unit as in War Establishment:—																									
Total																									
War Establishment																									
Wanting to complete (Detail of Personnel and Horses below)																									
Surplus																									
*Attached (not to include the details shown above)																									
Civilians:— Employed with the Unit Accompanying the Unit																									
TOTAL RATIONED ...																									

* In the case of field ambulances, hospitals or depots, the number of patients are to be included here, the names being shown in A. F. A. 36.

_____ Signature of Commander.

_____ Date of Despatch.

For information of the A.G.'s Office at the Base.

Officers and men who have become casuals, been transferred or joined since last report.

Place _____ Date 4/12/15

Regtl. Number	Rank	Name	Corps	Nature of casualty, or name of unit from or to which transferred	Date of being struck off or coming on the ration return	Remarks*
102	S/S²/B	Rea W.G.	1st Bty	To hospital	4/12/15	
3258	Dr	Fletcher E.W.	Posted to	2nd Bty	27/11/15	
2916	"	Kimberly J.	2nd Bty	from hosptl	27/11/15	
2855	"	Williams R.B.	"	" "	28/11/15	
2956	Gr	Paxton W.	"	" "	1/12/15	
2242	Dr	Wedgly H.	3rd "	" "	28/11/15	
3262	Gr	Freeman L.	Posted to	3rd Bty	29/11/15	
2999	"	Shambrook H.	3rd Bty	to hosptl	1/12/15	
2648	Dr	Micklewright H.	" "	" "	" "	
1041	"	Mallins W.	" "	" "	" "	
2nd	Lieut	Adshead F.	" "	Proceed on Arty course	2/12/15	
2064	S/a/B₃	Newman P.	" "	to hospl	4/12/15	
2000	Dr	Briggs W.	Am. Col	" "	1/12/15	
2080	"	Duffield G.	" "	" "	" "	

* State whether absence is of a permanent or temporary nature, adding, in the case of casuals from wounds or disease, any available information for communication to the relatives.

Army Form B. 213.

FIELD RETURN.

(To be furnished by all arms, services, and departments (except A.S.C. units) to the A. G.'s Office at the Base in accordance with Field Service Regulations, Part II.)

No. of Report _____

RETURN showing numbers RATIONED by, and Transport on charge of, _____ at _____ Date. _____

DETAIL.	Personnel			Animals.								Guns, carriages, and limbers and transport vehicles										REMARKS
	Officers	Other ranks	Natives	Horses			Mules		Camels	Oxen		Guns, carriages and limbers, showing description	Ammunition wagons and limbers	Machine guns	Aircraft, showing description	Horsed		Motor Cars	Tractors	Mechanical			
				Riding	Draught	Heavy Draught	Pack	Large	Small								4 Wheeled	2 Wheeled			Lorries, showing description	Trucks, showing description	Trailers	Motor Bicycles	Bicycles	

Effective Strength of Unit

Details, by *Arms* attached to unit as in War Establishment :—

Total

War Establishment

Wanting to complete
(Detail of Personnel and Horses below)

Surplus

*Attached (not to include the details shown above)

Civilians :—
Employed with the Unit
Accompanying the Unit

TOTAL RATIONED ...

* In the case of field ambulances, hospitals or depots, the number of patients are to be included here, the names being shown in A. F. A. 36.

_____ Signature of Commander.

_____ Date of Despatch.

2 S.M. قحط A.F.A.

Jam

vol XI

WAR DIARY
or
INTELLIGENCE SUMMARY

(Erase heading not required.)

Army Form C. 2118

Place	Date	Hour	Summary of Events and Information	Remarks and references to Appendices
BAYENCOURT	1/1/16		Uneventful	
	2/1/16	4.30 p.m	Germans shewed SAILLY-au-BOIS. heavier. Heavies replied.	W.P.b.
	3/1/16		Ordinary retaliations.	W.P.b.
	4/1/16		" "	W.P.b.
			G.O.C. R.A. inspected Wagon lines. Commander-in-chief inspected positions. Lt-Col. E.C. Burrow to one Major. g.w. Taylor, 2 W ov. Bty. Sgt-Major Winger A.J., 12th W ov. Bty. Waverley in dugouts.	W.P.b.
	5/1/16	10.00 a.m	Germans shelled 2nd W ove. Bty. position K.1. ½. 2. 3. (Sheet 57 D. N.E. 1:20,000).	W.P.b.
	6/1/16	—	Ordinary retaliations. Party doing musketry course in trenches	W.P.b.
	7/1/16		" " " "	W.P.b.
	8/1/16	3.30 pm	Germans shelled SAILLY-AU-BOIS severely. Heavies replied.	W.P.b.
	9/1/16		Ordinary retaliations. Party in trenches doing musketry	W.P.b.
		4.45 pm	Course	
	10/1/16		Ordinary retaliations.	W.P.b.
	11/1/16		" "	W.P.b.
	12/1/16		" "	W.P.b.

Army Form C. 2118

WAR DIARY
or
INTELLIGENCE SUMMARY
(Erase heading not required.)

Instructions regarding War Diaries and Intelligence Summaries are contained in F. S. Regs., Part II. and the Staff Manual respectively. Title Pages will be prepared in manuscript.

Place	Date	Hour	Summary of Events and Information	Remarks and references to Appendices
BAYENCOURT	13/1/16		Ordinary retaliations	WD.6.
	14/1/16		"	WD.6.
	15/1/16		"	WD.6.
	16/1/16		C.O. went to Senior Officers' Course BEAUVAL. Lt. Col. W. E. Walker	WD.6.
	17/1/16		"	WD.6.
	18/1/16		have Bde. attached to Brigade for 4 days. Ordinary retaliations	WD.6.
	19/1/16		"	WD.6.
	20/1/16	4.30pm	Germans shelled heavily round 3rd Wor. Bty position at K 3 a. 8. 2. (51 D NE 1/20000)	WD.6.
	21/1/16		(ordinary retaliations)	WD.6.
	22/1/16		C.O. returned from course.	WD.6.
	23/1/16	2.30pm	Continued Bombardment of enemy's trenches, works & village. Wire cutting.	WD.6.
	24/1/16		"	WD.6.
	25/1/16	2.0am	Heavy bombardment by enemy along whole Bde. front, 8th W. Div. alignment of Trenches from enemy evident.	WD.6. WD.6. WD.6.
	26/1/16		Ineffectual	
	27/1/16	7.20 pm	G.A.S. alarm received. Batteries "Stood to" "Green" "Red" "Orange" "Stood to"	WD.6. WD.6.
		8.10		

WAR DIARY
INTELLIGENCE SUMMARY
(Erase heading not required.)

Army Form C. 2118

Place	Date	Hour	Summary of Events and Information	Remarks and references to Appendices
BAYENCOURT	27/1/16	8.55 p.m.	"Stand down" received	W.P.C.
	29/1/16	2.30 a.m.	Continued Bombardment of enemy's trenches. Began Co-operated with 3rd S.M.F.A. Bde.	
		7.25 a.m.	"G.A.S." alarm received. "Began" Stood to.	W.P.C.
		8.15 "	"Stand Down" received	
	29/1/16	6.45 "	"G.A.S." alarm received. Began Stood to again	W.P.C.
		7.40 "	"Stand Down" received	
	30/1/16	4.0 a.m.	Continued bombardments of enemy trenches with 3rd S.M.F.A.Bde. 6th Gloucester Fusiliers went into German trenches at Souchez and at GOMMECOURT WOOD 5th Warwicks made to go over owing to mist. Major Lottery went on Senior Officers course at BEAUVAL	W.P.C.
	31/1/16		Muscetive	W.P.C.

31/1/16.

P.C. Bullock
Lieut Colonel,
Comdg. 2nd South Midland F.A. Bde.

Army Form O. 1810.
All Arms.

Each issue of orders will be numbered consecutively throughout the year. A fresh series will be commenced with the first issue in each year.

Unit _____

DAILY ORDERS. Part II.

No. _____

Station _____
Date 1st January 1916

Imp. Hav. — 5,000

Sub. No. of Order.	Subject.	Regimental No., Rank and Name.			Sqdn. Batty or Co.	Particulars of Casualties &c., and date
		No	Rank			
		Surg	Major	Oldham A.B.	H Qrs	
		2/Lieut.		Thacker W.J	3rd Bty	
		1076	Dr	Bright A.B	1st "	
		1078	Gr	Davis W.H.	" "	
		2767	"	Stanton. W.W.	" "	
		2041	"	Scott W.	2nd "	Granted Leave from 2-1-16 to 10-1-16
		863	Bdr	Chidgey H.	" "	
		878	Gr.	Gwilliam. A	" "	
		2209	Dr.	Bennett. G.	3rd "	
		2946	Gr.	Colman G.	" "	
		2414	a/Bdr	Coombs. J.	" "	
		2908	Gr.	Jines. G.	A.Col	
		2183	Bdr	Davis J.S.	" "	
		3014	Dr.	Baldwin W.	" "	
		864	Sgt	Hurons. B.	" "	
		2215	Dr	Bowers F.	H.Qrs	
		2811	Gr	Tranter. F.	2nd Bty	26-12-15
		2642	Dr	Oliver E.W	" "	28-12-15
		1034	Bdr.	Bramwich A.	1st "	30-12-15	Discharges from Hospital
		3258	Dr	Fletcher. E.W	2nd "	31-12-15
		2853	"	Whitehouse E.	" "	31-12-15
		2605	Gr.	Lawley. G.	1st "	26-12-15
		747	Sgt	Darke. A.	" "	1-1-16
		308	"	Warby. H.	3rd "	24-12-15
		3243	Dr	Smith. A	A.Col	28-12-15
		3050	"	Bishton. G.	" "	30-12-15

Officer Commanding *or* Adjutant.

Army Form O. 1810.
All Arms.

Each issue of orders will be numbered consecutively throughout the year. A fresh series will be commenced with the first issue in each year.

Unit _____

DAILY ORDERS. Part II.

No. _____

Station _____

Date _1st January 1916_

Imp. Hav. — 5,000

Sub. No. of Order.	Subject.	Regimental No., Rank and Name.		Sqdn. Batty or Co.	Particulars of Casualties &c., and date
		No	Rank		
		747	Sgt.	Darke. A.	1st Bty	— 28-12-15
		1022	a/Bdr	Raby A.W.	"	1-1-16
		893	Bdr	Haughton G.	2nd "	Admitted 29-12-15
		3258	Dr.	Fletcher E.W.	" "	to 28-12-15
		2853	"	Whitehouse E.	" "	28-12-15
		1024	Cpl.	Hood A.G.	" "	Hospital 30-12-15
		2651	Gr.	Morris G.	3rd "	29-12-15
		997	"	Grubb F.	" "	31-12-15
		2/Lieut. —		Lines. H.D.	A. Col.	Joined from 3/2nd S.M.B. RFA 28/12/15.
		308.	Sgt.	Warby H.	3rd Bty	Awaiting Disposal on finding of Court of enquiry Re injury caused by neglect
		2/	Lieut	Edwards A.B.	1st Bty	Returned from Artillery School, HAVERNAS. 1-1-16.
		963	Cpl.	Cameron H.J.R.	2nd "	
		2941	Gr	Evans H.C.	3rd Bty	Evacuated to Base 4-12-15
		834	"	Taylor. H.	2nd "	" ENGLAND 15-12-15
		962	A/Bdr	Ashwin R.	" "	" BASE 19-11-15
		2489	Gr	Smith. F.	HQrs	" 26-11-15
		850	Bdr.	Caldwell. G.A.	2nd Bty	Sent to Base 2-1-16 for discharge 16-1-16 Struck off Strength

Officer Commanding or Adjutant.

Army Form O. 1810.
All Arms.

Each issue of orders will be numbered consecutively throughout the year. A fresh series will be commenced with the first issue in each year.

Unit _____

DAILY ORDERS. Part II.

No. _____

Station _____
Date 8th January 1916

Imp. Hav. — 5.000

Sub. No.of Order.	Subject.	Regimental No., Rank and Name.	Sqdn. Batty or Co.	Particulars of Casualties &c., and date
		No / Rank		
		2835 / Dr. / Wintle C.	1st Bty	7-1-16 ⎫
		428 / Sgt Fit / Bicks J.	2nd "	2-1-16 ⎪
		347 / Bdr / Allen	" "	2-1-16 ⎬ To Hospital
		2018 / Dr. / Saunders J.	" "	6-1-16 ⎪
		2243 / a/Bdr / Hicks C.	3rd "	4-1-16 ⎪
		2221 / Dr. / Grainger A.	HQrs	5-1-16 ⎭
		499 / Gr. / Maullin W.	2nd Bty	2-1-16 in ENGLAND
		2/Lieut. / Perrins C.F.D.	1st Bty	Date 3-1-16 – Discharged from Highland 868
		2945 / Gr. / Maynard J.	2nd "	7-1-16 from hospital
		2651 / " / Morris G.	3rd "	6-1-16 "
		3057 / Gr. / Trehearn P.A.	HQ	transferred from Am Col. 8-1-16
		2/Lieut. / Lane W.V.	A Col	Joined from 3/2nd SMFA Bde 7-12-15
		308 / Sgt / Warby H.	3rd Bty	Tried by F.G.C.M. (acquitted) 3-1-16
		2425 / Gr. / Cooke J.	" "	transferred from 48th SM Div Sub. Park 13-11-15

Officer Commanding or Adjutant.

Army Form O. 1810.
All Arms.

Each issue of orders will be numbered consecutively throughout the year. A fresh series will be commenced with the first issue in each year.

Unit _____

DAILY ORDERS. Part II.

No. _____

Station _____
Date 8th January 1916

Imp. Hav. — 5,000

Sub. No. of Order	Subject	Regimental No., Rank and Name	Sqdn. Batty or Co.	Particulars of Casualties &c., and date
		No / Rank		
		949 / Gr / Smart E.H.	1st Bty	Rejoined from Arty Course 2-1-16
		1020 / Bdr / Bacon G.P.	" "	Reduced to ranks by FGCM 3-1-16
		519 / Sgt / Boulton G.	2nd "	Allotment of Pay 3d incrd to Mother - 6d for wife 6-11-15
		850 / Bdr / Caldwell G.	" "	Sent to Base pending discharge 2-1-16
		2/Lieut / Smith S.H.	3rd "	} Proceeds on Civil Administration 4-1-16
		1058 / Gr / Beaman F.	" "	
		2/Lieut / Smith S.H.	" "	} return from ditto 6-1-16
		1058 / Gr / Beaman F.	" "	
		2686 / SS / Howes	Ambol	} Re-inforcements Joined from DAC 6-1-16
		3249 / Dr / Birch	"	
		3316 / " / Badham	"	
		3286 / Dr / James		
		3498 / " / Parks		
		3246 / " / Prior	Ambol	} Reinforcements Joined from 4th Bde 6-1-16
		3290 / " / Reeves		
		3245 / " / Smith		
		3230 / " / Thompson		

Officer Commanding or Adjutant.

Army Form O. 1810
All Arms.

Each issue of orders will be numbered consecutively throughout the year. A fresh series will be commenced with the first issue in each year.

Unit _____

DAILY ORDERS. Part II.

No. _____

Station _____
Date 15th January 1916

Imp. Hav. — 5,000

Sub. No. of Order.	Subject.	Regimental No., Rank and Name.			Sqdn. Batty or Co.	Particulars of Casualties &c., and date
		No	Rank			
		946	Cpl	Dowey R.P.C	1st Bty	
		949	Gr	Smart E.H.	"	
		1085	"	Reynolds W.H.	"	
		2435	"	Rowbotham	2nd	
		881	"	Hart F.W.	"	
			2/Lieut	Adshead H.H.	3rd	Granted Leave
		2255	Bdr.	Canty H.	"	from 10/1/16 to 17/1/16
		113	Dr	Wharriad. H	"	
		2413	a/Bdr	Potter. W	"	
		2450	Bdr	Elt. E.	A Col	
		2444	Gr	Steward H	"	
		2206	Dr	Morris H	HQ.	
		2303	Bdr.	Stroud. E	A Col	
		864	Sgt.	Truscon G.C.	2nd Bty	Granted 1 months 3-2-16 leave on Completion of AFW. 3126 = 26-2-16
		862	Dr	McCann C	"	
						leave 10-1-16 to 9-2-16
		2488	Gr	Gillam J.W.	Am Col	13-1-16 to Hospital
		2828	Dr	Thorn C	"	13-1-16
		2064	Gr	Newman P.	3rd Bty	evacuated struck off strength. TO ENGLAND 27/12/15 per H.S. St George 23-12-15
		2243	Bdr	Hicks. E.	3rd	appointed Pay Sergt 30-11-15

Officer Commanding or Adjutant.

Army Form O. 1810.
All Arms.

Each issue of orders will be numbered consecutively throughout the year. A fresh series will be commenced with the first issue in each year.

Unit _____

DAILY ORDERS. Part II.

No. _____

Station _____
Date _____

Imp. Hav. — 5,000

Sub. No. of Order.	Subject.	Regimental No., Rank and Name.	Sqdn. Batty or Co.	Particulars of Casualties &c., and date	
	✓	No Rank			
		2606 Dr Lewis W.E.	1st Bty	to hospital	11-1-16
		3049 Gr Leppard W.J.	"	" "	13-1-16
		2405 Dr Cookson J.G.	"	" "	14-1-16
		2640 Gr McLean J.	2nd	" "	9-1-16
		2264 Dr Meale	"	" "	14-1-16
		2068 Gr Field E.	3rd	" "	11-1-16
		1059 a/Bdr Wood J.G.R.	1st	Promoted to Bdr in place of No 1020 Bdr Bacon G.P. reduced to ranks	4-1-16
		2009 S/a/Bdr Collinson E.V.	1st	To be paid a/Bdr in place of a/Bdr Wood, promoted Bdr from	4-1-16
		2495 Gr Hart A.W.	1st	Transferred to ENGLAND (Struck off strength)	29-11-15
		2842 Gr Wright L.O.	1st	Struck off Strength Authority A.G. G.H.Q. of/443/dated 8-1-16	15-1-16
		850 Bdr Caldwell G.	2nd	Struck off Strength time expired to BASE pending discharge	15-1-16
		799 Gr Hamlin	2nd	retd from leave & hospital in ENGLAND	14-1-16
		803 Bdr Vale E.	3rd	Re-engaged completed A.F.W. 3126	4-1-16
		2046 Cpl Crow J.	3rd	evacuated struck off strength. To ENGLAND 23/12/15 per H.S. "St. George"	23-12-15

Officer Commanding or Adjutant.

Army Form O. 1810.
All Arms.

Each issue of orders will be numbered consecutively throughout the year. A fresh series will be commenced with the first issue in each year.

Unit _____

DAILY ORDERS. Part II.

No. _____

Station _____

Date 15th January 1916

Sub. No. of Order.	Subject.	Regimental No., Rank and Name.			Sqdn. Batty or Co.	Particulars of Casualties &c., and date	
		No	Rank				
		2221	Dr.	Grainger A	HQ.	from hospital	9-1-16
		1022	a/Bdr	Raby W.A.	1st Bty	" "	14-1-16
		3079	Gr.	Leppard W.J.	" "	" "	14-1-16
		893	Bdr.	Haughton G.	2nd -	" "	9-1-16
		344	"	Allen W.R.	" "	" "	14-1-16
		2243	"	Hicks E.	3rd -	" "	9-1-16
		2068	Gr.	Field E.	" "	" "	15-1-16
		323	Cpl.	Pulley G.	3rd -	Promoted Sgt vice Lissetter	30-11-15
		1041	Bdr.	James A	" "	" Cpl vice Pulley	" "
		2243	a/Bdr	Hicks E	" "	" Bdr - James	" "
		940	S/a/Bdr	Grubb W	" "	" " " Yates	11-12-15
		2356	Gr.	Bantam W.	" "	" a/Bdr - Grubb	30-12-15
		2944	Dr.	Jones A	" "	" " " Hicks	6-11-15
		858	Dr.	Roberts E.	A Col.	Struck off Strength (time expired) (BASE pending discharge)	8-1-16
		206	Cpl.	Evans W	" "	Struck off strength evacuated	To ENGLAND 24/12/15 per H.S. St George
		3470	Gr.	Pagett H.W.	" "	Struck off strength authority a/ GHQ D/443/ dated 8-1-16	15-1-16
		3100	Dr.	Morris	" "	Re-inforcement joined from 4th Bde (in hospital)	6-1-16
		541	Dr.	Harbrow W	HQ.	Struck off strength (time expired)	14-1-16

Officer Commanding or Adjutant.

Army Form O. 1810.
All Arms.

Each issue of orders will be numbered consecutively throughout the year. A fresh series will be commenced with the first issue in each year.

Unit _____

DAILY ORDERS. Part II.

No. _____

Station _____
Date 22nd January 1916

Imp. Hav. — 5,000

Sub. No. of Order.	Subject.	Regimental No., Rank and Name.			Sqdn. Batty or Co.	Particulars of Casualties &c., and date	
		No	Rank				
		2835	Dr.	Wintle C.	18 Bty	from hospital	19-1-16
		3041	Gr.	Freeman	2nd	" "	14-1-16
		2254	Dr.	Stanley W.	A Col	" "	19-1-16
		2828	—	Thorn E.	"	" "	18-1-16
		2606	Dr.	Lewis W.	1st Bty	Transferred to C.C.S. 16=1=16	
			Major	Lattey J.C.	"	Granted leave	
		2009	a/Bdr	Collinson E.A.	1st Bty	14-1-16	
		2014	Sptr	Ruff F.	"	to	
		950	Gr.	Astings C.	2nd		
		2243	Bdr	Hicks E.	3rd	24-1-16	
		1054	Gr.	Fox J.	"		
		1040	Bdr	Sector A.	A Col		
		2364	Gr.	Blick J.	"		
		3061	Dr.	Barnett H.	"		
		2626	Gr.	Terry S.	"		
		24885	BSM	Sinclair B.	HQrs		
		2214	Dr.	Burrows L.	"		
		1038	Cpl.	James A.			
		2021	Sd	Howles A.		Granted Proficiency Pay Class II from 5=8=15	
		2022	Sd	Palfrey S.	A Column		
		1099	Gr.	Booton C.			
		3052	—	Boucher W.G.			

Officer Commanding or Adjutant.

Army Form O. 1810.
All Arms.

Each issue of orders will be numbered consecutively throughout the year. A fresh series will be commenced with the first issue in each year.

Unit _____

DAILY ORDERS. Part II.

No. _____

Station _____
Date 22nd January 1916

Imp. Hav. — 5,000

Sub. No. of Order.	Subject.	Regimental No., Rank and Name.	Sqdn. Batty or Co.	Particulars of Casualties &c., and date	
		120 Rank Capt Dicey J.C.	HQ.	appointed adjutant as from Authority 3rd Army AMS/914.	16-10-15
		494 Bdr Cox W	1st Bty	To hospital	18-1-16
		2059 Gr Tyler J	2nd	"	18-1-16
		2548 Dr Jennings J	"	"	19-1-16
		2924 " Partridge R	"	"	"
		2313 " Allsopp W	"	"	"
		424 Gr Hayter W.H	3rd	"	16-1-16
		1000 Dr Willis F	"	"	22-1-16
		924 a/Bdr Elcock R.W	HQ.	"	20-1-16
		Lieut Col Bullock C.C.	HQ.	Proceeds on Senior Officers Course	16-1-16
		2221 Dr Grainger A	"		
		Lieut Col Bullock C.C.	"	retd from	21-1-16
		2221 Dr Grainger A	"		
		2nd/Lieut Gascoyne G	3rd	Joined from 3/2nd SMFA Bde.	22-1-16
		2430 Dr Rusburn W.H	1st	Attached to 48th Divl Hdqrs. R.A.	21-1-16
		54 BSM Hayward W.H	2nd	6 months leave. Struck off strength, Authority AG GHQ A/9411/d/ 29/11/15 Completed A.F.W.3126	15-1-16

Officer Commanding or Adjutant.

Army Form O. 1810.
All Arms.

Each issue of orders will be numbered consecutively throughout the year. A fresh series will be commenced with the first issue in each year.

Unit _____

DAILY ORDERS. Part II.

No. _____

Station _____
Date 22nd January 1916

Imp. Hav. — 5,000

Sub. No. of Order.	Subject.	Regimental No., Rank and Name	Sqdn. Batty or Co.	Particulars of Casualties &c., and date	
		No.	RANK			completed AFW 3126
		481	Gr. Wilcox A.	2nd Bty	on months leave struck off strength Authority Ag. GHQ A/9711/d/29/11/15	21-1-16
		66	BSM Heath R.	3rd	ditto	14-1-16
			2/Lieut. Williams C	..	} Proceeds on Arty Course.	14-1-16
		323	Sgt. Pulley G	..		
		—	Gr. Waldron	..		
		308	Sgt. Warby H.	..	} Proceeds on Munition test	18-1-16
		2144	Cpl. Harris S	..		
		2488	Dr. Kite F S	A Bty	} Re-inforcements Joined.	19-1-16
		3116	" Watkins E. J	—		
		3201	" Baylis G.	—		
		3243	" Harmer R J	—		
		3226	" Joyner R J	—		

Officer Commanding *or* Adjutant.

Army Form O. 1810.
All Arms.

Each issue of orders will be numbered consecutively throughout the year. A fresh series will be commenced with the first issue in each year.

Unit _____

DAILY ORDERS. Part II.

No.

Station
Date 29th January 1916

Imp. Hav. — 5,000

Sub. No. of Order.	Subject.	Regimental No., Rank and Name.			Sqdn. Batty or Co.	Particulars of Casualties &c., and date	
		No	Rank				
		2606	Dr.	Lewis W.H.	1st Bty	Sent to C.C.S 16/1/16 (Struck off strength)	28-1-16
		2015	a/Bdr	Underhill H.	"	To ENGLAND 1/1/16 per H.S. St. PATRICK. (Struck off strength)	28-1-16
		3315	Dr.	Hopkins J.H.	"	Reinforcements joined.	24-1-16
		763	a/Bdr	Chidgey H.	2nd	Promoted to Bdr vice Bdr Caldwell (discharged)	24-1-16
		2248	Gr	Rogers W.	"	Appointed a/Bdr vice a/Bdr Chidgey	24-1-16
		428	Sergt	Bick J.		to C.C.S. 3-1-16	
		1024	Cpl	Hoond A.G.	2nd Bty	" " 9-1-16	28-1-16
		2313	Dr	Allsopp W.		" " 20-1-16	
		2264	"	Keale A.		" " 22-1-16	
						all Struck off strength	
		3481	Dr	Wilde F	2nd Bty	Reinforcement joined	24-1-16
		929	Cpl	Franklin H.	3rd Bty		
		1041	"	James A.	"	Proceeds on Trench Mortar Course	26-1-16
		2951	Gr	Hales F.			
		425	"	Carpenter J.			

Officer Commanding or Adjutant.

Army Form O. 1810.
All Arms.

Each issue of orders will be numbered consecutively throughout the year. A fresh series will be commenced with the first issue in each year.

Unit _____

DAILY ORDERS. Part II.

No. _____

Station _____

Date 29th January 1916

Sub. No. of Order.	Subject.	Regimental No., Rank and Name.		Sqdn., Batty. or Co.	Particulars of Casualties, &c., and date.	
		No	Rank			
		3391	Dr	Watts T.B.	3rd Bty	Reinforcements Joined	24-1-16
		3396	"	Baddeley E.H.	"		
		554	BSM	Hayward M.J.	A. Bat.	Proceeded to Base pending discharge (Struck off Strength)	25-1-16
		1054	Bdr	Heath G.	3rd Bty	Granted Leave 24-1-16 to 31-1-16	
		2583	"	Jay W.W.	"		
		2947	a/Bdr	Jones. A.	"		
		2006	Bdr	Gwilliams H.	A Bat.		
		2023	Gr	Hardeman J			
		2989	Dr	Darnsley L.H.			
		435	Sgt	Kettle H.	A Bat.	in ENGLAND Authority GHQ. (Struck off Strength)	25-1-16
		2/	Lieut	Williams C.	3rd Bty	Retd from Arty Course	28-1-16
		323	Sgt	Pulley G.	"		
			Gr	Waldron			
		3244	Gr	Crowther H.	A Bat.	transferred to H.Q.	29-1-16
		2013	Dr	Ratcliffe D	H.Q.	To 66 Stn. (Struck off Strength)	29-1-16

Officer Commanding or Adjutant.

Army Form O. 1810.
All Arms.

Each issue of orders will be numbered consecutively throughout the year. A fresh series will be commenced with the first issue in each year.

Unit _____

DAILY ORDERS. Part II.

No. _____

Station _____

Date 29th January

Sub. No. of Order.	Subject.	Regimental No., Rank and Name.			Sqdn. Batty or Co.	Particulars of Casualties &c., and date	
		No.	Rank				
		2221	Dr	Grainger A	HQ	To Hospital	24-1-16
		2052	Gr	Rea. A E	2nd Bty	"	23-1-16
		2292	"	Delahey J.W.	"	"	26-1-16
		2068	"	Field. E	3rd	"	24-1-16
		3064	Dr	Barnett H	A Col	(while on leave ENGLAND)	
		466	"	Sollars F	ASC	"	24-1-16
		2221	Dr	Grainger. A	HQ	From Hospital	27-1-16
		2640	Gr	McLean F	2nd Bty	"	23-1-16
		2059	"	Tyler. J	"	"	27-1-16
		2287	"	Baylis A	A Col	"	22-1-16
		2/Lieut		Woods W A	2nd Bty	Granted Leave from 24-1-16 to 31-1-16	
		2/Lieut		Turpin J A	A C		
		259	Gr	Keyte C E	HQ		
		2016	Dr	Wall P	1st Bty		
		2024	Gr	Evans H G	"		
		2030	Dr	Hall G.	"		
		2664	Gr	Holt H	2nd		
		1016	"	Evans G	"		

Officer Commanding or Adjutant.

CONFIDENTIAL

WAR DIARY.

of

2nd S.M.F.A. Bde.

From 1/2/16 to 29/2/16.

(Volume ~~XIII~~ XII)

48

1/2 S M Bde R.F.A
Vol XIII

WAR DIARY
or
INTELLIGENCE SUMMARY

Army Form C. 2118

Place	Date	Hour	Summary of Events and Information	Remarks and references to Appendices
BAYENCOURT	1/2/16	2.30pm	1st WORC BTY shelled enemy's system of trenches in conjunction with howitzers uneventful enemy retaliation	W.S.6.
	2/2/16		" " "	W.S.6.
	3/2/16		" " "	W.S.6.
	4/2/16		Major Hartley returned from Course at BEAUVAL	W.S.6.
	5/2/16		Ranging with aeroplane	W.S.6.
	6/2/16		" " "	W.S.6.
	7/2/16		" " "	W.S.6.
	8/2/16		German artillery active. Doing much ranging.	W.S.6.
	9/2/16		" " "	W.S.6.
	10/2/16		" " "	W.S.6.
	11/2/16		" " " Gun Brooks. 2nd Bty kicked	W.S.6.
	12/2/16	2.30 am	Brigade Bombarded enemy trenches	W.S.6.
		of hr	" " "	W.S.6.
	13/2/16		Artillery active on both sides	W.S.6.
		12midnight	Brigade bombarded enemy trenches	W.S.6.
	14/2/16		Continual shelling on intercommunication trenches throughout the day. Casualties in 1st Bty.	W.S.6.
	15/2/16		Fairly quiet.	W.S.6.

Army Form C. 2118

WAR DIARY
or
INTELLIGENCE SUMMARY
(Erase heading not required.)

Instructions regarding War Diaries and Intelligence Summaries are contained in F. S. Regs., Part II. and the Staff Manual respectively. Title Pages will be prepared in manuscript.

Place	Date	Hour	Summary of Events and Information	Remarks and references to Appendices
BAYENCOURT.	16/2/16	11.30 pm	2 nd Worc. Bty bombarded enemy system of trenches in front of GOMMECOURT	W.R.C.
	17/2/16		Fairly quiet.	W.R.C.
	18/2/16	11.35 am	Heavy hostile bombardment on Brigade front. Germans attacked Brigade on our left. 2 nd worc. Bty came into action.	W.R.C.
	19/2/16	6.45	Heavy hostile Bombardments on part of our Zone. Some shells passed forward Bde H.Q. K.T.C. (Sheet 57 d NE 20000)	W.R.C.
	20.2.16.		Quiet day.	J.C.D
	21.2.16.	10.38 pm	Brigade bombarded Rosdel and trenches round GOMMECOURT.	J.C.D
	"		Quiet day.	J.C.D
	22.2.16	11.30 pm	Uneventful day. Brigade bombarded enemies front- and 2nd line trenches - 1st howitz Battery assisted. German reply feeble	J.C.D
	23.2.16.	-	Uneventful.	J.C.D
	24.2.16	-	Uneventful.	J.C.D
	25.2.16	-	Uneventful.	J.C.D
	26.2.16.	-	Uneventful	J.C.D
	27.2.16	-	Uneventful.	J.C.D
	28.2.16	-	Enemy shelled FONQUEVILLERS during day.	J.C.D
	29.2.16.	-	German Artillery Action. Several German aeroplanes	J.C.D

Army Form C. 2118

WAR DIARY
or
INTELLIGENCE SUMMARY
(Erase heading not required.)

Instructions regarding War Diaries and Intelligence Summaries are contained in F.S. Regs., Part II. and the Staff Manual respectively. Title Pages will be prepared in manuscript.

Place	Date	Hour	Summary of Events and Information	Remarks and references to Appendices
SAILLY.	1.3.16		2's Womens Battery moved one section to front W9 FONQUEVILLERS. Enemy artillery quiet.	W.S.E.
	2.3.16.	7 pm	Enemy artillery more active 16 day. 1st Battery dummy position heavily shelled. 2d Battery moved manning section to new position.	W.S.E.
	3.3.16		Uneventful. Both sides quiet. Major Harvey commanding Bty. 2nd Bty registering new position. Major Harvey commanding Bty. this leave being extended.	W.S.E.
	4.3.16		Uneventful on both sides	W.S.E.
	5.3.16		" " " None retaliation.	W.S.E.
	6.3.16		" " " 2/Lt B.H.B. Ames went to 36 th Division on being appointed to regular commission.	W.S.E.
	7.3.16		Uneventful. None retaliation.	W.S.E.
	8.3.16	6 pm	1 American Div Wounded Brig. under orders to move to new position S.E. of CHATEAU LA NIEPE.	W.S.E.
	9.3.16	8 pm	Uneventful. Remaining section of 2 nd Bty returned to original position.	W.S.E.
	10.3.16	10.30 pm	Uneventful. Batteries regaining section to the limit of their arc. To be able to concentrate Barrage if necessary on enemy bombardment on our nights. Has nature unknown	W.S.E.

Army Form C. 2118

WAR DIARY
or
INTELLIGENCE SUMMARY
(Erase heading not required.)

Instructions regarding War Diaries and Intelligence Summaries are contained in F. S. Regs., Part II. and the Staff Manual respectively. Title Pages will be prepared in manuscript.

Place	Date	Hour	Summary of Events and Information	Remarks and references to Appendices
BAYENCOURT	11.3.16		Uneventful. Usual retaliations and registerings. Batteries all working hard on alternative positions and wire cutting positions.	W.P.C.
	12.3.16		Uneventful. New instruments for positions allocated by G.O.C. R.A.	W.P.C.
	13.3.16		Uneventful.	W.P.C.
	14.3.16		" Choosing O.P.s for 2nd & D. handing over positions to 2nd Divisional line.	
		3.6 p.m.	Lt.-Col. J.R. Colville D.S.O. 83rd Bde. arrived and assumed command; Lt.-Col. E.C. Balfour C.B. being gazetted to T.F. Reserve.	W.P.C.
	15.3.16		Uneventful. Forward H.Q. at K 7 c 4.5. given up. Scheme concentrated on BAYENCOURT	W.P.C.
	16.3.16		Uneventful. Work on communications for a progress rais	W.P.C.
	17.3.16		Uneventful	W.P.C.
	18.3.16		"	W.P.C.
	19.3.16	10.0 p.m. 2-3 am	Bombardment of enemy trenches in preparation for raid. Heavy bombardments to nights of our being raided on enemy raid on left given information	W.P.C.
	20.3.16	12.0 midnight	proved this to be an enemy raid. Bombardments of enemy trenches	W.P.C.
	21.3.16	1 am	" " " Uneventful uneventful	W.P.C.

Army Form C. 2118

WAR DIARY
or
INTELLIGENCE SUMMARY
(Erase heading not required.)

Instructions regarding War Diaries and Intelligence Summaries are contained in F.S. Regs., Part II. and the Staff Manual respectively. Title Pages will be prepared in manuscript.

Place	Date	Hour	Summary of Events and Information	Remarks and references to Appendices
BAYENCOURT	22-3-16		Inconspicuous. Finishing trenches being made to preparations for projected raid.	W.S.6.
	23-3-16	1.15	Bombardment opened for raid.	
			1) Trenches E.28.b. Central	
			2) " K.4.d. "	
		2.25 am	Party from 8th Royal Warwick Regt. entered trenches in E.28.b. Central and secured one prisoner (one Pte Ke.L. party being of 8 Bavs). Bombardments ceased. (See separate report.)	
		2.45 am	Heavy German bombardment of trenches in front of FONQUEVILLERS the village itself.	
		1.0 pm	3 or big movements in conjunction with Heavies, GOMMECOURT PARC and trenches in front. Inconspicuous. communication trenches and listed firing.	W.S.6. W.S.6. W.S.6. W.S.6. W.S.6.
	24-3-16		" "	W.S.6.
	25-3-16		" "	
	26-3-16		" "	
	27-3-16		" "	
	28/3/16		Inconspicuous	W.S.6
	29-3-16		Arrival of drafts from what is known as "D" vacancy of Mr. Burnsley, 2nd Lu Gregory J.B.C. & A. from no Battery to Billeted at THIEVRES, & 2nd Lu Cole arrived with drafts.	W.S.6.

Army Form C. 2118

WAR DIARY
or
INTELLIGENCE SUMMARY
(Erase heading not required.)

Instructions regarding War Diaries and Intelligence Summaries are contained in F. S. Regs., Part II. and the Staff Manual respectively. Title Pages will be prepared in manuscript.

Place	Date	Hour	Summary of Events and Information	Remarks and references to Appendices
BAYENCOURT	30/3/16		Capt Sutherland (Am. Col. 3rd S.M.[?].B.[?].) assumed command of D. Bty. B.Cy composed of 1 ammunition from 1, 2, 3 infre. Bty's from Am Col. directed being taken in to Batterie to complete.	WSL
	31/3/16	1.30.	Germans shelled FONQUEVILLERS. No casualties. No. 15 complete transfers of men to complete Battery effected.	WSL

Appended.
1) Casualties.
2) Report on raid.

31/3/16

9 [signature]
Lieut. Colonel,
Comdg. 2nd South Midland F.A. Bde.

Report of action of 2nd S.M.F.A.Bde. and 1st Batt: 3rd S.M.F.A.
Bde. in support of 143rd Inf:Bde on night of 22/23rd March 1916.
===

RIGHT ATTACK.
The 3/2nd Batt.and 1/3rd Batt.were detailed in support
of right attack. Major Thompson commanded the 2 Batts.and remained
with the Officer Commanding the attack at Post 5. This Post was
connected by telephone with both batts. with my own post,and with
Hdqrs. of left attack, in each case by several alternative lines.

As the 2 attacks were timed to start simultaneously, the order for
all guns to commence was issued direct to all batts. by the Officer
Commanding the Artillery of the left attack.

1st Phase. At 1-15 a.m. the order "Fire" was given. The 3/2nd batt.
and 1 section 1/3rd batt.fired for 6 minutes,at section fire 5
seconds,with shrapnel on proposed point of entry and front line trenche
North and South of it,while the remaining section of 1/3rd batt.fired
shrapnel and H.E.,at section fire 10 seconds,on the support trenches
behind point of entry.

2nd Phase. At the conclusion of 6 minutes,the 1 section of the 1/3rd
batt.lifted it's fire and reinforced the barrage on support trenches,
at section fire 10 seconds,while 2 guns of the 3/2nd batt.kept up a
fire at 3 rounds per minute on Machine gun emplacements north and
south of point of entry. The remaining section ceased firing.

3rd Phase. At 2-15 a.m. the Officer Commanding the attack reported to
Major Thompson that his men were clear of the trenches and the 3/2nd
batt.re-opened it's original barrage at section fire 5 seconds,
dropping to 10 seconds after 2 minutes,when 1 section 1/3rd batt.
reinforced this barrage,while the remaining section continued to fire
on support trenches at section fire 30 seconds. A few minutes later the
officer commanding the attack requested Major Thompson to cease
firing as he thought if he did so that the German fire might also
cease. At 2-25 a.m. both batts. ceased firing.
    Direct telephonic communication to both batts.was cut by shell
fire towards end of 2nd phase but communication,by previously
arranged channels through 1/2nd batt.,was kept up. This was satisfactor
except that there was a slight delay in ceasing firing.
    During the right attack the 2 batts. fired, in the 1st phase,252
shrapnel,and in the 2nd and 3rd phases 650 shrapnel and 278 H.E.

LEFT ATTACK.
The 1/2nd and 2/2nd batts.were detailed to support the
left attack. Major Lattey commanded the 2 batts. and remained with
the Officer Commanding the attack at the 1/2nd batt.observation post
in No.3 Communication trench. This post was connected by telephone
to both batts,to my own post,and to Hdqrs of right attack,in each
case by several alternative lines. As the two attacks were timed to
commence simultaneously when O.C.right attack informed the O.C.left
attack that he was ready,I arranged for Major Lattey to give the order
for all batts. to open fire.

1st Phase. At 1-15 a.m. the order to commence was given. The 1/2nd
Batt.and 1 section of 2/2nd Batt.fired for 3 minutes at the point
of entry and at the front line trenches north and south of it with
shrapnel at section fire at 5 seconds,while the remaining section of
the 2/2nd batt.fired at the junctions of communication and support
trenches behind point of entry with shrapnel and H.E. at section fire
10 seconds.
    After 3 minutes the section of 2/2nd batt.which was firing near
point of entry was lifted and reinforced the barrage on support
trenches.

2nd Phase. At 6 minutes from commencement of fire the 1/2nd Batt. ceased firing. The 2/2nd Batt. quickened it's fire for 2 minutes to section fire 5 seconds and then dropped back to 10 seconds.

3rd Phase. At 1-37 a.m. the officer commanding the attack reported his men clear of enemy front line trenches. The 1/2nd Batt. re-opened it's fire on front line trenches at section fire 5 seconds, after 2 minutes being reinforced by 1 section of the 2/2nd batt. and dropping it's rate of fire to section fire 10 seconds, while the other section of the 2/2nd batt. remained on support trenches at section fire 30 seconds. The whole ceased when infantry were reported safely returned

Telephonic communication was unimpaired throughout over all lines. During the 1st phase the 2 batt. fired 252 shrapnel, during the 2nd and 3rd phases 370 shrapnel and 122 H.E.

During the second phase 1 gun of B/125 Batt. fired 30 rounds shrapnel at intervals of 40 seconds as a curtain on the left of the attack.

During the affair my post was with the G.O.C.143rd Inf.Bde and I was in telephonic communication with the Os.C. the Artillery of both attacks.

(sd) J.R.Colville, Lieut-Colonel

Commanding 2nd S.Mid. F.A.Brigade.

For information of the A.G.'s Office at the Base.

Officers and men who have become casuals, been transferred or joined since last report.

Place _____ Date 4th March 1916

Regtl. Number	Rank	Name	Corps	Nature of casualty, or name of unit from or to which transferred	Date of being struck off or coming on the ration return	Remarks*
	Major	Taylor G.A.	2nd Battery	To ENGLAND to take command of 2/4th Warwick Howitzer Bde	28/2/16	
	2/Lieut.	Clements W.G.	Hd Qrs	Detained one day at SOUTHAMPTON when returning from leave	29/2/16	
	2/Lieut.	Williams A.B.	2nd Battery		1/3/16	
906	Cpl	Powell R.G.	ditto	Proceeded on Arty Course	27/2/16	
2811	Gr.	Tranter F.	ditto	To No 19 CCS	26/2/16	Struck off strength
3493	Gr.	Boswell D.C.	ditto	To No 19 CCS	1/3/16	ditto
	Captain	Penny A.F.	1st Battery	Returned from course of ranging instruction in ENGLAND	3/3/16	-
997	a/Bdr	Saunders H.	3rd Battery	To No. 19 CCS	26/2/16	Struck off strength
2360	Gr.	Bowley W.	ditto	To No 19 CCS	1/3/16	ditto
2862	Gr.	Williams W.	ditto	To No 19 CCS	2/3/16	ditto
924	a/Bdr	Elcock W.	Hd Qrs	To No. 4 CCS	23/1/16	ditto
1069	Dr.	Brewer C.A.	ditto	To be Temporary paid a/Bdr vice a/Bdr Elcock	from 24/1/16	

* State whether absence is of a permanent or temporary nature, adding, in the case of casuals from wounds or disease, any available information for communication to the relatives.

No. of Report _____

Army Form B. 213.

FIELD RETURN.

(To be furnished by all arms, services, and departments (except A.S.C. units) to the A. G.'s Office at the Base in accordance with Field Service Regulations, Part II.)

RETURN showing numbers RATIONED by, and Transport on charge of, _____ at _____ Date _____

DETAIL	Personnel			Animals								Guns, carriages, and limbers and transport vehicles										REMARKS
	Officers	Other ranks	Natives	Horses			Mules		Camels	Oxen	Guns, carriages and limbers, showing description	Ammunition wagons and limbers	Machine guns	Aircraft, showing description	Horsed		Motor Cars	Tractors	Mechanical			
				Riding	Draught	Heavy Draught	Pack	Large	Small							4 Wheeled	2 Wheeled			Lorries, showing description	Trucks, showing description	Trailers	Motor Bicycles	Bicycles	
Effective Strength of Unit																									
Details, by *Arms* attached to unit as in War Establishment:—																									
Total																									
War Establishment																									
Wanting to complete																									
(Detail of Personnel and Horses below)																									
Surplus																									
*Attached (not to include the details shown above)																									
Civilians:— Employed with the Unit Accompanying the Unit																									
TOTAL RATIONED ...																									

* In the case of field ambulances, hospitals or depots, the number of patients are to be included here, the names being shown in A. F. A. 36.

_____Signature of Commander.

_____Date of Despatch.

For information of the A.G.'s Office at the Base.

Officers and men who have become casuals, been transferred or joined since last report.

Place _____ Date 4th March 1916

Regtl. Number	Rank	Name	Corps	Nature of casualty, or name of unit from or to which transferred	Date of being struck off or coming on the ration return	Remarks*
567	Sgt	Parker J	Am Column	Rejoined from HQ 48th Div Arty	28/2/16	
2416	Dr	Cole G	ditto	Transferred to Divl Salvage Corps Authority GRO 1408 dated 15/2/16	23/2/16	Struck off strength
866	Gr	Humphries S	ditto	To BASE pending discharge — TIME expired 13/3/16	3/3/16	Struck off strength
3493	Gr	Boswell D.E	2nd Battery	To Hospital	26/2/16	
2974	Dr	Spires H.E	do	" "		
2614	Gr	Lane W	do	" "	28/2/16	
2996	Gr	Green J	3rd Battery	" "	1/3/16	
2865	Cpl Fitter	Wright	do	" "	3/3/16	
2966	Gr	Holt H	do	" "	4/3/16	
2471	Dr	Griffin J	Am Column	" "	29/2/16	
2287	Gr	Baylis A	do	" "		
3224	Gr	Redding J	do	" "	1/3/16	
1029	2/Cdr	Wise E	do	" "	2/3/16	
2296	Dr	Jones S	do	" "	" "	
3100	"	Morris R	do	" "	" "	
2793	"	Slade H	do	" "	3/3/16	
2369	Gr	Ball J	do	" "	29/2/16	
2369	"	do	do	" "	3/3/16	
3050	Dr	Bishton G	do	" "	1/3/16	

* State whether absence is of a permanent or temporary nature, adding, in the case of casuals from wounds or disease, any available information for communication to the relatives.

Army Form B. 213.

FIELD RETURN.

No. of Report. _____

(To be furnished by all arms, services, and departments (except A.S.C. units) to the A. G.'s Office at the Base in accordance with Field Service Regulations, Part II.)

Date. _____

RETURN showing numbers RATIONED by, and Transport on charge of, _____ at _____

DETAIL	Personnel			Animals.							Guns, carriages, and limbers and transport vehicles										REMARKS
				Horses			Mules							Horsed		Motor Cars	Tractors	Mechanical			
	Officers	Other ranks	Natives	Riding	Draught	Heavy Draught	Pack	Large	Small	Camels	Oxen	Guns, carriages and limbers, showing description	Ammunition wagons and limbers	Machine guns	Aircraft, showing description	4 Wheeled	2 Wheeled			Lorries, showing description	Trucks, showing description	Trailers	Motor Bicycles	Bicycles	
Effective Strength of Unit																									
Details, by Arms attached to unit as in War Establishment :—																									
Total																									
War Establishment																									
Wanting to complete (Detail of Personnel and Horses below)																									
Surplus																									
*Attached (not to include the details shown above).																									
Civilians:— Employed with the Unit Accompanying the Unit																									
TOTAL RATIONED ...																									

* In the case of field ambulances, hospitals or depots, the number of patients are to be included here, the names being shown in A. F. A. 36.

_____ Signature of Commander.

_____ Date of Despatch.

For information of the A.G.'s Office at the Base.

Officers and men who have become casuals, been transferred or joined since last report.

Place _____ Date _4th March 1916_

Regtl. Number	Rank	Name	Corps	Nature of casualty, or name of unit from or to which transferred	Date of being struck off or coming on the ration return	Remarks*
528	Dr	Weavers A	2nd Battery	From hospital	28/2/16	
914	"	Millichip Ea	do	" "	3/3/16	
3396	"	Baddeley EH	3rd "	" "	3/3/16	
2591	Gr	Keyte CC	Hd Qrs	Allotment to FATHER increased from 6 to 9d perday	from 14/2/16	necessary papers forwarded

* State whether absence is of a permanent or temporary nature, adding, in the case of casuals from wounds or disease, any available information for communication to the relatives.

Army Form B. 213.

FIELD RETURN.

No. of Report _____

(To be furnished by all arms, services, and departments (except A.S.C. units) to the A. G.'s Office at the Base in accordance with Field Service Regulations, Part II.)

RETURN showing numbers RATIONED by, and Transport on charge of, _____ at _____ Date _____

DETAIL.	Personnel			Animals.								Guns, carriages, and limbers and transport vehicles											REMARKS
				Horses				Mules		Camels	Oxen	Guns, carriages and limbers, showing description	Ammunition wagons and limbers	Machine Guns	Aircraft, showing description	Horsed		Motor Cars	Tractors	Mechanical		Trailers	Motor Bicycles	Bicycles
	Officers	Other ranks	Natives	Riding	Draught	Heavy Draught	Pack	Large	Small							4 Wheeled	2 Wheeled			Lorries, showing description	Trucks, showing description				
Effective Strength of Unit																									
Details, *by Arms* attached to unit as in War Establishment:																									
Total																									
War Establishment																									
Wanting to complete (Detail of Personnel and Horses below)																									
Surplus																									
*Attached (not to include the details shown above)																									
Civilians: Employed with the Unit Accompanying the Unit																									
TOTAL RATIONED ...																									

* In the case of field ambulances, hospitals or depots, the number of patients are to be included here, the names being shown in A. F. A. 36.

_____ Signature of Commander.

_____ Date of Despatch.

For information of the A.G.'s Office at the Base.

Officers and men who have become casuals, been transferred or joined since last report.

Place _____ Date 11th March 1916

Regtl. Number	Rank	Name	Corps	Nature of casualty, or name of unit from or to which transferred	Date of being struck off or coming on the ration return	Remarks*
	Capt	Penney A.F.	1st Worc Bty	Rejoined from Course of Ranging Instruction	5/3/16	
	2/Lieut	Allen B.A.B.	ditto	TRANSFERRED to 36th Div Authority A.G./2524/224. Regular Commission vide LONDON GAZETTE 26/2/16	7/3/16	Struck off Strength
2276	Sgt	Arnold H.	2nd Battery	Proceeded on Gas Course	6/3/16 to 11/3/16	
332	Bdr	Cook L.	ditto	Promoted to Cpl vice Cpl Hoond. evacuated 12/2/16	13/2/16	
2133	a/Bdr	Oakley H.	ditto	Promoted to Bdr vice Bdr Cook L.	13/2/16	
1093	Dr	Godfrey J.	ditto	Promoted to a/Bdr vice a/Bdr Oakley H.	13/2/16	
906	Bdr	Powell R.G.	ditto	Returned from Arty Course	10/3/16	
1031	Dr	Powell J.	ditto	Allotment of Pay 6d per day to wife. This cancels allotment to Dependant	from 26/2/16	

wife's address:—
Powell, Annie Beatrice
Ombersley
Nr Droitwich
WORCESTERSHIRE

* State whether absence is of a permanent or temporary nature, adding, in the case of casuals from wounds or disease, any available information for communication to the relatives.

FIELD RETURN.

Army Form B. 213.

No. of Report _____

(To be furnished by all arms, services and departments (except A.S.C. units) to the A.G.'s Office at the Base in accordance with Field Service Regulations, Part II.)

RETURN showing numbers RATIONED by, and Transport on charge of, _____ at _____ Date. _____

DETAIL	Personnel			Animals							Guns, carriages, and limbers, and transport vehicles.										REMARKS
	Officers	Other ranks	Natives	Horses			Mules		Camels	Oxen	Guns, carriages and limbers, showing description	Ammunition wagons and limbers	Machine guns	Aircraft, showing description	Horsed		Motor Cars	Tractors	Mechanical			Motor Bicycles	Bicycles.
				Riding	Draught	Heavy Draught	Pack	Large	Small							4 Wheeled	2 Wheeled			Lorries, showing description	Trucks, showing description	Trailers		
Effective Strength of Unit Details, *by Arms* attached to unit as in War Establishment:—																							
Total																							
War Establishment																							
Wanting to complete (Detail of Personnel and Horses below)																							
Surplus																							
*Attached (not to include the details shown above)																							
Civilians:— Employed with the Unit Accompanying the Unit																							
TOTAL RATIONED ...																							

* In the case of field ambulances, hospitals or depots, the number of patients are to be included here, the names being shown in A. F. A. 36.

_____ Signature of Commander.

_____ Date of Despatch.

For information of the A.G.'s Office at the Base.

Officers and men who have become casuals, been transferred or joined since last report.

Place _____   Date 11th March 1916

Regtl. Number	Rank	Name	Corps	Nature of casualty, or name of unit from or to which transferred	Date of being struck off or coming on the ration return	Remarks*
102	S.Sgt	S'dr Rea W.G.	1st Worcs Bty	To. BASE - 18/12/15 struck off strength		
2066	Gr	Holt W	2nd Worcs Bty	To. C.C.S.	5/3/16	Struck off strength
940	S'dr	Grubb W	ditto	Proceeded on Anti gas course	6/3/16 to 11/3/16	
2287	Gr	Baylis. A.	Am Column	To. C.C.S.	5/3/16	Struck off strength
465	Sgt	Stooke W	ditto	Completed Army Form W 3126		Papers to RECORDS.
33	BQMS	Summers. A	ditto			
567	Sgt.	Parker J.I.	ditto.	Allotment of Pay 1/8 per day to wife	from 2/2/16	
2781	Dr	Adams W	Hd Qrs	Transferred to 1st S.M.F.A. Bde authority 48th Div arty dated 7/3/16	10/3/16	
3492	Gr	Holbeche S.	Hd Qrs	Reinforcements Collected from 3rd Bde. R.F.A.	9/3/16	
3126	Dr	Holmes. A.E.				
3361	"	Dyson A.L.				
3332	"	Litt W	Am Column			
3103	"	Price C.L.				
3218	"	Jones E.F.	3rd Battery			
3093	"	Guyatt F.				

*State whether absence is of a permanent or temporary nature, adding, in the case of casuals from wounds or disease, any available information for communication to the relatives.

Army Form B. 213.

FIELD RETURN.

No. of Report _____

(To be furnished by all arms, services and departments (except A.S.C. units) to the A. G.'s Office at the Base in accordance with Field Service Regulations, Part II.) Date. _____

RETURN showing numbers RATIONED by, and Transport on charge of, _____ at _____

DETAIL	Personnel			Animals						Guns, carriages, and limbers, and transport vehicles.											REMARKS
				Horses			Mules							Horsed		Mechanical					
	Officers	Other ranks	Natives	Riding	Draught	Heavy Draught	Pack	Large	Small	Camels	Oxen	Guns, carriages and limbers, showing description	Ammunition wagons and limbers	Machine guns	Aircraft, showing description	4 Wheeled	2 Wheeled	Motor Cars	Tractors	Lorries, showing description	Trucks, showing description	Trailers	Motor Bicycles	Bicycles.	
Effective Strength of Unit																									
Details, *by Arms* attached to unit as in War Establishment:—																									
Total																									
War Establishment																									
Wanting to complete (Detail of Personnel and Horses below)																									
Surplus																									
*Attached (not to include the details shown above)																									
Civilians:— Employed with the Unit Accompanying the Unit																									
TOTAL RATIONED ...																									

* In the case of field ambulances, hospitals or depots, the number of patients are to be included here, the names being shown in A. F. A. 36.

Signature of Commander. _____

Date of Despatch. _____

For information of the A.G.'s Office at the Base.

Officers and men who have become casuals, been transferred or joined since last report.

Place _____   Date 11th March 1916

Regtl. Number	Rank	Name	Corps	Nature of casualty, or name of unit from or to which transferred	Date of being struck off or coming on the ration return	Remarks*
2402	Gr	Priest CW	} 1st Battery			
3501	"	Powell C.J.				
962	BdR	Ashwin R.	} 2nd Battery			
3154	Gr	Wilde G.				
3214	"	Green A.H.				
2292	"	Delahay G.	}	Reinforcements Joined from S.a.Bob 9/3/16		
3494	"	Trump G.				
3224	"	Watkins H.G.				
3294	"	Woodward Wa				
3114	"	Warrender JL	} 3rd Battery			
3120	"	Radcresh				
3246	"	Dowler J.				
2938	Dr	Pitcher H.				
3192	"	Porter L.B.				
3476	"	Shutt W.				
803	BdR	Vale E.	3rd Battery	} Returned from 1 months leave	9/3/16	
874	Gr	Gwilliam A.	2nd "			
499	Gr.	Maullin W.	" "			
880	Sgt	Hughes H.	" "			

* State whether absence is of a permanent or temporary nature, adding, in the case of casuals from wounds or disease, any available information for communication to the relatives.

Army Form B. 213.

FIELD RETURN.

No. of Report _____

(To be furnished by all arms, services and departments (except A.S.C. units) to the A. G.'s Office at the Base in accordance with Field Service Regulations, Part II.)

RETURN showing numbers RATIONED by, and Transport on charge of, _____ at _____ Date _____

DETAIL	Personnel			Animals								Guns, carriages, and limbers, and transport vehicles.						Horsed		Mechanical			Motor Bicycles	Bicycles.	REMARKS
	Officers	Other ranks	Natives	Horses			Pack	Mules		Camels	Oxen	Guns, carriages and limbers, showing description	Ammunition wagons and limbers	Machine guns	Aircraft, showing description	4 Wheeled	2 Wheeled	Motor Cars	Tractors	Lorries, showing description	Trucks, showing description	Trailers		
				Riding	Draught	Heavy Draught		Large	Small														
Effective Strength of Unit																							
Details, *by Arms* attached to unit as in War Establishment:—																							
Total																							
War Establishment																							
Wanting to complete (Detail of Personnel and Horses below)																							
Surplus																							
*Attached (not to include the details shown above)																							
Civilians:— Employed with the Unit Accompanying the Unit																							
TOTAL RATIONED ...																							

* In the case of field ambulances, hospitals or depots, the number of patients are to be included here, the names being shown in A. F. A. 36.

_____ Signature of Commander.

_____ Date of Despatch.

For information of the A.G.'s Office at the Base.

Officers and men who have become casuals, been transferred or joined since last report.

Place _____ Date 11th March 1916

Regtl. Number	Rank	Name	Corps	Nature of casualty, or name of unit from or to which transferred	Date of being struck off or coming on the ration return	Remarks*
2385	Dr.	Brompton R.C.	1st Worc Bty	To Hospital	8/3/16	
2491	Gr	Hill J	ditto	" "	9/3/16	
2565	Dr	Inglis J	2nd "	" "	9/3/16	
2142	Gr	Aston T	3rd "	" "	9/3/16	
	2/Lieut	Smith S.H.	ditto	" "	6/3/16	
3046	Gr	Munn S.E.	1st Battery	From Hospital	6/3/16	
2243	"	Gunster J	2nd "	" "	5/3/16	
2614	"	Lane W	" "	" "	6/3/16	
2341	"	Buckley A.E.	" "	" "	6/3/16	
2924	Dr	Partridge L	" "	" "	9/3/16	
2974	"	Spiers A.E.	" "	" "	7/3/16	
2996	Gr	Green J	3rd "	" "	9/3/16	
2441	Dr	Griffin J	Am Column	" "	8/3/16	
3100	"	Morris R	" "	" "	5/3/16	
3224	Gr	Redding J	" "	" "	10/3/16	

* State whether absence is of a permanent or temporary nature, adding, in the case of casuals from wounds or disease, any available information for communication to the relatives.

Army Form B. 213.

FIELD RETURN.

No. of Report _____

(To be furnished by all arms, services and departments (except A.S.C. units) to the A.G.'s Office at the Base in accordance with Field Service Regulations, Part II.)

RETURN showing numbers RATIONED by, and Transport on charge of, _____ at _____ Date _____

DETAIL	Personnel			Animals							Guns, carriages, and limbers, and transport vehicles.									REMARKS
	Officers	Other ranks	Natives	Horses			Mules		Camels	Oxen	Guns, carriages and limbers, showing description	Ammunition wagons and limbers	Machine guns	Aircraft, showing description	Horsed		Motor Cars	Tractors	Mechanical			Motor Bicycles	Bicycles	
				Riding	Draught	Heavy Draught	Pack	Large	Small								4 Wheeled	2 Wheeled			Lorries, showing description	Trucks, showing description	Trailers		
Effective Strength of Unit																								
Details, *by Arms* attached to unit as in War Establishment:—																								
Total																								
War Establishment																								
Wanting to complete																								
(Detail of Personnel and Horses below)																								
Surplus																								
*Attached (not to include the details shown above):—																								
Civilians:—																								
Employed with the Unit																								
Accompanying the Unit																								
TOTAL RATIONED ...																								

* In the case of field ambulances, hospitals or depots, the number of patients are to be included here, the names being shown in A. F. A. 36.

Signature of Commander _____

Date of Despatch _____

For information of the A.G.'s Office at the Base.

Officers and men who have become casuals, been transferred or joined since last report.

Place _____ Date 18th March, 1916

Regtl. Number	Rank	Name	Corps	Nature of casualty, or name of unit from or to which transferred	Date of being struck off or coming on the ration return	Remarks*
	Lieut. Col.	Bullock E.C.	H.Q.rs.	RETAINED in ENGLAND (while on leave for duty with the T.F. RESERVE	Struck off strength	Authority GHQ 7/3/16
	Lieut. Col.	Colville J.R. DSO	ditto	Joined from 83rd BDE. RFA.	14/3/16	
2/2429	Gr.	Herring J (servant)	ditto	ditto	14/3/16	
(RAMC)	Major	Oldham A.C.	ditto	Granted Leave from 18/3/16 to 25/3/16		
	2/Lieut	Foster H.J.A.	1st Battery	Transferred to No. 20. A.A. Section on 12th November 1915	Struck off Strength	Authority 48th Dw 13/3/16
102	S.Sgt Sdlr	Rea W.	ditto	Rejoined from DAC	16/3/16	
102	"	ditto	ditto	Proceeded to BASE TIME - EXPIRED	18/3/16	Struck off strength
105	Sgt	Tolley E.H.	2nd. Battery	ditto	18/3/16	ditto
2/23	Sgt Ftr	Dick J.	ditto	Rejoined from DAC	16/3/16	
2296	Sgt	Arnold H.	ditto	Returned from Gas Course	12/3/16	
940	Bdr	Grubb W.	3rd Battery	" "	12/3/16	
2996	Gr.	Green J.	ditto	Proceeded to BASE (for Dental treatment)	14/3/16	

*State whether absence is of a permanent or temporary nature, adding, in the case of casuals from wounds or disease, any available information for communication to the relatives.

Army Form B. 213.

FIELD RETURN.

(To be furnished by all arms, services, and departments (except A.S.C. units) to the A. G.'s Office at the Base in accordance with Field Service Regulations, Part II.)

No. of Report _____

Date _____

RETURN showing numbers RATIONED by, and Transport on charge of, _____ at _____

DETAIL	Personnel			Animals.							Guns, carriages, and limbers and transport vehicles										REMARKS
	Officers	Other ranks	Natives	Horses			Mules		Camels	Oxen	Guns, carriages and limbers, showing description	Ammunition wagons and limbers	Machine guns	Aircraft, showing description	Horsed		Motor Cars	Tractors	Mechanical			Motor Bicycles	Bicycles	
				Riding	Draught	Heavy Draught	Pack	Large	Small							4 Wheeled	2 Wheeled			Lorries, showing description	Trucks, showing description	Trailers			
Effective Strength of Unit																									
Details, *by Arms* attached to unit as in War Establishment:—																									
Total																									
War Establishment																									
Wanting to complete (Detail of Personnel and Horses below)																									
Surplus																									
*Attached (not to include the details shown above)																									
Civilians:— Employed with the Unit Accompanying the Unit																									
TOTAL RATIONED																									

* In the case of field ambulances, hospitals or depots, the number of patients are to be included here, the names being shown in A. F. A. 36.

_____ Signature of Commander.

_____ Date of Despatch.

For information of the A.G.'s Office at the Base.

Officers and men who have become casuals, been transferred or joined since last report.

Place _____ Date 18th March 1916

Regtl. Number	Rank	Name	Corps	Nature of casualty, or name of unit from or to which transferred	Date of being struck off or coming on the ration return	Remarks*
2142	Gr.	Aston F.	3rd Battery	to No 4 CCS	11/3/16	Struck off Strength
2865	Cpl	Wright A.B.	ditto	ditto	15/3/16	ditto
2904	Bdr	Garbutt B.	Am Column	Retd from Sick Leave	14/3/16	
2296	Dr.	Jones S.	ditto	To No 29 CCS	12/3/16	Struck off Strength
564	Sgt.	Parker J.F.	ditto	Posted to 3rd Bty	12/3/16	
3324	Whlr S.Sgt	Watts A.	ditto	Joined from DAC	16/3/16	
2/4	Sgt	Chatterly W.H.	ditto	Proceeded to BASE (time expired)	18/3/16	Struck off Strength
2514	Gr.	Hollingshead J.	1st Battery	To Hospital	16/3/16	
2085	Dr.	Rimmer C.J.	2nd "	" "	13/3/16	
3339	Gr.	Barrow R.	" "	" "	14/3/16	
2341	"	Buckley A.E.	" "	" "	14/3/16	
994	Dr.	Read A.	3rd "	" "	14/3/16	
1000	"	Willis F.	" "	" "	15/3/16	
2244	a/Bdr	Whitford H.	" "	" "	16/3/16	
424	Gr.	Hayward G.	" "	" "	14/3/16	
2385	Dr.	Crompton R.C.	1st "	From Hospital	18/3/16	
2565	"	Inglis J.	2nd "	" "	13/3/16	
2085	"	Rimmer C.J.	" "	" "	18/3/16	
1000	"	Willis F.	3rd "	" "	16/3/16	
1029	a/Bdr	Wise E.	Am Column	" "	14/3/16	
2793	Dr.	Slade H.	" "	" "	13/3/16	

* State whether absence is of a permanent or temporary nature, adding, in the case of casuals from wounds or disease, any available information for communication to the relatives.

Army Form B. 213.

FIELD RETURN.

No. of Report _____

(To be furnished by all arms, services, and departments (except A.S.C. units) to the A. G.'s Office at the Base in accordance with Field Service Regulations, Part II.)

RETURN showing numbers RATIONED by, and Transport on charge of, _____ at _____ Date _____

DETAIL.	Personnel			Animals.								Guns, carriages, and limbers and transport vehicles										REMARKS
				Horses			Mules				Guns, carriages and limbers, showing description	Ammunition wagons and limbers	Machine Guns	Aircraft, showing description	Horsed		Motor Cars	Tractors	Mechanical			
	Officers	Other ranks	Natives	Riding	Draught	Heavy Draught	Pack	Large	Small	Camels	Oxen					4 Wheeled	2 Wheeled			Lorries, showing description	Trucks, showing description	Trailers	Motor Bicycles	Bicycles	

Effective Strength of Unit

Details, *by Arms* attached to unit as in War Establishment:—

Total

War Establishment

Wanting to complete
(Detail of Personnel and Horses below)

Surplus

*Attached (not to include the details shown above)

Civilians:—
Employed with the Unit
Accompanying the Unit

TOTAL RATIONED ...

* In the case of field ambulances, hospitals or depots, the number of patients are to be included here, the names being shown in A. F. A. 36.

_____ Signature of Commander.

_____ Date of Despatch.

For information of the A.G.'s Office at the Base.

Officers and men who have become casuals, been transferred or joined since last report.

Place _____ Date 25th March 1916

Regtl. Number	Rank	Name	Corps	Nature of casualty, or name of unit from or to which transferred	Date of being struck off or coming on the ration return	Remarks*
2239	Dr	Blizzard A	Hd Qrs	To 4 CCS	23/3/16	Struck off Strength
	Lieut	Cross H.P.	1st Battery	Joined from DAC probatory attached	21/3/16	
2095	Dr	Harris J	48th DAC	Attached to 1st Bty	21/3/16	
39	Gnr	Fyfe A	do			
2496	Dr	Harris J	1st Battery	Awarded		
2016	"	Wall F	ditto	7 days F.P.	24/3/16	
985	"	Wigley W	ditto	No. 2		
2283	Dr	Twenberrow G.W.	2nd Battery	Granted Leave from	21/3/16 to 28/3/16	
3047	Dr	Stock G.J.	Am Column	To No 4 CCS	23/3/16	Struck off Strength
631	Sgt	Whitmore J	ditto	To BASE TIME-EXPIRES 6/4/16	24/3/16	ditto
323	Sgt	Pulley G	3rd Battery	RE-ENGAGED		
13	SQSgt	Jeynes W.E.	Am Column	Completed A.F.W 3126	23/3/16	Papers to RECORDS
898	Bdr	Garbutt J				
892	Bp.Fit	Cotterell A.H.	2nd Battery			
332	Bp.	Cook L.				
899	Dr	Crouch W				
533	S.Ftr Sgt	Sheward A	2d Battery	REFUSED To RE-ENGAGE	23/3/16	Papers to RECORDS
893	A/Bdr	Haughton G				
428	Sgt Fit	Dick J				

* State whether absence is of a permanent or temporary nature, adding, in the case of casuals from wounds or disease, any available information for communication to the relatives.

Army Form B. 213.

To be made up to and for Sunday in each week.

No. of Report _____

FIELD RETURN.

(To be furnished by all arms, services, and departments (except A.S.C. units) to the A. G.'s Office at the Base in accordance with Field Service Regulations, Part II.)

RETURN showing numbers (a) Effective strength of Unit.
(b) Rationed by Unit. at _____ Date _____

DETAIL	Personnel			Animals.							Guns, carriages, and limbers and transport vehicles										REMARKS
	Officers	Other ranks	Natives	Horses			Mules		Camels	Oxen	Guns, carriages and limbers, showing description	Ammunition wagons and limbers	Machine guns	Aircraft, showing description	Horsed		Motor Cars.	Tractors	Mechanical			
				Riding	Draught	Heavy Draught	Pack	Large	Small							4 wheeled	2 wheeled			Lorries, showing description	Trucks, showing description	Trailers	Motor Bicycles	Bicycles	

Effective Strength of Unit

Details, *by Arms* attached to unit as in War Establishment:—

Total

War Establishment

Wanting to complete

Surplus
(Detail of Personnel and Horses below)

*Attached (not to include the details shown above)

Civilians:—
Employed with the Unit
Accompanying the Unit

TOTAL RATIONED...

* In the case of field ambulances, hospitals or depots, the number of patients are to be included here, the names being shown in A. F. A. 36.

_____ Signature of Commander.

_____ Date of Despatch.

For information of the A.G.'s Office at the Base.

Officers and men who have become casuals, been transferred or joined since last report.

Place _____ Date 25th March 1916

Regtl. Number	Rank	Name	Corps	Nature of casualty, or name of unit from or to which transferred	Date of being struck off or coming on the ration return	Remarks*
2230	Dr	Blizzard A	H. Qrs	To Hospital	23/3/16	
2389	Gr	Clarke A	1st Bty	" "	24/3/16	
2855	Dr	Whitehouse S	2nd Bty	" "	18/3/16	
2212	"	Morgan C	" "	" "	20/3/16	
2695	"	Perkins W	" "	" "	21/3/16	
2281	Gr	Doughty G	" "	" "	24/3/16	
3431	"	Weavers W	" "	" "	21/3/16	
842	Dr	Reeves C	3rd "	" "	19/3/16	
2342	"	Wedgbury H	" "	" "	20/3/16	
2514	Gr	Hollingshead T	1st Bty	From Hospital	21/3/16	
2212	Dr	Morgan C	2nd "	" "	23/3/16	
2341	Gr	Buckley AC	" "	" "	24/3/16	
994	Dr	Reed A	3rd "	" "	23/3/16	
842	Dr	Reeves C	" "	" "	20/3/16	
2244	a/Bdr	Whitford H	" "	" "	20/3/16	
2370	Dr	Lane H	48th DAC attached to 1st Bty	To Hospital	25/3/16	
2232	Gr	Merrick JW	Am Column	Proceeded to HAVRE for Munitions	24/3/16	struck off strength
2664	"	Morris JA	" "			
3050	Dr	Bushton GL	" "			
				AUTHORITY:- Hd Qrs 3rd Army No. AC/1322 dated 16/3/16		

*State whether absence is of a permanent or temporary nature, adding, in the case of casuals from wounds or disease, any available information for communication to the relatives.

To be made up to and for Sunday in each week.

Army Form B. 213.

FIELD RETURN.

No. of Report _____

(To be furnished by all arms, services, and departments (except A.S.C. units) to the A. G.'s Office at the Base in accordance with Field Service Regulations, Part II.)

RETURN showing numbers (a) Effective strength of Unit.
(b) Rationed by Unit.

Date _____ at _____

DETAIL	Personnel			Animals.								Guns, carriages, and limbers and transport vehicles										REMARKS
				Horses				Mules		Camels	Oxen	Guns, carriages and limbers, showing description	Ammunition wagons and limbers	Machine guns	Aircraft, showing description	Horsed		Motor Cars	Tractors	Mechanical			
	Officers	Other ranks	Natives	Riding	Draught	Heavy Draught	Pack	Large	Small							4 wheeled	2 wheeled			Lorries, showing description	Trucks, showing description	Trailers	Motor Bicycles	Bicycles	

Effective Strength of Unit

Details, *by Arms* attached to units as in War Establishment:—

Total

War Establishment

Wanting to complete

Surplus

(Detail of Personnel and Horses below)

*Attached (not to include the details shown above)

Civilians:—
Employed with the Unit
Accompanying the Unit

TOTAL RATIONED…

* In the case of field ambulances, hospitals or depôts, the number of patients are to be included here, the names being shown in A. F. A. 36.

Signature of Commander.

Date of Despatch.

Reg No.	Rank.	Name.	Corps.	Remarks.	Date.
3455.	Dr.	Butcher. G. H.			
827.	"	Cantrell. J. W.			
2418.	"	Christian. W.			
2435.	"	Dyer. E.			
730.	Sgt.	Lane. H.			
2907.	Bmr	Garbutt. B. H.			
912.	"	Porter. J. E.			
2230.	Cpl	Willis. A. E.			
3172.	Gnr.	Homer. A. E.			
3231.	"	Michael. S. J.		Transferred from Amm. Col.	
2747.	"	Reed. R.		to "D" Worcester Bty.	31/3/16
2197.	"	Waldron. G.			
2265.	"	Harris. F.			
2254.	"	Stanley. W.			
2805.	"	Till. A. R.			
2305.	"	Westwood. S. H.			
3498.	"	Parkes. H.			
3276.	"	Prior. F.			
3230.	"	Thompson. G. W.			
126.	Cpl	Hardiman. H.	Amm. Col.	Transferred to 1st Worcs Bty.	31/3/16

Reg. No.	Rank.	Name.	Corps.	Remarks.	Date.
2192	Dr.	Cassell. E. W.		Transferred from 3rd Worcester	
2402	"	Churchill. A.		Battery to "D" Worcester Battery	
3426	Gnr.	Dowler. J.			31/3/16
3294	Gnr	Woodward. W. A.		Transferred from 3rd Worcester	
2366	"	Weaver. T.		Battery to Amm. Column.	31/3/16
2002	Cpl	Newey W. G.	Amm. Col.	Transferred to Hd Qrs	31/3/16

Reg. No.	Rank	Name	Corps	Remarks	Date
758	Sgt	Sealy. H.			
1054	Bom	Heath. G.			
2861	S/S	Westwood. T.			
2067	Gnr.	Griffin. E.			
2919	"	Gammon. H.			
2985	"	Harber. T.			
3090	"	Hobbs. W.			
2819	S/a/Bom.	Taylor. W.			
2478	Dr.	Giddins. E.			
1041	"	Malins. W.			
2960	"	Norcott. T.			
999	"	Ramsay. E.			
842	"	Reeves. C.			
2987	a/Bom	Shacklock. J.		Transferred from 3rd Worcester	
1000	Dr.	Willis. F.		Battery, to "D" Worcester	
2859	S/a/Bom	Webb. D.		Battery.	31/3/16
2977	Gnr.	Gill. P.			
3391	Dr.	Watts. T.C.			
3494	Gnr.	Trump. G.			
3227	"	Watkins. G.H.			
3120	"	Radevecht. F.			
3710	S/a/Bom	Preston. W.			
2999	Gnr.	Shambrook. H.			
2938	Dr.	Pitcher. H.			
3397	"	Belcher. C.			
2926	Gnr.	Birch. C.			
2255	Cpl.	Canty. H.			
2905	Sadr.	Cockell. W.			

Reg. No.	Rank	Name	Corps.	Remarks.	Date.
835	Cpl	Green. W.			
2084.	a/Bom	Stanton. W.			
2854.	Sadl Sgt	Wilcox. F.			
2917.	Dr.	Hall. A. E.			
881.	Gnr.	Hart. F. V.			
2555.	Dr.	Hiles. A.			
2164.	Gnr.	Jackson. E. R.			
2050.	"	Knowles. G.			
2635.	"	Mallard. J.			
2284.	"	Martin. H.			
2964.	"	Oliver. L. G.			
932.	Dr.	Pardoe. E.			
928.	Sgt Hr.	Bicks. J.			
2340.	Gnr.	Bradley. C. F.			
2083	Bom	Cottrell. T. E.		Transferred from 2nd Worcester Bty to "D" Worcester Bty.	31/3/16.
1899.	Dr.	Crouch. W.			
2292.	Gnr.	Delahay. T.			
1016.	"	Evans. G. H.			
3032.	Dr.	Foster. J. W. E.			
50	Sgt	Goodyear. N. G.			
2694.	Dr.	Payne. G.			
2701.	Gnr.	Penger. G. H.			
1031.	Dr.	Powell. J.			
2048	"	Pullen. J. E.			
2738.	Gnr.	Reese. P			
2735.	"	Rowbotham.			
2815.	Dr.	Tolley. W.			
2283.	"	Twinberrow. G.W.			

Reg. No.	Rank.	Name.	Corps	Remarks.	Date
2875	Dr.	Weaver. C.			
985	"	Wigley. W.		Transferred from 1st Worcester	
2835	"	Wintle. C.		Bty. to "D" Worcester Bty 31/3/16.	
3315	"	Hoskins. J.S.			
2853	Dr.	Whitehouse. C.		Transferred from 2nd Worcester	
3431	Gnr.	Weaver. W.		Bty. to "D" Worcester Bty 31/3/16.	
3214	"	Green. A.H.			

Reg. No.	Rank	Name	Corps	Remarks	Date
808	Cpl	Higgs. W	Hd Qrs	Transferred to Amm. Col.	
2324	Gunner	Burgess. P. H.	1st Bty	" " D. Bty.	
2405	Dr	Cookson. T. V.	"	" " " " "	
747	Sgt	Darke. A	"	" " " " "	
2027	Gnr	Evans. F. J.	"	" " " " "	
2447	Dr	Edwards. G.	"	" " " " "	
2480	"	Goodman. H.	"	" " " " "	
220	Sgt	Willetts. A. M.	"	" " " " "	
559	Bom	Winwood. W.	"	" " " " "	
955	"	Stallard. A. H.	"	" " " " "	
1059	"	Wood. T. G. R.	"	" " " " "	
2334	S/S	Taylor. S.	"	" " " " "	
2514	Gnr	Hollingshead. T.	"	" " " " "	
3079	"	Leppard. W. T.	"	" " " " "	
2634	"	Mackie. H.	"	" " " " "	
2116	"	Miles. S. A.	"	" " " " "	
1096	"	Powell. L.	"	" " " " "	31/3/16
2767	"	Stanton. W. W.	"	" " " " "	
3041	"	Stinton. J. A.	"	" " " " "	
2807	"	Turner. C.	"	" " " " "	
2212	"	Widdus. H.	"	" " " " "	
980	"	Williams. W.	"	" " " " "	
1094	Dr	Harris. G. H.	"	" " " " "	
2496	"	Harris. F.	"	" " " " "	
2511	"	Hassell. B.	"	" " " " "	
2602	"	Lea. W.	"	" " " " "	
2129	"	Smith. F.	"	" " " " "	
2016	"	Wall. P.	"	" " " " "	

Reg. No.	Rank.	Name.	Corps.	Remarks.	Date.
2868	Dr.	Hawkins. C.C.			
2602	"	Hearn. L.			
548	"	Howard. W.H.		Reinforcements posted to Amm. Col.,	
3198	"	Hooper. T.M.			31/3/16
1734	"	Johnson. H.			

Reg. No.	Rank	Name	Corps	Remarks	Date
2790	Dr	Stovold. J.J.			
3109	"	Willis. C.			
2880	"	Yoxall. R.			
3432	Gnr.	Adkins. J.A.F.			
3520	"	Bryant. H.G.			
675	"	Barett. J.J.			
664	"	Pearson. W.C			
663	"	Powell. A.			
3079	"	Thomas. L.			
580	"	Wheatley. J.			
3538	"	Wilkes. J.			
2200	"	Warr. J.			
548	Dr	Arrowsmith. B.			
2215	"	Bray. W.			
2709	"	Brettle. E.			
3173	"	Bowling. N.			
2244	"	Boyd. E.		Reinforcements posted to Amn. Col.	31/3/16
3085	"	Cross. A.			
167	"	Clarke. G.			
3495	"	Cooper. H.			
2813	"	Cacott. J.			
2216	"	Elgar. F.			
2844	"	Francombe. C.R.			
2850	"	Forest. F.			
2607	"	Godwin. E.			
2134	"	Harford. C.W.			
2731	"	Hambridge. A.S.			
3084	"	Greenslade. J.			

Reg. No.	Rank.	Name.	Corps.	Remarks.	Date.
659	Bom.	Thornton. R.			
2827	Gnr.	Bartlett. A. E.			
2799	"	Brownsey. H. A.			
2977	"	Brooks. W			
604	"	Pickman. H.			
2753	"	Cruse. E.		Reinforcements posted to "D" Worcester Battery. 31/3/16.	
2753	Dr	Walker. G. J.			
2251	Gnr.	Clarke. E.			
2576	"	Godsell. A. V.			
3280	"	Griffiths. O. S.			
3499	Ftr.	Cook. G. H.			
541	Gnr.	Yarrington. W.			
3006	"	Yeates. E.			

Reg. No.	Rank.	Name	Corps	Remarks.	Date.
581.	Gnr.	Ashford. J.			
3281.	Cpl	Bach. P. H.			
2581.	Bom.	Binding. L. T.			
3503.	Dr.	Beasley. A. E.			
3185.	Gnr.	Chambers. N. V.			
3138.	Dr.	Chambers. G. W. L.			
3088.	a/Bom	Davis. H. W.			
3040.	Dr.	Evans. W. C.			
547.	Sadr.	Gilks. W. L.			
2724.	Dr.	Giles. C.			
2277.	Sgt.	Green. F.			
2444.	Gnr.	Griffiths. A. T.			
2492.	"	Hale. C.		Reinforcements posted to "D" Worcester Bty.	31/3/16.
530.	Ftr.	Humphreys. J. N.			
3295.	S/S.	Lampitt. J.			
1317.	Cpl	Lucas. A. H.			
334.	"	Munday D.			
181.	Bom.	Nicklin. W. L.			
680.	"	Norman. E. G. M.			
603.	Gnr.	Pardfield. S.			
3144.	Dr.	Russell. L. W.			
382.	Bom.	Stokes. R.			
632.	Ftr.	Stokes. W. M.			
3438.	Gnr.	Steer. E.			
2101.	a/Bom	Smith. G. V.			
3440.	Bom.	Tromans. J. W.			
668.	S/S	Wyatt. F.			
2604.	Dr.	Werrett. F. E. T.			

Reg No	Rank	Name	Corps	Remarks	Date
1112	Cpl	Spencer. H			
677	S/S	Lambourne. G.A.			
3208	Gnr	Morgan. C.H.			
668	"	Smith. J.H.			
3504	"	Swift. E.M.			
2759	"	Stokes. C.			
3118	"	Taylor. W.H			
2657	Dr.	Cooper. A.			
2838	"	Huntley. R.W.			
2359	Gnr	Banfield. H.J			
583	"	Beeson. F.			
526	"	Cox. G.S.			
3118	"	Cross. P.S.			
3090	"	Fox. C.D.			
3284	"	James. A.		Reinforcements posted to	
2683	"	Lee. H.		3rd Worcester Bty.	31/3/16
3070	"	Maddick. S.			
2130	Dr.	Hallett. A.C.			
529	"	Husson. B.G.			
655	"	Hughes. G.			
2815	"	Holmes. T.C.			
2580	"	Jones. C.			
2218	"	Loveridge. G.			
2788	"	Loder. A.C.			
2908	"	Martin. A.H.			
2578	"	Turvey. A.C.			

Reg. No	Rank	Name	Corps	Remarks	Date
3089	Sadr.	Ebb. A. H.			
3259	Gnr.	Burston. A. H.			
3061	Dr.	Barrett. H.			
3005	Gnr.	Cording. A.			
2701	"	Cook. W.			
2040	"	Clarke. W. J.			
1428	"	Coles. W.			
2087	"	Gales. F. R.			
3094	"	Hales. J. W.			
675	"	James. A. W. R.			
3082	"	Jeffrey. H.			
532	"	Lewis. H. W.			
676	"	Lea. H.			
1637	"	Le Tissier. C.		Reinforcements posted to 2nd Worcester Battery	31/3/16
649	"	Mee. B. V.			
695	"	Mills. G. W.			
3270	"	McHarg. W. J.			
2206	Dr.	Miles. W. P.			
2205	"	Mitchell. F.			
601	"	Nott. F.			
3362	"	Perkins. A.			
2235	"	Pope. A. F.			
3252	"	Pidgeley. W.			
3081	"	Richards. T.			
2861	"	Saunders. J. G.			
2212	"	Smith. C.			
605	"	Strong. F. W.			

Reg No.	Rank	Name	Corps.	Remarks	Date
2198	Dr.	Woolford. H.			
3436	Cpl	Hill. J.J.			
3133	a/Bom	Best. H.			
3248	S/S	Cooke. J.			
3311	Gnr.	Barker. F.F.G.			
682	"	Beech. E.J.			
3075	"	Billing. W.			
3176	"	Brace. W.			
661	"	Breedon. F.			
3293	"	Browning. A.W.			
585	"	Burman. A.E.			
3131	"	Canty. J.			
589	"	Corcoran. T.			
600	"	Hunt. C.J.			
2062	"	Morris. D.C.			
1489	"	Oliver. C.			
690	"	Wright. T.P.		Reinforcements posted to 1st Worcester Battery.	31/3/16
2820	Dr.	Baynes. W.			
8279	"	Brind. C.B.			
2917	"	Bunn. G.H.			
3087	"	Denner. H.			
2766	"	Knight. H.			
3371	"	Shuck. T.			
2905	"	Titcombe. H.			
3144	"	Turner. F.			
597	"	Viner. J.H.			
2690	"	Walker. A.E.			
3394	"	Wilson. F.A.			
2756	"	Windsor. A.A.			

Reg No	Rank	Name	Corps	Remarks	Date
2917	Dr.	Bunn. G.H.	}		
3185	Gnr.	Chambers. N.V.			
3138	Dr.	Chambers. G.M.L			
2753	Gnr.	Creese. E.			
2657	Dr.	Cooper. A.			
2251	Gnr.	Clarke. E.			
3087	Dr.	Denner. H.		Reinforcements joined on 31/3/16	
2607	a/Bom	Godwin. E.V.			
2576	Gnr.	Godsell. A.V.			
2444	"	Griffiths. A.T.			
3499	Ftr.	Cook. G.A.			
1317	Cpl	Lucas. A.H.			
1112	"	Spencer. L.			
2790	Dr.	Stovold. J.			
2578	"	Turvey. A.E.			
2604	"	Werrett. F.E.T.	}		

Reg No.	Rank	Name	Corps	Remarks	Date
3118	Gnr	Taylor. W. H.			
659	Sgt	Thornton. R.			
3440	Cpl	Tromans. J. W.			
2905	Dr.	Titcombe. H.			
3079	Gnr	Thomas. L. F. J.			
3144	Dr.	Turner. F.			
597	"	Vivier. J. W. H.			
3394	"	Wilson. F. A.			
2756	"	Windsor. A. H.			
2200	Gnr	Watt. J.			
2198	Dr.	Woolford. H.			
2753	"	Walker. G. J.			
2690	"	Walker. A. G.			
580	Gnr	Wheatley. J.			
3538	"	Wilkes. J. F.		Reinforcements joined on 31/3/16.	
3109	a/Bom	Willis. C.			
690	Bom.	Wright. T. P.			
668	S/S.	Wyatt. F.			
541	Gnr.	Yarrington. W.			
2880	a/Bom.	Yoxall. R.			
3006	Gnr.	Yeates. C.			
2277	Sgt.	Green. F.			
2581	Cpl.	Binding. S. T.			
2827	Gnr.	Bartlett. A. C.			
2799	"	Brownsey. H. A.			
2977	"	Brooks. W.			
2820	Dr.	Baynes. W.			
3371	"	Shuck. T.			

Reg No.	Rank.	Name.	Corps.	Remarks.	Date.
3270	Gnr.	McHarg. W. J.			
3208	"	Morgan. C. H.			
334	Cpl	Munday. D.			
2062	Gnr.	Morris. D. C.			
181	Bom	Nicklin. W. L.			
680	"	Norman. C. J. M.			
601	Dr.	Nott. L. P.			
1489	Gnr.	Oliver. C.			
664	"	Pearson. W. C.			
604	"	Pickman. H.			
603	"	Pandfield. L.			
3392	Dr.	Perkins. A.			
663	Gnr.	Powell. A.			
2225	Dr.	Pope. A. F.			
8252	"	Pidgeley. W.			
3061	"	Barnett. H.		Reinforcements joined on 31/3/1916.	
3081	Gnr.	Richards. T.			
3414	a/Bom	Russell. L. W.			
606	Dr.	Strong. F. W.			
2212	"	Smith. C.			
2861	"	Saunders. J. G.			
382	Cpl	Stokes. A.			
668	Gnr.	Smith. J. H.			
632	Ftr.	Stokes. W. M.			
3438	Gnr.	Steer. C.			
3504	"	Swift. C. M.			
2101	a/Bom	Smith. G. V.			
2759	Gnr.	Stokes. C.			

Reg No	Rank	Name	Corps	Remarks	Date
3198	Dr.	Hooper. T. M.			
2815	"	Holmes. T. C.			
600	Gnr.	Hunt. C. J.			
655	Dr.	Hughes. C.			
529	"	Husson. B. G.			
530	Ttr.	Humphreys. J. A.			
2130	Dr.	Hallett. E. A.			
2838	"	Huntley. A. W.			
675	Gnr.	James. A. W. R.			
3284	"	James. A.			
3580	Dr.	Jones. C.			
1734	"	Johnson. H.			
3082	Gnr.	Jeffrey. H.			
2766	Dr.	Knight. H.			
677	S/S	Lambourne. G. A.			
3295	S/S	Lampitt. J.		Reinforcements joined on 31/3/16	
532	Gnr.	Lewis. A. W.			
676	"	Lea. H.			
1687	"	Le Tissier. C.			
2768	Dr.	Loder. H.			
2218	"	Loveridge. G.			
2623	Gnr.	Lee. H.			
2908	Dr.	Martin. A. H.			
2205	"	Mitchell. F.			
3070	a/Bom	Maddick. L.			
649	Gnr.	Mee. B. V.			
695	"	Mills. G. W.			
2206	Dr.	Miles. W. P.			

Reg.No.	Rank	Name.	Corps.	Remarks.	Date.
3118	Gnr.	Cross. P.S			
3085	Dr.	Cross. A.			
3005	Gnr.	Cording. A.			
1428	"	Coles. W.			
2040	"	Clarke. W.J.			
167	Dr.	Clarke. G.			
3495	"	Cooper. A.			
3088	Cpl	Davis. A.W.			
3089	Sadr.	Elt. A.A.			
2813	Dr.	Eacott. J.			
2216	"	Elgar. F.			
3040	"	Evans. W.C.			
3090	Gnr.	Fox. C.D.			
2850	Dr.	Forest. F		Reinforcements joined on 31/3/16.	
2844	"	Francombe. R			
2087	Gnr.	Gales. F.R.			
547	Sadr.	Gilks. W.L.			
2724	Dr.	Giles. C.			
3584	"	Greenslade. J.			
8280	Gnr.	Griffiths. C.J.			
3094	a/Bom	Hale. J.W.			
2492	Gnr.	Hale. E.			
2134	Dr.	Harford. C.W.			
2731	"	Hambridge. A.			
2868	"	Hawkins. C.C.F.			
2602	"	Hearne. L.			
3436	Sgt	Hill. J.J.			
548	Dr.	Howard. W.A.			

Reg. No.	Rank.	Name.	Corps.	Remarks.	Date.
3432	Gnr.	Adkins. J. A.			
581.	"	Ashford. J.			
548.	Dr.	Arrowsmith. B.			
3281	2.m.S	Back. R. E.			
3135.	Bom.	Best. H.			
661.	"	Breedon. F.			
675.	Gnr.	Barrett. J. J.			
3293.	a/Bom.	Browning. A. W.			
683.	Gnr.	Beeson. F.			
682.	"	Beech. C. J.			
585.	"	Burman. A. E.			
2359.	a/Bom.	Banfield. A. J.			
3311.	Gnr.	Barker. F. G.			
3503.	Dr.	Beasley. A. E.			
3075.	Gnr.	Billing. W.			
3520.	a/Bom.	Bryant. A. G.			
3176.	Gnr.	Brace. W.		Reinforcements joined on	31/3/16
2215.	Dr.	Bray. W.			
12709.	"	Brettle. E.			
8279.	"	Brind. C. D.			
3259.	Gnr.	Burston. A. H.			
3173.	Dr.	Bowling. N.			
2244	"	Boyd. E. F.			
3131.	Gnr.	Canty. J.			
3348.	S/S.	Cook. J.			
589.	Gnr.	Corcoran. J.			
826.	"	Cox. G. S			
2791.	"	Cook. W.			

Reg. No	Rank	Name	Corps	Remarks	Date
982	Cpl	Evans. A. E.	1st Battery	Promoted to Sgt, vice Sgt Willetts to "D" Battery.	31/3/16
696	"	Hoyle. T. M.	" "	Promoted to Sgt, vice Sgt Darke, to "D" Battery.	31/3/16
963	Cpl	Cameron. H. J. R.	2nd. Battery	Promoted to Sgt, vice Sgt Goodyear, to "D" Battery.	31/3/16
906	"	Powell. R. G.	" "	Promoted to Sgt, vice Sgt Tolley, to Base, time expired.	31/3/16
962	Bom	Ashwin. R.	" "	Promoted to Cpl, vice Corporal Powell.	31/3/16
861	"	Bawcutt. J.	" "	Promoted to Cpl, vice Corporal Cameron.	31/3/16
856	Cpl	Duggins. A.	3rd Battery	Promoted to Sgt, vice Sgt Sealy, to "D" Battery.	31/3/16

Reg. No	Rank	Name	Corps	Remarks	Date
		Reversions of reinforcements joined 31/3/16.			
3281	2 m.S	Bach. R.E.	D. Battery	Reverted to Corporal.	
3436	Sgt.	Hill. J.J.	1st "	" " "	
3440	Cpl	Tromans. J.W.	D "	" " Bom.	
382	Cpl a/Sgt	Stokes. A.	" "	" " "	
2581	" "	Binding. S.T.	" "	" " "	
3133	Bom a/Cpl	Best. H.	1st "	" " a/Bom.	
3088	Cpl	Davis. H.W.	D "	" " "	
181	Bom a/Cpl	Nicklin. W.L.	" "	" " Bom.	
659	Sgt	Thornton. R.	" "	" " "	
661	Bom	Breedon. F.	1st "	" " Gunner	31/3/16
3293	a/Bom	Browning. A.W.	" "	" " "	
2359	" "	Banfield. H.J.	3rd "	" " "	
3520	" "	Bryant. H.G.	Amm. Col.	" " "	
3094	" "	Hale. J.W.	2nd Bty	" " "	
3070	" "	Maddick. S.	3rd "	" " "	
3414	" "	Russell. L.W.	D "	" " "	
3109	" "	Willis. C.	Amm. Col.	" " Driver	
690	Bom	Wright. T.P.	1st Bty.	" " Gunner	
2880	a/Bom	Yoxall. R.	Amm. Col.	" " Driver	
2607	" "	Godwin. C.V.	" "	" " "	

Reg No.	Rank	Name.	Corps.	Remarks.	Date.
1038	Cpl	James. A.	Amm. Col.	Transferred to 2nd Worcs. Bty.	31/3/16
3324	Sgt Whr	Watts. A.	" "	" " " "	" "
3324	Sgt Whr	Watts. A.	2nd Bty.	Reverts to permanent grade of "wheeler" on joining B.E.F.	23/2/16
1087	Cpl	Edwards. J	} Amm. Column.	Transferred to 3rd Worcester Battery.	31/3/16
2006	Bom	Gwilliam. H.			
2367	Gnr.	Blick. J.			
2488	"	Gillam. J.W.			

48 Vol 15

— CONFIDENTIAL —

WAR DIARY

OF

2nd. S.M.F.A. Bde.

(Volume ~~XVIII~~ XIV)

from 1.4.16   to 30.4.16.

Army Form C. 2118

WAR DIARY
or
INTELLIGENCE SUMMARY
(Erase heading not required.)

Instructions regarding War Diaries and Intelligence Summaries are contained in F. S. Regs., Part II. and the Staff Manual respectively. Title Pages will be prepared in manuscript.

Place	Date	Hour	Summary of Events and Information	Remarks and references to Appendices
BAYENCOURT	1/4/16	—	Murenitfur	4.5.16
	2/4/16	—	" Completion of I.D. training continued	4.5.16
	3/4/16	10.30	Conference by GOC RA "	4.5.16
		11.30	" GOC 48th Divn	
	4/4/16	—	Murenitfur	4.5.16
		2.30pm	Conference by GOC 48th Divn.	
	5/4/16	1.0pm	German shells near Murenitfur	4.5.16
	6/4/16		Murenitfur weather very changeable	4.5.16
	6/4/16	2.30pm	Conference by GOC 48th Division.	4.5.16
	7/4/16		Murenitfur little snowing	4.5.16
	8/4/16		"	4.5.16
	9/4/16	2.30pm	GOC held another Conference	4.5.16
	10/4/16		Murenitfur. Enemy artillery quiet	4.5.16
	11/4/16		" weather improved	4.5.16
	12/4/16		"	4.5.16
	13/4/16		"	4.5.16
	14/4/16		Trouble experienced from Murenwerfers nearly every day	4.5.16

WAR DIARY
or
INTELLIGENCE SUMMARY

(Erase heading not required.)

Army Form C. 2118

Place	Date	Hour	Summary of Events and Information	Remarks and references to Appendices
CAYENCOURT	16/4/16		Uneventful. Conference by G.O.C.	w/e
	16/4/16	9.30 p.m.	"Jerichos" German airman Machine gunned night flying. Capt. Hay J.C. Query on leave received to leave 16th inst.	w/e
	17/4/16		Uneventful. Weather very changeable.	w/e
	18/4/16		Uneventful. Smoke from Minenwerfers seen rear of Fonquevillers	w/e
		11.30 am	Enemy shelling by 2nd More. Brig in front of CHATEAU de la HAIE & Brunemont quiet. Brigade composing positions for 2nd Wore Bde (& I Brig).	w/e
	19/4/16		Enemy artillery fairly active along whole front. Uneventful.	w/e
	20/4/16			w/e
	21/4/16	8.20 am	Enemy shelling with 15 c.m. shells in front of CHATEAU de la HAIE.	w/e
		3.0 pm	Conference by G.O.C. Division	
	22/4/16		Uneventful	w/e
	23/4/16	3.30 pm	Enemy shelling in neighbourhood of 1st Worcester Bty; two explosions were heard	w/e

WAR DIARY
or
INTELLIGENCE SUMMARY

Army Form C. 2118

(Erase heading not required.)

Place	Date	Hour	Summary of Events and Information	Remarks and references to Appendices
BAYENCOURT	24/4/16		and on gun damaged so that it had to be taken to I.O.M's workshop. 3 casualties	W.S.G.
	25/4/16		Rearrangements of infantry covering like Bty now covering 8th wores & 1/R WarR. 3rd wores still working left sector.	W.S.G.
	26/4/16		Nothing of interest. Some shelling of Bienvillers.	W.S.G.
	27/4/16	3 a.m.	3rd wores Brig moved to K 7 a 15.60. (57 d. N.E.)	W.S.G.
	28/4/16	2.0 a.m.	Day spent in registration of new installation where howitzers on 2nd K.W. have moved.	W.S.G.
	29/4/16	11.30 p.m.	Registration of my 2 guns moved. Enemy generally quiet any activity. Answers movements to night of Bngadr. shelling on our trenches and houses & military in Bienvillers.	W.S.G.
	30/4/16		Nothing of interest	W.S.G.

Lieut. Colonel,
Comdg. 2nd South Midland H.A. Bde.

Reg. No.	Rank	Name	Corps	Remarks	Date
1060	Sgt.	Roberts. W.	1st Worc Bty	To HOSPITAL	7.4.16
2051	Bom	Nicklin. W. H.	" "	" "	8.4.16
1078	Gnr	Davis. H. J.	" "	" "	2.4.16
2764	Dr.	Sharpe. C.	" "	" "	3.4.16
2756	"	Windsor. R. H.	" "	" "	3.4.16
2503	Gnr.	Hale. A.	" "	" "	4.4.16
3017	"	Munn. R.	3rd " "	" "	27.3.16
1090	Dr.	Twining. C.	1st Worc Bty	From HOSPITAL	8.4.16
2764	"	Sharpe. C.	" "	" "	8.4.16
2152	Tptr	Saward. C.	2nd " "	" "	2.4.16
2281	Gnr	Doughty. G.	" "	" "	5.4.16
1027	a/Bom	Griffin. S.	3rd " "	" "	4.4.16
2960	Dr.	Norcott. T.	" "	" "	4.4.16
2243	Bom	Hicks. C.	" "	" "	7.4.16
1039	a/Bom	Pritchard. W.	Amm. Col.	" "	4.4.16
2539	a/Bom	Hall. R.	" "	" "	6.4.16
2853	Dr	Whitehouse. C.	2nd Bty	" "	3.4.16
3244	Gnr	Crowther. H.	Hd Qrs.	" "	4.4.16
2764	Dr.	Sharpe. C.	1st Worc Bty	" "	7.4.16
3017	Gnr	Munn. R.	3rd " "	" "	5.4.16

Reg. No.	Rank	Name	Corps	Remarks	Date
	Capt.	Smith Carrington	N. C H.ᵈ Amm Col.		
2693	Gnr.	Mills. W.	Hd 2ⁿᵈ		
2038	"	Brant. F	1st Bty.		
1020	"	Bacon. G	" "		
2273	"	Gunster. J	2nd "		
2356	a/Bom.	Bantom. W	3rd "		
888	S/Bom	Chester. H	" "	Leave Granted	
2103	Gnr.	Berry J. W	" "	8.4.16, to 15.4.16.	
932	Dr.	Pardoe. E	D "		
3032	"	Foster. J. W. E	" "		
980	Gnr.	Williams. W	" "		
2435	Dr.	Dyer. E	" "		
2688	Ftr.	Parker. W. R.	Amm. Col.		
2298	Dr.	Lee. H.	" "		
898	Bom.	Garbutt. J	2nd Bty.	Completed A.F. W.3126.	
1730	Sgt	Kite. H.	Amm. Col.	Leave granted from to	8.4.16. 7.5.16.
2089	Dr.	Beaman. W	Amm. Col.	To No. 4. C.C.S. struck off strength. (was shown last week, but not taken off strength)	31/3/16.

Reg. No.	Rank	Name	Corps	Remarks	Date
2667	Gnr.	Nott. H.	2nd Bty.	To C.C.S. struck off strength	1/4/16
2164	"	Jackson. G.R.A.	" "	" " " " "	1/4/16
334	Cpl	Potts. A.	Amm. Col.	TRANSFERRED TO 48th DIV. HD. QRS. struck off strength	28/2/16
1029	a/Bom	Griffin. S.	3rd Bty.	allotment 5d per day to mother 18/11/1914 to 31/1/16. now deceased, onwards to Father from 1/2/1916.	
	Captain	Sutherland. J. M.	D. Bty.	Joined from 3rd S.M.F.A BDE	31/3/16
	Lieut.	Gregory. S. D.	D. Bty. }	Joined from reinforcements.	31/3/16
	2/Lieut.	Cole. R. C.	1st " }		
	2/Lieut.	Brindley. H.	2nd " }		
	Lieut	Gregory. S. D.	D. Bty.	Reverted to permanent grade on joining	31/3/16
756	Sgt.	Duggins. A	3rd Bty }	Proceeded on Arty Course	3/4/16
	2/Lieut.	Sellars. G. V.	Amm. Col. }		
2760	Dr.	Paxton. P. }		attached from 3rd S.M.F.A. BDE	31/3/16
322	"	Read. J. F. } (Officer's servant & groom)			

15th April 1916.

Reg. No.	Rank.	Name.	Corps.	Remarks.	Date.
323.	Sgt.	Pulley. G.	3rd Battery.	Granted leave	10-4-16. to 9-5-16.
1504	Cpl.	Pearle. W.	(R.A.M.C. attached.)	" "	" "
900.	Sgt. Whr.	Wood. C.	1st Battery.	" "	12-4-16. to 11-5-16.
465.	Sgt.	Stooke. W.	Amm. Column	" "	" "
332.	Cpl.	Cook. L.	2nd Battery.	" "	13-4-16. to 12-5-16.
892.	Cpl Ftr	Cottrell. A.	" "	" "	" "

COMPLETED A.F. W.3126.

	Capt. & Adjt.	J.C. Dixey.	Hd Qrs.	Granted leave from	13-4-16 to 20-4-16.
319.	Gnr.	Baynton. T.	Amm. Column.	REFUSED TO RE-ENGAGE. PAPERS TO RECORDS.	11-4-16.

15th/April 1916.

Reg. No.	Rank.	Name.	Corps.	Remarks	Date.
2219.	Dr.	Dowler. C.	1st. Battery.	To Hospital.	10-4-16.
2126.	Gnr.	Mills. A. E.	" "	" "	11-4-16.
2973.	"	Jones. F.	" "	" "	12-4-16.
2764.	"	Sharp. E.	" "	" "	12-4-16.
3082.	"	Jeffery. H.	2nd "	" "	8-4-16.
3210	"	Ricketts. T. D.	" "	" "	8-4-16.
2367.	"	Blick. J.	3rd "	" "	11-4-16.
2243.	Bom.	Hicks. E.	" "	" "	12-4-16.
3004.	Gnr.	Vale. J. F.	" "	" "	13-4-16.
2767.	"	Stanton. W. W.	D. "	" "	10-4-16.
764.	Sgt.	Gittins. S.	Amm. Column.	" "	9-4-16.
1060.	Sgt.	Roberts. W.	1st. Bty.	From Hospital.	9-4-16.
2503.	Gnr.	Hale. A.	" "	" "	9-4-16.
2051.	Bom.	Nicklin. W. L.	" "	" "	11-4-16.
3323.	Gnr.	Page. A.	2nd "	" "	10-4-16.
2846.	Dr.	Wall. J.	" "	" "	11-4-16.
1089.	"	Kings. J.	3rd "	" "	9-4-16.
3431.	Gnr.	Weaver. W. H.	2nd "	" "	13-4-16.
2265.	Dr.	Harris. F.	Amm. Column.	" "	11-4-16.
3082.	Gnr.	Jeffery. H.	2nd Bty.	" "	13-4-16.

15th April 1916.

Reg No	Rank	Name	Corps	Remarks	Date
370.	S.Sgt. Sdr.	Sillitoe. H.	Amm. Column.	Posted to 1st Worc Battery.	10-4-16.
126.	Cpl.	Hardiman. H	1st Battery.	TIME EXPIRED. TO BASE pending discharge. struck off strength.	14-4-16.
3210.	Gnr	Ricketts. J.D.	2nd. B.ty.	To C.C.S. struck off strength.	12-4-16.
2284.	"	Martin. A.	"D" "	Posted to 2nd. Bty.	13-4-16.
1881.	"	Hart. J.V.	"D" "	TIME EXPIRED. TO BASE pending discharge. struck off Strength.	13-4-16.
857.	"	Harrison J.J.	2nd. "	Completed A.F. W.3126. Granted leave from to	4-12-15 3-1-16.
	2/Lieut. (Temp.Lt.)	A.C.W. Hobson	3rd "	(Promoted to Temp Capt.)	17-10-15.
	2/Lieut.	C.F.D. Perrins	"D" "	Promoted to Temp Lieut.	17-10-15.
	2/Lieut.	W.A. Woods	2nd "	" " " "	26-11-15.
	2/Lieut.	J.K. Turpin.	Amm. Column.	" " " "	10-2-16.

(Authority Lt. Genl. Director. Genl. of the Terr: Force. 5-4-16.)

15th April 1916.

Reg No.	Rank	Name	Corps	Remarks	Date
2221	Dr.	Grainger. A.	Hd Qrs.	Granted Proficiency Pay Class II from	5-8-15.
1040	Bom.	Sexton. A.	Amm. Column.	Posted to 2nd Battery.	15-4-16
2963.	Gnr.	Allard. F.	1st Battery	}	
1489.	"	Oliver. C.N.	" "	}	
3317.	"	Warrender J.	3rd "	} Proceeded to School of	
583.	"	Beeson. F.	" "	} Mortars for course of	14/4/16.
181.	Bom.	Nicklin. W.J.	D. "	} training.	
2492	Gnr.	Hale. E.	" "	}	
2205	a/Bom	Hughes. W.	2nd Bty.	To be Bom. vice Bom Ashwin promoted.	18-3-16
2278	a/Bom	Rogers. W.	" "	" " " " " Bowcott "	31-3-16
2052	Gnr.	Rea. A.E.	" "	" a/Bom. " a/Bom. Hughes "	18-3-16
2909	"	Wright. J.	" "	" " " " " Rogers "	31-3-16.
2967	"	Bicknell. F.	" "	" " " " " Stanton transferred to D. Battery	31-3-16.

22/4/1916.

Reg. No.	Rank	Name	Corps	Remarks	Date
512.	Gnr	Hayward. G. (number should read	3rd Worcs Bty 512 not 427 -	Joined from D.A.C. please amend)	13/11/15.

22/4/1916.

Reg No.	Rank.	Name.	Corps.	Remarks.	Date.
2492.	Gnr.	Hall. E	"D" Worcs Bty.	Returned from School of Mortars. 4th Army.	21/4/16.
2492.	Gnr.	Hall. E	" " "	Posted to 48th D.A.C. struck off strength (Authority 48th Div. Arty)	22/4/16. 21/4/16.
181.	Bom	Nicklin. W.J.	D. Worcs Bty.	Posted to T.M. Battery struck off strength (Authority T.M.O. 48th Div R.A.	20/4/16. 20/4/16.
2277	Sgt.	Green. F.	"D" Worcs Bty.	Transferred to G.H.Q. BASE struck off strength	21/4/16.
1317.	Cpl	Lucas A.H.			
2581.	Bom	Binding S.T.			
2251.	Gnr.	Clarke G.			
2576.	"	Godsall A.V.		"D" Worcs Bty. Attached to T.M. Bty.	21/4/16.
3120.	"	Raderecht H.			
3214.	"	Green. A.H.			
3414.	"	Russell L.W.			
3438.	"	Steer. E.			

22/4/1916.

Reg No.	Rank.	Name.	Corps.	Remarks.	Date.
2195.	a/Bom.	Harris. J.	3rd Worcs Bty.	Joined from D.A.C.	17-4-16
2760	Gnr.	Paxton. P.P.	"D" Worcs Bty.	Joined from 3rd S.M.F.A Bde	30/3/16
1322.	Dr.	Reid. J.J.	" " "	" " " " taken on strength.	
	2/Lieut	Sellers. V.G.	Amm. Column	Returned from Arty course	15/4/16.
	Captain	Chandler. A	"D" Worcs Bty.	Joined from 48th Div. Arty. H.Q.	18/4/16.
126.	Cpl	Hardiman. H.	1st Worcs. Bty.	Refused to re-engage. Papers to RECORDS.	16/4/16.
728.	Sgt Ftr.	Bick. J	"D" " "	Re-engaged. Papers to RECORDS	18/4/16.
115.	S.S. Far	Rose F. W.	3rd " "	Re-engaged. Papers to RECORDS.	18/4/16.
2273	Gnr.	Gunster. J.H	2nd " "	Married, and placed on separation allowance from that date. allotment 6d per day. Wife's name and address. Flora. D. Gunster. 16. Farley Street. Comer Gardens. Worcester.	10/4/16.

22/4/1916.

Reg. No.	Rank	Name.	Corps.	Remarks.	Date.
2963.	Gnr.	Allard. F.	1st Worcs Bty	Returned from School of Mortars. 4th Army	21/4/16.
1489.	"	Oliver. C.N.	" " "		
2963.	Gnr.	Allard. F.	1st Worcs Bty	Posted to 48th. D.A.C. struck off strength. Authority 48th Div. Arty. 21/4/16	22/4/16
1489.	"	Oliver. C.N.	" " "		
874.	Gnr.	Avery. W.	1st Worcs Bty	Transferred to "D" Battery.	18/4/16.
2779.	Dr	Smith. J.D.	" " "		
3094.	Gnr.	Hales. J.	2nd Worcs Bty	To 29. C.C.S. struck off strength.	19/4/16.
756.	Sgt.	Duggins. A.	3rd Worcs Bty	Returned from Arty Course	17/4/16.
3317.	Gnr.	Warrender. J.	3rd Worcs Bty	Returned from School of Mortars. 4th Army	21/4/16.
583.	"	Beeson. J.	" " "		
583.	Gnr.	Beeson. J.	3rd Worcs Bty	Posted to 48th D.A.C. struck off strength. (Authority 48th Div. Arty. 21/4/1916.	22/4/16.

22/4/1916

Reg No.	Rank	Name.	Corps.	Remarks.	Date.
2962	Gnr.	Hughes. W.	Hd Qrs.	TO HOSPITAL	12.4.16
3126	Dvr.	Holmes. A. C.	" "	" "	18.4.16
2327	Gnr.	Bragg. G.	1st Worc Bty.	" "	16.4.16
2682	Ftr.	Price C J.	" " "	" "	16.4.16
2493	Gnr.	Holt W H.	" " "	" "	18.4.16
3311	"	Barker F F G.	" " "	" "	22.4.16
66	B.S.M.	Heath. R.	3rd "	" "	19.4.16.
993	Dvr.	Field. J.	" "	" "	19.4.16.
1072	Bom.	Martin J G.	" "	" "	19.4.16.
2651	Gnr.	Morris. G.	" "	" "	21.4.16.
2067	"	Griffin. E.	"D" "	" "	20.4.16.
3103	Dvr.	Pryke C L.	Amm. Column.	" "	19.4.16.
2962	Gnr.	Hughes. W.	Hd Qrs	FROM HOSPITAL.	16.4.16.
3126	Dvr.	Holmes. A. C.	" "	" "	21.4.16.
1078	Gnr.	Davis. H J.	1st Worc Bty.	" "	16.4.16.
2219	Dvr.	Dowler. C.	" " "	" "	18.4.16.
2126	Gnr.	Miles. A. C.	" " "	" "	19.4.16.
2764	Dvr.	Sharp. E.	" " "	" "	21.4.16.
2327	Gnr.	Bragg. G.	" " "	" "	22.4.16.
2370	Dvr.	Lane C H (48th D.A.C. attached)	" " "	" "	17.4.16.
2367	Gnr.	Blick. J.	3rd "	" "	17.4.16.
2242	Dvr.	Wedgbury G H	" "	" "	17.4.16.
3004	Gnr.	Vale. J J.	" "	" "	19.4.16.
764	Whr Sgt	Gittins. S.	Amm. Column.	" "	19.4.16.
2814	Gnr.	Tooley L.	2nd Worc Bty	TO HOSPITAL	19.4.16.
3094	"	Hales. J	" " "	" "	16.4.16.

29/4/16

Reg no.	Rank	Name	Corps	Remarks	Date
72429	Gnr.	Herring. J.	Hd Qrs.	To Hospital.	24-4-16
8279	Dr.	Baird. C. B.	1st Battery	" "	26-4-16
1017	"	Hodges J.	" "	" "	24-4-16
2198	"	Woolford. H	" "	" "	26-4-16
2838	B.S.M.	Winzar. A. J.	" "	" "	24-4-16
2312	Gnr.	Allen. G.	" "	" "	24-4-16
3293	"	Browning. A.W.	" "	" "	24-4-16
2729	"	Raybould. W.G.	" "	" "	24-4-16
2370	Dr.	Lane. H. (48th D.A.C. attached)	" "	" "	26-4-16
3156	Gnr.	Tarpey H. (")	" "	" "	28-4-16
532	"	Lewis. H.W.	2nd "	" "	22-4-16
2074	"	Grey. W.	3rd "	" "	25-4-16
3023	"	Dolphin. V.	" "	" "	28-4-16
2356	a/Bdr.	Bantam. W.	" "	" "	29-4-16
3016	" "	Harper. A. E.	" "	" "	29-4-16
68	Gnr.	Kingsly (48th D.A.C. attached)	" "	" "	29-4-16
2101	a/Bdr.	Smith. G. V.	D	" "	22-4-16
2283	Dr.	Twinberrow. G.	" "	" "	25-4-16
3397	"	Belcher. C.	" "	" "	25-4-16
2305	"	Westwood S.	" "	" "	26-4-16
581	Gnr.	Ashford. J.	" "	" "	25-4-16
2682	Ftr.	Price. E. J.	1st "	From "	26-4-16
2312	Gnr.	Allen. G.	" "	" "	25-4-16
2973	"	Jones. J.	" "	" "	25-4-16
2814	"	Tooley. L. A.	2nd "	" "	24-4-16
532	"	Lewis. H.W.	" "	" "	25-4-16
1072	Bdr.	Martin. G.	3rd "	" "	23-4-16

29/4/1916.

Reg No	Rank	Name	Corps	Remarks	Date
993	Dr.	Field, J.	3rd Battery.	From Hospital.	25/4/16
66	B.S.M.	Heath, R.	" "	" "	27/4/16
2194	a/Bdr	Daniels, L.	" "	" "	28/4/16
2101	" "	Smith, G. V.	D. "	" "	24/4/16
2767	Gnr.	Stanton, W.	" "	" "	24/4/16
2067	"	Griffin, C.	" "	" "	26/4/16
	2/Lieut.	Lane, W. K.	1st "	To "	28/4/16
2838	B.S.M.	Wingat, A. J.	" "	To No. 4 C.C.S.	23/4/16
3293	Gnr.	Browning, A. W.	" "	To No. 29 C.C.S.	24/4/16
8279	Dr.	Bind, C. B.	" "	To No. 29 C.C.S.	27/4/16
1034	Bdr.	Bramwich, A. W.	" "	Proceeded on Anti Gas Course.	23/4/16
1034	"	"	" "	Rejoined from Anti Gas Course.	28/4/16
906	Sgt.	Powell, R. G.	2nd. "	Proceeded on Anti Gas Course.	21/4/16
906	"	"	" "	Rejoined from Anti Gas Course	25/4/16

29/4/16.

Reg No.	Rank	Name.	Corps.	Remarks.	Date
1317.	Cpl	Lucas. A. H			
2581.	Bdr.	Binding. S. J.			
2251.	Gnr.	Clarke. F.			
2576.	"	Godsall. A V			
3120.	"	Radevecht. F	"D" Battery.	Transferred to Heavy Trench Mortar Battery.	21/4/16
3214.	"	Green. A. H.		struck off strength	
3414.	"	Russell. L. W.		authority T.M.O. 48th Div R.A.	18/4/16.
3438.	"	Steer. E.			
3103.	Dr.	Price. C.	Amm Column.	To No. 4.C.C.S. struck off strength	22/4/16
	2/Lieut.	Sankey H. B.	2nd. Battery.	Granted extension of leave by War Office to 26/4/16. authority D.A.A. & Q.M.G.	24/4/16.
	Capt. & Adjt.	Dixey. J C	Head Qrs.	Granted leave from to Recalled from leave	13-4-16 20-4-16. 16-4-16
888.	Bdr.	Chester. H.	3rd Battery.	To Hospital.	24-4-16
888	"	"	"	From "	26-4-16.

29/4/16

Reg. No.	Rank	Name	Corps	Remarks	Date
519	Sgt	Boulton. G.	2nd Battery.	Increase in allotment of pay from 10d to 1/10d	24/4/16
962	Cpl	Ashwin. A. R.	" "	Increase in allotment of pay from 1/- to 1/6	24/4/16
2414	Bdr	Coombs. J	3rd "	Proceeded on Anti Gas Course	23/4/16
2414	Bdr	Coombs. J	" "	Rejoined from Anti Gas Course	27/4/16
803	Cpl	Vale. E	" "	Proceeded on Anti Aircraft course	24/4/16
2074	Gnr.	Grey. W.	" "	To Highland C.C.S. struck off strength.	24/4/16
113	Dr.	Wharrad. H	" "	To Base. Time Expires — struck off strength.	28/4/16 12/5/16
3093	Dr.	Guyatt. F.	" "	Discharged from Hospital to Base. struck off strength.	4/4/16
465	Dr.	Collett. A. E. D.	" "	Joined from Div Arty H.Q. taken on strength.	18/4/16
73801	"	Bloomfield. H.	" "		

29/4/1916.

Reg. No.	Rank	Name	Corps	Remarks	Date
2919	Gnr.	Gammon. H	"D" Battery.	allotment of Pay from 6d per day to mother (Mrs. J. Gammon) Paid by Command Paymaster from 8/2/16, to 24/4/16. Payment recommended by Worcestershire Territorial Association 25/4/16. Mother's address :- Mrs. J. Gammon, Tadpole Cottage. Spetchley. Worcestershire.	16-1-16
2435	Dr.	Dyer. G	"D" Battery.	Married. allotment of 6d per day to wife, from 12/4/16. Wife's name and address :- Florence Dyer. 5. Prospect Hill. Kidderminster.	12/4/16

29/4/1916

Reg No.	Rank	Name.	Corps	Remarks.	Date.
	Captain.	Meacher. E.	2nd Battery		
	Capt. & Adjt.	Dixey. J. C.	Hd Qrs		
2441	Dr	Edwards. F. S.	1st Battery.		
2406.	"	Cooke. W.	" "		
2405.	"	Cookson. J. G.	"D" Bty.		
1033.	"	King. A. D.	2nd "		
1051.	"	Crisp. A. R.	" "		
466.	BQMS	Parker. A	3rd "		
3017.	Gnr	Munn. R.	" "	Granted Leave from	29/4/16
994	Dr.	Read. A.	" "	to -	6/5/16
2913.	S.S.	Tyler. B	Amm. Col.		
2104	Tptr.	Hardiman. E	" "		
2254	Dr	Stanley. W	" "		
3064	"	Tomkins. W. A	" "		
1728.	Sgt Ftr	Bick. J	"D" Bty.	Completed A.F. W.3126 Granted leave from to	29/4/16 28/5/16
115	SSgt Far	Rose. F. W.	3rd Battery.	Completed A.F. W.3126 Granted leave from	28/4/16
658.	Cpl	Johnson. A. H	Amm. Col.	to	27/5/16
808.	Cpl	Higgs. W.	"D" Battery.	Completed A.F. W.3126 Granted leave from to	26/4/16 25/5/16

Promotions.   29/4/1916.

Reg. No.	Rank	Name.	Corps.	Remarks.	Date.
494.	Bdr.	Cox. W.	1st Battery.	To be Corporal from — vice Cpl Hardiman to BASE. Time expired.	14-4-16.
1022	a/Bdr	Raby. W. A.	" "	To be Bdr from vice Bdr Winwood transferred to "D" Bty.	31-3-16.
1061.	" "	Merriman. W.	" "	To be Bdr from vice Bdr. Stallard transferred to "D" Bty.	31-3-16.
1097.	" "	Ratcliffe. E. A	" "	To be Bdr from vice Bdr Wood transferred to "D" Bty.	31-3-16.
3133.	" "	Best. H.	" "	To be Bdr from vice Bdr. Cox. promoted Corporal.	14-4-16.
2312.	Gnr	Allen. G.	" "	To be a/Bdr from vice a/Bdr Raby promoted Bdr.	31-3-16
690.	"	Wright, J.P.	" "	To be a/Bdr from vice a/Bdr Merriman promoted Bdr.	31-3-16
661.	"	Breedon. F.	" "	To be a/Bdr from vice a/Bdr Ratcliffe promoted Bdr.	31-3-16.

29/4/1916

Reg No.	Rank	Name	Corps	Remarks	Date
		Promotions contd.			
940	Bdr	Grubb. W.	3rd Bty	To be Cpl from — vice Cpl Franklin transferred to T.M.B	27-1-16
2244	a/Bdr	Whitford H	" "	To be corporal from vice Cpl Lucas transferred to T.M.B.	18-4-16
2975	Gnr	Spencer. F.	" "	To be Bdr from vice Bdr. Heath transferred to D. Bty.	31-3-16
1058	"	Beaman. F.	" "	To be a/Bdr from vice a/Bdr Whitford promoted Corporal	18-4-16
3016	"	Harper. A. E.	" "	To be temp: paid a/Bdr from vice a/Bdr Saunders to 19. CCS	31-3-16

Reg. No.	Rank	Name	Corps	Remarks	Date
3244	Gnr.	Crowther. H.	Hd Qrs.	TO HOSPITAL	29/3/16
1090	Dr.	Twining. E.	1st Bty.	" "	28/3/16
2846	"	Wall. J.	2nd "	" "	28/3/16
2152	Tptr.	Saward. C.	" "	" "	31/3/16
2846	Dr.	Wall. J.	" "	" "	31/3/16
3223	Gnr.	Page. P.	" "	" "	31/3/16
2243	Bom.	Hicks C.	3rd. "	" "	27/3/16
3016	Gnr.	Harper. A. E.	" "	" "	27/3/16
3246	"	Dowler. J.	" "	" "	29/3/16
1089	Dr.	King. J.	" "	" "	" "
2259	"	Dicks. J.	" "	" "	" "
2960	"	Norcott. T.	" "	" "	" "
1027	a/Bom.	Griffin. S.	" "	" "	31/3/16
2194	" "	Daniels. S.	" "	" "	" "
2089	Dr.	Beaman. W. C.	Am. Col.	" "	30/3/16
1039	a/Bom.	Pritchard. W.	" "	" "	" "
2539	"	Hall. R.	" "	" "	31/3/16
2265	Dr.	Harris. F.	" "	" "	" "
2389	Gnr.	Clarke. A.	1st Bty.	FROM HOSPITAL	30/3/16
3339	"	Barrows. R.	2nd "	" "	25/3/16
2698	Dr.	Perkins. W.	" "	" "	" "
2846	"	Wall. J.	" "	" "	30/3/16
512	Gnr.	Hayward. P.	3rd "	" "	27/3/16
2259	Dr.	Dicks. J.	" "	" "	30/3/16
3016	Gnr.	Harper. A. E.	" "	" "	1/4/16
3246	"	Dowler. J.	" "	" "	" "

Reg No.	Rank.	Name.	Corps.	Remarks.	Date
2126	Gnr.	Miles. A.E.	1st Bty.		
2129	Dr.	Smith. F.	" "		
752	Sgt.	Aston. H.	3rd "		
2068	Gnr.	Field. E.	" "	} Granted leave from	28/3/16
	Major	Thompson. S.J.	3rd "	to	4/4/16.
	2/Lieut.	Sankey H.B.	2nd "		
894	Gnr.	Griffiths. C.J.	1st Bty.		
50	Sgt.	Goodyear. W.G.	2nd "	Completed A.F. W.3126.	
13	F.Q.M.S.	Jeynes. W.	Amm. Col.	Granted one months	
33	2.M.S.	Summers. A.J.	" "	leave from	28/3/16
891	Cpl.	Shephard. W.	Hd Qr.	to	27/4/16
2996	Gnr.	Green. J.	3rd Bty.	to BASE for Dental treatment. (struck of strength.)	16/3/16
2164	Gnr.	Jackson. E.R.A.	2nd Bty	TO HOSPITAL	31/3/16.
2667	"	Nott. H.	" "	" "	" "

Reg. No.	Rank	Name	Corps	Remarks	Date
	Major	Taylor. G. H.	2nd Bty.	In command of Brigade.	20/2/16, to 26/2/16
	"	Lattey. J. C.	1st Bty.	" " " "	27/2/16, to 13/3/16
	2/Lieut	Thacker. W. T.	3rd "	TO ENGLAND to report to WAR OFFICE. (struck off strength.)	28/3/16
	2/Lieut.	Smith. S. H.	" "	TO ENGLAND sick, per "H.S. St. George." (struck off strength.)	11/3/16
900.	Sgt Whr.	Wood. C.	1st "	RE-ENGAGED, papers to RECORDS.	29/3/16
894.	Gnr.	Griffiths. E. G.	" "		
812	a/Bom	French. J	" "	REFUSED TO RE-ENGAGE. papers to RECORDS.	29/3/16
1319.	Gnr.	Baynton. T.	Amm. Col.	TO BASE TIME EXPIRES (struck off strength.)	30/3/16 13/4/16
2622.	Dr.	Louch. G	" "	Discharged from Southern General Hospital. ENGLAND	20/3/16
				Granted extension of furlough from to Authority O.I/c Tel. Force Records. 19485.	21/3/16 24/3/16 18/3/16
				Rejoined unit	28/3/16

Vol 15

· CONFIDENTIAL ·

WAR DIARY

OF

241st. (S. M.) Bde. R.F.A.
late 1/2 SM Bde

(VOLUME ~~XIX~~)

From 1/5/16   To 31/5/16

Army Form C. 2118

WAR DIARY
or
INTELLIGENCE SUMMARY
(Erase heading not required.)

Instructions regarding War Diaries and Intelligence Summaries are contained in F.S. Regs., Part II. and the Staff Manual respectively. Title Pages will be prepared in manuscript.

Place	Date	Hour	Summary of Events and Information	Remarks and references to Appendices
BAYENCOURT	1/5/16		Uneventful. Artillery inactive.	WSC
	2/5/16		" " Manoeuvres ensuing	WSC
	3/5/16		Manoeuvres. Visit from members (C.R.A. etc) of North Midland Divisional Artillery prior to proposed relief.	WSC
	4/5/16		Artillery active in trenches	WSC
	5/5/16		Further visits from C.O. & Battery Commanders of 1st North Midland Brigade R.F.A. to take over. Infantry relieved	WSC
	6/5/16		Artillery inactive. 5th & 6th S. Stafford Regts. Reliefs now covering Brigade	WSC
	7/5/16		Further details of relief were arranged with 1st N.M. Bde R.F.A.	WSC
	8/5/16	8.0 am	1st Howr. Bty shelled. Material and personnel damage nil.	WSC
		8.45	Relief of 1 gun 1st Howr Bty by 1 gun D Bty 1st N.M. Bde.	WSC
		9.15 pm	" " " 1 section 2nd " " 1 section 2 Lincoln Bty	WSC
			" " " 1 " 3rd " " Minute relieved retire to wagon lines	WSC

WAR DIARY
or
INTELLIGENCE SUMMARY

Army Form C. 2118

(Erase heading not required.)

Place	Date	Hour	Summary of Events and Information	Remarks and references to Appendices
BAYENCOURT				
	9/5/16	9.0 am	Ammunition Return of 1 gun 1cu wave Bty by Gen B Bty 1st N.M. Bde RFA	W.T.6
	10/5/16	8.45	Review of renumbered Brigades. CRA reviewed 46th (NM) Divisn	W.T.6
		9.15	Review of Bde H.Q. by H.Q. 1st N.M. Bde RFA.	
	11/5/16	9.0 am	Whole Brigade now concentrated on lines	W.T.6
COUIN	12/5/16		in COUIN Training.	W.T.6
	13/5/16		" " "	W.T.6
	14/5/16		" " "	W.T.6
	15/5/16		An Coe reassume 2nd section 4 6th D.A.C.	W.T.6
	16/5/16			W.T.6
	17/5/16	9.0 am	Inspection by C.R.A. Training	W.T.6
	18/5/16	10.0 am	Reorganisation of Bde. D Bty joined 4th S.M. (How) Bde and 5th Warwick (How) Bty joined as Bengals. 24 Dv (SM) Bde RFA now consists A Bty 24 Dv Bde (1st Warwick Bty) B " " " " (2nd " ") C " " " " (3rd " ") D " " " " (5th Warwick How Bty)	W.T.6

Army Form C. 2118

WAR DIARY
or
INTELLIGENCE SUMMARY
(Erase heading not required.)

Instructions regarding War Diaries and Intelligence Summaries are contained in F. S. Regs., Part II. and the Staff Manual respectively. Title Pages will be prepared in manuscript.

Place	Date	Hour	Summary of Events and Information	Remarks and references to Appendices
COUIN	19/5/16	—	Training	wste.
	20/5/16	"	"	wste.
	21/5/16	"	"	wste.
	22/5/16		"	wste.
	23/5/16		"	wste.
	24/5/16		"	wste.
	25/5/16		"	wste.
	26/5/16	5.30 am	Field operations in conjunction with 143rd Inf Bde	wste.
		1.0 pm	"	
	27/5/16		Reconnaissance of rearward line positions continued	wste.
	28/5/16	9.30	Divl Arty Church Parade at St LEGER	wste.
	29/5/16		Training	wste.
	30/5/16		"	wste.
	31/5/16		"	wste.

OC MG. 241 SOUTH MIDLAND FIELD ARTILLERY BRIGADE
LIEUT. COLONEL,

May 6th/1916

No.	Rank	Name	Corps	Remarks	Date
929	Cpl	Franklin. H.			
1071	"	James. A		Transferred to Trench Mortar Battery. (now taken on strength again) but treated as detached only. Authority G.R.O. 1461.(2)	26-1-16.
2951	Gnr	Halls. F.			
425	"	Carpenter. J			
181	Bdr	Nicklin. W.J.		Transferred to Z 48th Trench Mortar Battery. (now taken on strength again) but treated as detached only. Authority G.R.O. 1461 (2)	20-4-16.
2492	Gnr	Hale. E			
2963	"	Allard. F.		Transferred to 48th. D.A.C. (for Trench mortar Battery.) (now taken on strength again) but treated as detached only. Authority G.R.O. 1461.(2)	22-4-16.
1489	"	Oliver. C.N.			
583	"	Beeson. F.			
1317	Cpl	Lucas. A.H.			
2581	Bdr	Binding. S.J.			
2251	Gnr	Clarke. G.			
2576	"	Godsall. A.V.		Transferred to Y. 48th Heavy Trench mortar Battery. (now taken on strength again) but treated as detached only. Authority G.R.O. 1461 (2)	21-4-16.
3120	"	Raderecht. F.			
3214	"	Green. A.H.			
3438	"	Steer. E.			
3414	"	Russell. L.W.			
567	Sgt	Parker. J.F.	3rd Battery		
—	Lieut.	Perrins. C.F.D.	D. "	Proceeded on Arty Course	1-5-16.
874	Dr.	Avery W. (Servant)	" "		

6/5/1916

No.	Rank.	Name	Corps.	Remarks.	Date.
	Major	Oldham. A.C.	(RAMC) Hd Qrs.	to Base. struck off strength. (Authority A.D.M.S. 48th Divn. 492.)	1-5-16
	Captain	Smith. H.	(RAMC) Hd Qrs.	Joined from 5th Royal Sussex Pioneers. taken on strength.	1-5-16
	2/Lieut.	Hustler. J. G.	Am. Column.	Joined from 3/2nd. S.M.F.A. Bde.	5-5-16
3246	Gnr.	Dowler. J.	"D" Battery.	Granted leave from to	5-5-16 12-5-16
	2/Lieut	A. Bonham Edwards.	2nd Bty.		
2732	Dr.	Rowley. A.	Hd Qrs.		
2535	"	Hinton. W.	1st Bty.		
519	Sgt.	Boulton. G.	2nd "		
2052	a/Bdr.	Rea. A. E.	" "		
2909	"	Wright. J.	" "		
2357	Gnr.	Booth. P.	3rd "		
997	"	Grubb. T.	" "		
2744	Dr.	Reynolds. R.	" "		
2480	"	Goodman. H.	" "	Granted leave from to	6-5-16 13-5-16
2197	Gnr.	Waldron. G.	" "		
3434	Bdr.	Woodings. F.	Am Column		
2000	Dr.	Briggs. W.	" "		
2034	"	Carpenter. G.	" "		
2802	Gnr.	Turner. W. F.	1st Bty.		

6/5/1916.

Reg No.	Rank	Name.	Corps.	Remarks.	Date.
2074	Gnr	Grey W.	3rd Battery.	Rejoined from Highland C.C.S. Taken on strength.	5-5-16.
2939.	"	Seabright. F.	" "	To Highland C.C.S. Struck off strength.	4-5-16.
842.	Dr.	Reeves. C.	" "	To No. 4. C.C.S. Struck off strength.	3-5-16.
1875	"	Weaver E.	" "	To No. 29. C.C.S. Struck off strength.	5-5-16
3032.	"	Foster. J.W.E	" "	Owing to death of wife on 23/3/16, has made an allotment of 3d per day from —	27-3-16.
				to Mrs. G. Knowles. 5. Drummond St. WOLVERHAMPTON, who has been appointed guardian for child. (boy).	
				also allotment of 3d per day from 27-3-16 to Mrs. E. Edwards. 11. Sherwood Terrace. Bushbury Lane. BUSHBURY, who has been appointed guardian for child. (girl.)	

6/5/1916.

Reg No.	Rank.	Name.	Corps.	Remarks.	Date.
812.	a/Bdr	Finch, J.	1st. Bty.	To Base — Time expired — struck off strength.	1-5-16. 16-5-16
3311.	Gnr.	Barker. F.F.G.	" "	To 29. C.C.S. struck off strength.	1-5-16.
3348.	S.S	Cook. J.	" "	Increased allotment to Wife from 6d to a 1/- per day from 12-4-16. Wife's name and address. Mrs. Clara Cook. 6. Blakebrook. Kidderminster.	
	2/Lieut.	Sankey. H.B.	2nd Bty.	Returned from sick leave	2-4-16.
803.	Cpl	Vale. E.	3rd "	Returned from anti-Aircraft Course	29-4-16.
764	Sgt Whlr.	Gittins. S.	Am. Column	Posted to 3rd Bty.	1-5-16.
530.	Ftr.	Humphries. J.H.	D. Bty.	Posted to 3rd Bty.	1-5-16.
547.	Sadlr.	Gilks. W.L.			
3088	a/Bdr	Davis. H.W.	D. Bty.	Performed duties of Pay Clerk from to	24-3-16 28-4-16

6/5/1916

Reg No	Rank	Name	Corps	Remarks	Date
3208	Gnr	Morgan. C.H	3rd Battery	TO HOSPITAL	1-5-16
2939	"	Seabright. F.	" "	" "	4-5-16
2240	Dr.	Chantler W.	" "	" "	4-5-16
2907	Bdr	Garbutt. B.	D	" "	3-5-16
3041	Gnr	Stanton. J.A	" "	" "	4-5-16
2875	Dr.	Weavers E	" "	" "	4-5-16
3074	Gnr	Davis G.	" "	" "	5-5-16
842	Dvr.	Reeves C.	" "	" "	2-5-16
2493	Gnr	Holt. W.H	1st "	FROM "	30-4-16
1017	Dvr.	Hodges. T.	" "	" "	1-5-16
2198	"	Woolford H.	" "	" "	2-5-16
2729	Gnr	Ragbourne. W.G	" "	" "	3-5-16
3208	"	Morgan. C.H	3rd "	" "	2-5-16
3016	a/Bdr	Harper. A.E	" "	" "	4-5-16
2651	Gnr	Morris G.	" "	" "	4-5-16
2243	Bdr	Hicks. E.	" "	" "	6-5-16
3397	Dvr.	Belcher C.	D "	" "	3-5-16
2305	"	Westwood. S.H.	" "	" "	3-5-16
72429	Gnr.	Herring J	Hd Qrs.	" "	1-5-16
2962	Gnr.	Hughes W.	Hd Qrs.	transferred to Am. Column	4-5-16
3155	Gnr.	Taylor. J.W	Amm. Column	transferred to Hd Qrs.	4-5-16

13/5/1916.

Reg No.	Rank	Name	Corps	Remarks	Date
	Captain	A. C. W. Hobson	3rd Bty.		
	Lieut.	H. Cross	2nd "		
2644	Dr.	Morris. A.	Hd. Qrs.		
2175	"	Smith. H. G.	1st Bty.		
1073	"	Postings. M.	2nd "		
2018	"	Saunders. J.	" "		
427	Gnr.	Hayter. W. H.	3rd "	Granted Leave from 13-5-16 to 20-5-16.	13-5-16 20-5-16
2822	Sptr.	Turvey. J.	" "		
2480	Dr.	Goodman. H.	" "		
2048	"	Pullen. C.	" "		
360	B.S.M.	Sheldon. W.	Am. Col.		
1099	Gnr.	Booton. E.	" "		
2036	Dr.	McDonough. J.	" "		
3004	Gnr.	Vale. J. F.	3rd Bty.	Proceeds on Signal Course at Hd Qrs, VIII Corps.	10/5/16

13/5/16

Reg No.	Rank	Name	Corps	Remarks	Date
2686	S.S.	Howes. G.H.	Amm Col.	Transferred to 4th S.M. (How.) Brigade. (Authority 48th. Div Arty. — 9/5/16)	11/5/16.
3145.	Gnr.	Northcott. F.J.			
1734.	Dr.	Johnson. H.			
2653.	Gnr.	Maiden. B.	Amm Col.	Transferred to "D" Bty.	13/5/16.
2915.	"	Stevens. W.H.			
2453.	"	Edwards. J.C.			
1008.	"	Stokes. B.			
3334.	Whlr.	Watts. W.	2nd Bty.	Allotment of Pay increased from 10d to 1/- from 23/2/16.	
893.	a/Bdr.	Haughton. G.	2nd Bty.	Re-engaged. completed A.F. W.3126. papers to records.	7/5/16.
407.	Bdr.	Preece. J.E.	Am Column	Re-engaged. Completed A.F. W.3126. papers to records.	10/5/16.

13th May 1916.

Reg No.	Rank.	Name.	Corps.	Remarks	Date.
220.	Sgt.	Willitts. A. M.	"D" Battery	Promoted to Bty Q.M.Sgt. from	11/5/16
2275.	Bdr.	Woodyatt. W. W.	2nd "	To. 29. C.C.S. struck off strength	11/5/16.
3332.	Dr.	Pitt. W.	Amm. Column	Transferred to 3rd. Battery.	10/5/16
2006.	Bdr.	Gwilliam. H.	3rd Bty	Transferred to Highland C.C.S. struck off strength.	12/5/16
2580.	Dr.	Jones. E.	" "		
3499.	Ftr.	Cook. G. A.	"D" "	Transferred to 3rd. S.M.F.A Bde struck off strength (Authority 48th Div. Arty. 9-5-16)	11/5/16.
2767.	Gnr.	Stanton. W.	"D" Battery	To. No. 4. C.C.S. struck off strength	7/5/16
39929	B.S.M.	Shelton. A.	"D" "	Joined from 12th Bty, 35th Brigade R.F.A. taken on strength.	30/4/16.
2186	Pte.	Church. W. J	"D" "	Joined from 2nd S.M.F.Amb: R.A.M.C. taken on attached strength.	9/5/16

13th May 1916.

Reg No.	Rank.	Name.	Corps.	Remarks	Date.
3004.	Cpl. S.S.	Williams. H.J.	1st Bty.	To Hospital	8/5/16.
3844.	Gnr.	Mills. G.W.	2nd "	" "	9/5/16
3825.	"	Jeffrey. H.	" "	" "	11/5/16.
2063.	Dr.	Long. N.	3rd "	" "	9/5/16.
2536.	"	Hogan. W.	" "	" "	10/5/16.
2580.	"	Jones. E.	" "	" "	12/5/16.
2006.	Bdr.	Gwilliam. W.	" "	" "	13/5/16.
2593.	Dr.	Knowles. S.	" "	" "	13/5/16.
2767.	Gnr.	Stanton. W.	" "	" "	5/5/16.
2101.	a/Bdr.	Smith. S.V.	" "	" "	6/5/16.
3079.	Gnr.	Leppard. W.J.	" "	" "	12/5/16.
39929.	B.S.M.	Shelton. A.	" "	" "	12/5/16.
2683.	Dvr.	Payne. W.	1st "	" "	7/5/16.
2683.	Dvr.	Payne. W.	1st Bty.	From Hospital	10/5/16.
2240.	"	Chantler. W.	3rd. "	" "	8/5/16.
3023.	Gnr.	Dolphin. V.	" "	" "	10/5/16.
2536.	Dr.	Hogan. W.	" "	" "	12/5/16.
3005.	Gnr.	Cording. A.	2nd. Bty.	Allotment of pay to Mother 6d per day from	22/7/15.

Mother's address
Mrs. E. Cording.
Glebe Farm.
Llandegveth.
Nr. Caerleon.
Newport.
Mon.

May 19th/1916

Reg No.	Rank.	Name.	Corps.	Remarks.	Date.
360.	B.S.M.	Sheldon. W.			
33.	Q.M.S.	Summers. A.J.			
730.	Sgt.	Kite. H.			
465.	"	Stooke. W.			
864.	"	Hirons. B.			
971.	"	Hickman. E.			
658.	Cpl	Johnson. A.H.			
2288.	"	Bourne. C.			
972.	"	Perry. J.			
773.	Bdr	Bird. W.			
2783.	"	Summers. H.E.			
2303.	"	Stroud. E.			
407.	"	Preece. F.			
2182.	"	Davis. J.T.			
2663.	a/Bdr.	Munslow. G.		B.A.C. transferred to	
1039.	"	Pritchard. W.		2nd Section B.A.C 15-5-16.	
2559.	"	Heaven. W.			
2539	"	Hall. R.			
1029.	"	Wise. E.			
3434	"	Woodings. F.			
13.	F.Q.M.S.	Jeynes. W.			
2913.	S.S.	Tyler. B.			
3083.	Cpl.S.S.	Wiltshire. C.			
2021.	S.S.	Howles. A.			
2022.	S.S.	Palfry. S.			
765	Whl.Sgt.	Jordan. J.			
2688.	Ftr.	Parker. W.R.			
2289	Ftr.Cpl.	Burton. W.			

May 19th/1916

Reg No.	Rank.	Name	Corps	Remarks.	Date.
2450	Sdr.	Elt. W.			
2104	Tptr	Hardiman. E.			
2881	"	Young. H.			
3432	Gnr.	Adkins. J.A.F.			
3520	"	Bryant. H. G.			
3810	"	Barett. J. J.			
1099	"	Booton. C.			
2371	"	Berry. L.			
365	"	Bulloch. C.			
3052	"	Boucher. W. C.			
2350	"	Baker. A.			
2921	"	Cave. D. P.			
2991	"	Cox. J. D.			
2990	"	Carter. C. F.			
3244	"	Crowther. H.		B.A.C. transferred to	
2434	"	Davis. W.		2nd. Section. B.A.C. 15-5-16.	
3074	"	Davis. G.			
2948	"	Duffett. A.			
2893	"	Gane. A.			
2023	"	Hardiman. J.			
2561	"	Hadland. A.			
2908	"	Jines. G.			
2597	"	Kenwrick. W.			
2626	"	Lerry. S.			
2610	"	Lewis. W.			
3338	"	Michael. A.H.			
2674	"	Oliver. J.			
1049	"	O'Shea. D.			

May 19th/1916.

Reg No.	Rank.	Name.	Corps.	Remarks.	Date.
3938.	Gnr	Pearson. W.G			
2962.	"	Hughes. W.			
2723.	"	Payne. W.			
3846.	"	Powell. A.			
3224.	"	Redding. J.			
2777.	"	Steward. H.			
3167.	"	Shaw. C.S.			
2881.	"	Thomasson. L.			
2831.	"	Vaux. J.			
3851.	"	Wheatley. J.			
2078.	"	Walker. W.			
3538.	"	Wilkes. J.			
3031.	"	Williams. E.			
3970.	"	Watt. J.			
3294.	"	Woodward. W.A.			
2866.	"	Weaver. J.		B.A.C. transferred to	
3883.	Dr	Arrowsmith. P.		2nd Section. D.A.C.	15/5/16
2320.	"	Ansell. A.			
3249.	"	Burch. E.			
3316.	"	Badham. W.J.			
3067.	"	Barber. J.			
3141.	"	Barnett. A.			
2215.	"	Bray. W.			
3179.	"	Boyward. W.			
3864.	"	Brettle. E.			
3173.	"	Bowling. N.			
2989.	"	Barnsley. J.H.			
3969.	"	Boyd. E.			

| Reg No. | Rank. | Name. | Corps. | Remarks. | Date. |

19th May 1916.

Reg No.	Rank.	Name.	Corps.	Remarks	Date.
3041.	Dr.	Baldwin. F.			
2371.	"	Blissett. F.			
2000.	"	Briggs. W.			
3201.	"	Baylies. G.			
830.	"	Caldwell. J.			
3063.	"	Cotterell. A.			
3875.	"	Cross. A.			
2034.	"	Carpenter. G.			
3937.	"	Clarke. G.			
3495.	"	Cooper. A.			
2088.	"	Duffield. G.			
3361.	"	Dyson. A. L.			
3855.	"	Eacott. J.			
3866.	"	Elgar. F.			
2465.	"	Fulcher. J.		B.A.C. transferred to	
3868.	"	Francombe. C.A.		2nd Section. DAC. 15/5/16.	
3856.	"	Forest. F.			
3512.	"	Garbutt. A.			
3876.	"	Greenslade. J.			
2471.	"	Griffin. J.			
3910.	"	Godwin. E.			
2479.	"	Grealey. M.			
3026.	"	Hardman. J.			
3508.	"	Hemming. J.			
2040.	"	Hawker. C.			
3273.	"	Harmer. R.J.			
3859.	"	Harford. C.W.			
3126.	"	Holmes. A.E.			

19th May 1916.

Reg.No.	Rank.	Name	Corps.	Remarks	Date.
2091.	Dr.	Homer. J			
3869.	"	Hambridge. A.S.			
3870.	"	Hawkins. C.C.			
2552.	"	Hanley. W.			
3871.	"	Hearn. L.			
3884.	"	Howard. W.H.			
3198.	"	Hooper. J.N.			
2560.	"	Hughes. C.			
3291.	"	Hopkins. N.W.			
3451.	"	Hames. C.			
3286.	"	James. R.W.			
2581.	"	Jones. J.			
2173.	"	Jones. A.H.			
2586.	"	Jeynes. H.			
3227.	"	Joyner. R.J.		B.A.C. transferred to	
2307.	"	Kelly. H.		2nd Section S.A.C. 15-5-16	
2488.	"	Kite. J.S.			
2998.	"	Lewis. G.H.			
2297.	"	Lampitt. W.			
2298.	"	Lee. H.			
2622.	"	Louch. G.			
3100.	"	Morris. R.			
2036.	"	McDonough. J.			
504.	"	Paget. W.			
2724.	"	Purnell. E.			
3290.	"	Rees. A.D.			
2751.	"	Restall. A.			
3249.	"	Shuker. G.			

May 19th/1916

Reg No.	Rank.	Name.	Corps.	Remarks.	Date.
2793.	Dr.	Slade. H			
3917.	"	Stovold. J.J.			
3219.	"	Smith. W.G.			
3243.	"	Smith. A.			
3245.	"	Smith. E.H.			
3064.	"	Tomkins. W.A.			
2929.	"	Tongue. C.			
3022.	"	Taylor. C.		B.A.C. transferred to 2nd. Section. D.A.C. 15-5-16.	
2135.	"	Taylor. V.			
2828.	"	Thorne. C.			
3116.	"	Watkins. E.J.			
2857.	"	Wright. C.			
3109.	"	Willis. C.			
2880.	"	Yoxall. R.			

19th. May 1916.

Reg no.	Rank.	Name.	Corps.	Remarks.	Date.
395.	Dr.	Judge. A.			
12.	"	Lamb. A.			
35.	"	Lamb. W.			
542.	"	Lorriman. A. E.			
636.	"	Masefield. A. W.			
545.	"	Mears. H.			
115.	"	Packwood. C.			
1227.	"	Pearsall. A. W.			
148.	"	Reid. J. W.			
199.	"	Redmayne. G. B.			
230.	"	Seymour. J. R. E.			
30.	"	Shilton. N. J.	"D" Howitzer Bty, joined from		
491.	"	Shufflebotham. F.	243rd. S. M. Bde, R.F.A. 18-5-16.		
746.	"	Stokes. E. B.			
259.	"	Tomes. C.			
138.	"	Tuckey. E. J.			
175.	"	Weston. H.			
637.	"	Whiteley. A.			
145.	"	Wolley. D. E.			
182.	"	Wood. J. F.			
847.	"	Woodhead. W.			
235.	"	Woodhouse. A. E.			

19th/May 1916.

Reg No.	Rank.	Name.	Corps.	Remarks.	Date.
656.	Gnr.	Shape. J.			
722.	"	Spicer. C.			
213.	"	Sutton. C. V.			
260.	"	Sutton. J.			
556.	"	Taylor. G.			
23.	"	Wallace. F.			
343.	"	Warner. J. J.			
612.	"	Welton. D.			
131.	"	Whittaker. F C			
1042.	"	Wood. A.			
47.	Dr.	Alsop. A.			
18.	"	Bayliss. J.			
62.	"	Bradley. H.			
1213.	"	Bullock. J.			
84.	"	Cave. F. E. W.			
94.	"	Coles. G.		"D" Howitzer Bty, joined from	
1124	"	Desborough. J.		243rd S. M. Bde. R.F.A. 18-5-16.	
587	"	Dyer. F.			
223	"	Flowers. R.			
222.	"	Frost. C. C.			
329.	"	Furness. P.			
116.	"	Groudle. A.			
625.	"	Hall. J.			
232.	"	Healey. H.			
123.	"	Hynes. W.			
1067	"	Hill. H.			
60.	"	Joyce. T. J.			
221.	"	Frost. C.			

Reg No.	Rank.	Name.	Corps.	Remarks.	Date.

May 19th/1916.

Reg No.	Rank	Name	Corps	Remarks	Date
196.	Gnr	Forrester. J.			
528.	"	Fowler. A. E.			
106.	"	Giddens. H.			
76.	"	Goode. A.			
256.	"	Goode. D. J.			
818.	"	Green. E. J.			
152.	"	Hamnett. A.			
134.	"	Hardman. C. H.			
733	"	Hawkins. C.			
69.	"	Hopkins. D.			
244.	"	Hughes. H.			
627.	"	Hunt. H.			
631	"	Ives. L.			
162.	"	Jeves. E. F.			
170.	"	Lee. G. R.			
239.	"	Long. V.			
153.	"	Nelson. L. A.			
140.	"	Owen. H.		"D" Howitzer Bty, joined from	
160.	"	Owen. J. S.		243rd. S. M. Bde R.F.A.	18-5-16.
197.	"	Packwood. A. M.			
548.	"	Pears. A.			
278.	"	Pilkington. A.			
1070.	"	Price. W. S.			
219.	"	Rodgers. O.			
14.	"	Russell. F.			
75.	"	Sargent. W.			
154.	"	Slator. H.			
46	"	Smith. S. G.			

19th May 1916.

Reg No.	Rank.	Name.	Corps.	Remarks.	Date.
220.	Sad. Cpl.	Yarwood. F.			
155.	Far. Sgt.	Stephens. J.			
129.	Cpl S.S.	Spriggs. F.			
173.	S.S.	Humphries. R.			
130.	S.S.	Hutton. A.			
194.	Tptr.	Shelley. F.			
26.	Gnr.	Alsop. W.			
598.	"	Anderson. J.			
1097.	"	Armstrong. J.			
195.	"	Asher. J. W.			
599.	"	Barker. R.			
1010.	"	Barnett. W. H.			
172.	"	Barnwell. A. W.			
33.	"	Blinco. J.			
233.	"	Bosworth. F. A.			
758.	"	Bryan. C. E.		"D" Howitzer Bty, joined from 243rd. S.M. Bde. R.F.A. 18-5-16.	
640.	"	Bullivant. H.			
255.	"	Cash. B.			
117.	"	Collier. J.			
99.	"	Collins. C.			
779.	"	Cooke. J. F.			
125.	"	Cope. P.			
453.	"	Cumberland. F.			
164.	"	Cutts. A. L.			
1058.	"	Dickenson. W.			
1059.	"	Dilnott. R.			
250.	"	Fenton. J.			
137.	"	Ford. A. J.			

19th May 1916

Reg No.	Rank.	Name.	Corps.	Remarks.	Date.
29.	B.S.M	Hopewell. J.			
143.	Whr.Q.M.S	Pryer. J.			
17.	Q.M.S.	Painter. P.			
40.	Sgt.	Millership. W.			
51.	"	Widdowson. O.			
177.	"	Lines. J.			
101.	"	Gibbons. H.			
110.	"	Heath. W.			
178.	Cpl	Neal. A.			
93.	"	Sparks. V.			
114.	"	Shepherd. J.			
198.	"	Hipwell. G.H.			
4.	"	Wetherington. S.			
38.	Bdr.	Parker. D.			
211.	"	Gilks. L. R.			
56.	"	Smith. D.	"D" Howitzer Bty. joined from		
108.	"	Barrett. J.	243rd S.M. Bde. R.F.A. 18-5-16.		
136.	"	Roberts. J.			
245.	"	Rixon. J.			
28.	"	Vears. W.			
174.	"	Battson. H.			
214.	a/Bdr.	Eaton. R.			
193.	"	Ainsley. H. R.			
133.	"	Cronin. A.			
143	"	Davis. J.			
144.	"	Wolley. R. J.			
54.	Whr.Cpl.	Watson. G.			
127.	Sadr.Sgt.	Dosher. L.			
Reg No.	Rank.	Name.	Corps.	Remarks.	Date.

19th May 1916.

Reg No.	Rank.	Name.	Corps.	Remarks.	Date.
39929	B.S.M.	Shelton. A.			
747	Sgt.	Darke. A.			
50.	"	Goodyear. W. G.			
730.	"	Lane. H.			
758.	"	Sealey. H.			
220.	Q.M.S	Willetts. A. M.			
3281.	Cpl	Back. R. E.			
2255.	"	Canty. H.			
835.	"	Green. W.			
3807.	"	Munday. D.			
2230.	"	Willis. A. E.			
808.	"	Higgs. W.			
2083.	Bdr.	Cottrell. J. E.			
2907.	"	Garbutt. B. H.		"D" Worcester Bty	
1054.	"	Heath. G.		transferred to	
3809.	"	Norman. E. G. M.		243rd. S.M. Bde. R.F.A.	18-5-16.
912.	"	Porter. J. E.			
3804.	"	Stokes. A.			
955.	"	Stallard. A. H.			
3440.	"	Tromans. J. W.			
559	"	Winwood. W.			
1059.	"	Wood. T. G. R.			
3803.	"	Thornton. R.			
3088.	a/Bdr.	Davis. H. W.			
2101.	"	Smith. G. V.			
2084.	"	Stanton. W.			
2987.	"	Shacklock. J.			
2710.	Sup a/Bdr.	Preston. W.			

May 19th/1916.

Reg No.	Rank.	Name.	Corps.	Remarks.	Date.
2819.	Sup a/Bdr.	Taylor. W.			
2859.	"	Webb. D.			
728.	Sgt Ftr.	Bick. J.			
2905.	Sadr.	Cockell. J. W.			
3295.	S.S.	Lampitt. J.			
3815.	Ftr.	Stokes. W. M.			
3813.	S.S.	Wyatt. J.			
2854.	Sad. Cpl.	Wilcox. J.			
2861.	S.S.	Westwood. J.			
2334.	S.S.	Taylor. S.			
3503.	Dr.	Beasley. A. E.			
3397.	"	Belcher. C.			
3455.	"	Butcher. G. H.			
3971.	"	Chambers. G. M. L.			
2405.	"	Cookson. J. V.			
899.	"	Crouch. W.		"D" Worcester Bty,	
2192.	"	Cassell. C. W.		transferred to	
2402.	"	Churchill. A.		243rd. S. M. Bde. R.F.A.	18-5-16
827.	"	Cantrell. J. W.			
2418.	"	Christian. W.			
2435.	"	Dyer. C.			
3877.	"	Evans. W. C.			
2447.	"	Edwards. J.			
3032.	"	Foster. J. W. C.			
3857.	"	Giles. C.			
2480.	"	Goodman. H.			
2478.	"	Giddins. E.			
1094.	"	Harris. G. H.			

Reg No.	Rank.	Name.	Corps.	Remarks.	Date.

19th May 1916.

Reg No.	Rank.	Name.	Corps.	Remarks.	Date.
2496.	Dr.	Harris. F.			
2511.	"	Hessell. B.			
3315.	"	Hopkins. J. S.			
2917.	"	Hall. A. E.			
2555.	"	Hiles. A.			
2265.	"	Harris. F.			
2602.	"	Lea. W.			
1041.	"	Malins. W.			
2960.	"	Norcott. J.			
2048.	"	Pullen. E.			
932.	"	Pardoe. E.			
2694.	"	Payne. G.			
1031.	"	Powell. J.			
2938.	"	Pitchers. H.			
3498.	"	Parkes. H.			
3276.	"	Prior. F.			
999.	"	Ramsey. E.		"D" Worcester Battery	
2129.	"	Smith. F.		transferred to	
2254.	"	Stanley. W.		243rd S. M. Bde. R. F. A.	18-5-16.
2283.	"	Twinberrow. G. W.			
2815.	"	Tolley. W.			
2805.	"	Till. A. R.			
3230.	"	Thompson. G. W.			
3923.	"	Werrett. F. E. J.			
2835.	"	Wintle. E.			
2016.	"	Wall. P.			
985.	"	Wigley. W.			
2853.	"	Whitehouse. E.			

19th May 1916.

Reg No.	Rank.	Name.	Corps.	Remarks.	Date.
3391	Dr.	Watts. T. C.			
1000	"	Willis. T.			
2305	"	Westwood. S. H.			
2779	"	Smith. T. D.			
1322	"	Reid. J. T.			
465	"	Collett. A. E.			
73801	"	Bloomfield. H.			
1734	"	Johnson. H.			
2653	"	Meaiden. B.			
2915	"	Stevens. W. H.			
2453	"	Edwards. J. E.			
1008	"	Stokes. B.			
3831	Gnr.	Ashford. J.			
2324	"	Burges. P. H.			
2340	"	Bradley. C. T.			
2926	"	Birch. C.	"D" Worcester Battery,		
3925	"	Bartlett. A. E.	transferred to		
3974	"	Brownsey. H. H.	243rd. S.M.Bde. R.F.A. 18-5-16.		
3892	"	Brooks. W.			
3927	"	Creese. E.			
3246	"	Dowler. J.			
2292	"	Delahay. T.			
2027	"	Evans. T. G.			
1016	"	Evans. G. H.			
3894	"	Griffiths. H. T.			
2067	"	Griffin. E.			
2977	"	Gill. P.			
2919	"	Gammon. H.			
Reg No.	Rank.	Name.	Corps.	Remarks.	Date.
3391	Dr.	Watts. T. C.			

19th May 1916.

Reg No.	Rank.	Name.	Corps.	Remarks.	Date.
3830.	Gnr.	Griffiths. O.S			
2514.	"	Hollingshead. T.			
3090.	"	Hobbs. W.			
2985.	"	Harber. T.			
3172.	"	Homer. A. E.			
2050.	"	Knowles. G.			
3079.	"	Leppard. W. T.			
2634.	"	Mackie. H.			
2116.	"	Miles. S. A.			
2635.	"	Mallard. J.			
3231.	"	Michael. S. J.			
2964.	"	Oliver. L. G.			
3845.	"	Pandfield. L.			
1096.	"	Powell. L.			
2701.	"	Penzer. G. H.			
2735.	"	Rowbotham. T.	"D" Worcester Battery		
2738.	"	Reece. P.	transferred to		
2747.	"	Reed. R.	243rd. S. M. Bde. R.F.A. 18-5-16.		
3041.	"	Straton. J. A.			
2999.	"	Shambrook. H.			
2807.	"	Turner. P.			
3494.	"	Trump. G.			
2212.	"	Widdus. H.			
980.	"	Williams. W. A.			
3431.	"	Weavers. W. H.			
3227.	"	Watkins. G. H.			
2197.	"	Waldren. G.			
3941.	"	Yarrington. W.			

19th May 1916

Reg No.	Rank.	Name.	Corps.	Remarks.	Date.
3006	Gnr.	Yeates. C.			
3939	"	Pickman. H.			
874	"	Avery. W.		"D" Worcester Bty, transferred to	
2760	"	Paxton. P.P.		243rd. S.M. Bde. R.F.A.	18-5-16.
3145	"	Northcott. F.J.			

19-5-1916.

Reg. No.	Rank.	Name.	Corps.	Remarks.	Date.
181.	Bdr.	Nicklin. W. L.	late "D" Bty 2nd Bde, now transferred to 243rd. S.M. Bde. R.F.A.	attached to Z. 48th T.M. Bty.	Taken on strength 18/3/16.
2492.	Gnr.	Hale. E.	(ditto)	attached to 48th D.A.C. as reinforcement.	
3889.	Cpl	Lucas A. H.			
3913.	Bdr.	Binding S. J.			
3893.	Gnr.	Clarke G.		attached to V. 48th T.M. Bty.	
3929.	"	Godsall A. V.	(ditto)		
3120.	"	Raderecht F.			
3214.	"	Green A. H.			
3438.	"	Steer E.			
3414.	"	Russell L. W.			
3214.	Gnr.	Green. A. H.	ditto.	To Hospital.	5-5-16.
3214.	"	Green. A. H.	ditto.	From do.	14-5-16.
3414.	Gnr.	Russell. L. W.	ditto.	To Hospital.	9-5-16.
	2/Lieut.	Hustler J. G.	B/241 Bty.	Transferred to D.A.C. struck off strength	14-5-16.
	Captain.	Smith Carrington N.E.H.	late Am Col.	Transferred to D.A.C.	15-5-16.
	2/Lieut.	Sellars. G. V.	ditto	struck off strength.	
3185.	Gnr.	Chambers. N. V.	late "D" Worcs Bty	Transferred to C/241st Battery.	18-5-16.

19th May 1916.

Reg No.	Rank.	Name.	Corps.	Remarks	Date.
2930.	Dr.	Farley. B.	A/241. Bty.	To Hospital.	14.5.16.
3887.	"	Husson. B. G.	C/241 "	" "	14.5.16.
2657.	"	Cooper. A.	ditto.	" "	15.5.16.
2271.	"	Yoxall. H.	ditto.	" "	17.5.16.
3090.	Gnr.	Fox. C. J.	ditto.	" "	18.5.16.
160.	"	Owen J. S.	D/241 Battery.	To Hospital. (teeth)	12.5.16.
29.	B.S.M.	Hopwell. G.	do do.	To Hospital	13.5.16.
3016.	a/Bdr.	Harper. A. E.	C/241. "	From Hospital.	16.5.16.
2356.	" "	Barton. W.	do "	" "	18.5.16.
160	Gnr.	Owen. J. S.	D/241 "	" "	14.5.16.
3041.	Gnr.	Stanton. J.	D. Bty. 2nd S.M. Bde. now 243rd S.M. Bde. R.F.A.	From Hospital.	14.5.16.
2457.	Gnr.	Farley J.	Hd Qrs.		
2839.	Gnr.	Wilton. C.	A./241. Bty.		
2309.	Sdlr.	Annis H.			
2050.	Gnr.	Knowles. G.		Granted leave from 19.5.16 to 26.5.16.	
2059.	"	Tyler. J.	B/241. Bty.		
2085.	Dr.	Rimmer C.J.			
2925.	Gnr.	Rumney. R.			
998.	Dr.	Evans. J.	C/241. Bty.		
2071.	Tptr.	Cotterell. G.			

19th May 1916.

Reg No.	Rank.	Name.	Corps	Remarks.	Date.
	Lieut.	Perrins. C.F.D.	Old "D" Bty 2nd. Bde, now transferred to 243rd Bde. R.F.A.	Returned from Arty Course	
874	Dr.	Avery. W. (servant)	ditto.		1.5.16.
567.	Sgt.	Parker. J.T.	C/241st Bde. R.F.A.		
	Captain	J. M. Sutherland			
	Captain.	A. L. Chandler.	"D" Battery 2nd Bde. R.F.A. transferred to 243rd. Bde. R.F.A.	struck off strength.	18.5.16.
	Lieut.	C.F.D. Perrins.			
	2/Lieut.	J. H. Brindley.			
1	2/Lieut.	L. D. Gregory.			
	Major.	Nickalls. C. P.	now D/241st Battery. R.F.A.	Joined from 243rd Bde R.F.A. taken on strength.	18.5.16.
	a/Captain.	Hayes. M. L.			
	Lieut.	Pridmore. R. G.			
	2/Lieut.	Bassett. D. D.			
	2/Lieut.	Withers. R. N. S.			
	2/Lieut.	Spencer. F. W.			
125.	Gnr.	Cope. P.	D/241 Bty.	proceeded on leave	13.5.16
491.	Dr.	Shufflebotham. F.	ditto.	" " "	13.5.16.
220.	Sad. Cpl.	Yarwood. F.	ditto.	" " "	17.5.16.
223.	Dr.	Flowers. R.	ditto.	" " "	17.5.16.

19th May 1916.

Regtl No.	Rank	Name	Corps	Remarks	Date
442.	Cpl S.S.	Stevenson. G	A. Battery.	Joined from 48th D.A.C.	19·5·16.
456.	Gnr.	Edmonds. J	A do.	taken on strength.	
2593.	Dr.	Knowles. S.	C Battery.	To No. 29. C.C.S. struck off strength	13·5·16
2939.	Gnr.	Seabright. F.	C Battery	Returned from Highland C.C.S. taken on strength.	15·5·16.
3088	Cpl	Davis. H.W.	D. Battery, now transferred to 243rd S.M. Bde. R.F.A. on joining from Reinforcements on 31·3·16, was reverted to Gunner.		
3088.	Gnr	Davis. H.W.	ditto.	Promoted to paid a/Bdr. 31·3·16	
12.	Dr.	Lamb. A.	4th S.M. Amm Col. now 243rd Bde.	Transferred to D. Bty. 241st Brigade	12·5·16.
	Lieut.	Pridmore. R.G.	D/241. Battery	Proceeded on Arty course. HAVERNAS.	14·5·16.
153.	Gnr.	Nelson. L.A (Servant)	" "	" " " "	14·5·16.
198.	Cpl.	Stipwell. G.A.	" "	Returned from ditto.	14·5·16

May 19th/1916

Reg No.	Rank.	Name.	Corps.	Remarks.	Date.
333	S.Sgt Farrier	Sheward. A.	B. Battery	Re-engaged. Completed A.F.W. 3126. Papers to RECORDS.	15·5·16
906	Sgt.	Powell. G.R.	B. Battery	Re-engaged. Completed A.F.W. 3126. Papers to RECORDS.	16·5·16
3823	Dr.	Maddick. S.	C. Battery	Allotment of pay 6d per day to Mother from 3·9·15. Paid by Devon. Terr. Assoc., up to — 8·5·16. Payment by Worc. Terr. Assoc. commenced 9·5·16.	

Mother's name and address:—

Mrs. Emma Maddick.
68. Fore Street.
TOTNES. Devon.

| 3112 | Gnr. | Cross. P.S. | C. Bty. | Allotment of pay 6d per day to Mother from 3·1·16. Payment by Worcs., Terr, Assoc, commencing 9·5·16 | |

Mother's name and address:—

Mrs. Sarah Ann Cross.
162 Florence Road.
WIMBLEDON. Surrey

19th May 1916.

Reg.No.	Rank.	Name.	Corps.	Remarks.	Date.
3126.	Dr.	Holmes. A.E.	Hd Qrs.	Transferred to Am. Col, now 2nd Section. D.A.C.	13·5·16
3244.	Gnr.	Crowther. H.			
3828.	Gnr.	Thomas. L.	Am. Col (now 2nd Section D.A.C.)	Transferred to Hd Qrs.	13·5·16
2369.	"	Ball. J.			
3436.	Cpl	Hill. J.J.	A. Battery.	Allotment decreased from 2/- to 6d a day from 27/4/16, to his wife, Mrs. Kate Elizabeth Hill, Police Station. 67. High St. EVESHAM	
3009.	Cpl.	Williams. H.F.	A. Battery	To. No. 4 C.C.S. struck off strength	16·5·16
	Major.	Lattey. J.C.	"	Posted to D.A.C. struck off strength	18·5·16.
2386.	Gnr.	Crump. W.J. (Groom)	"	Attached to 48th D.A.C.	18·5·16.
2761.	"	Saunders. W. (Servant)	"		
	Captain	Saunders. G.N.	"	Joined from D.A.C. taken on strength	
11872	B.S.M.	Cowland. H.S.	"	" " " "	
125.	Dr	Jones. W. (Groom)	"	" " " "	
1691.	Gnr.	Mutter. G.	"	" " " "	18-5-16.

May 26th/1916.

Reg No.	Rank	Name.	Corps.	Remarks	Date
	2/Lieut.	Bassett. D. D.	D/241. Battery	Posted to R.A. Std 2n. struck off strength	21/5/16
219.	Gnr.	Rodgers. O. (servant)	do.		
23.	"	Wallace. F. (groom)	do.		
134.	Sgt	Miles. G. W.	A.V.C.	joined for duty with A/241 Bty.	taken on attached strength 24.5.16
181.	"	Manton. H. H.	"	" " " " B/241 "	
139.	"	Barwell. S.	"	" " " " C/241 "	
194.	"	Beeson. C. J.	"	" " " " B/241 "	
	2/Lieut.	Sellars. G.	B/241 Bty.	Joined from D.A.C.	temporarily attached. 25.5.16.
	2/Lieut.	Mottram. F.	A/241 "	" " " "	
	2/Lieut.	Flowers. H. F.	C/241 "	" " " "	
	2/Lieut.	Lines. H. D.	Late Am. Col.	Transferred to D.A.C. struck off strength	15.5.16.
2975	Bdr.	Spencer. F.	C/241. Bty.	To be Pay Clerk from	21.2.16.
994.	Dr.	Read. A.	ditto	To be Roughrider from	31.3.16.

26th May 1916.

Reg No.	Rank.	Name.	Corps.	Remarks.	Date.
108.	Bdr.	Barrett. F.	D/241. Battery.		
136.	"	Roberts. F.	" "		
129.	Cpl. S.S	Spriggs. J.	" "		
155.	Far Sgt.	Stephens. J.	" "		
127.	Sdlr. Sgt.	Dosher. L. A.	" "		
140.	Gunner	Owen. H.	" "	Re-engaged.	
138.	Dvr.	Tuckey. C. C.	" "	Completed. AFW. 312-6.	
133.	a/Bdr.	Cronin. A. H.	" "		
134.	Gnr.	Hardman. C. H.	" "	Papers to Records. 26.5.16.	
117.	"	Collier. J.	" "		
2243.	Bdr.	Hicks. C.	C/241. Bty.	Re-engaged. Completed A.F. W.312.6. Papers to Records. 25.5.16.	
1489.	Gnr.	Oliver. C. N.	A/241. Bty. attached to 480th. D.A.C. as reinforcement for T.M. BATTERIES	Allotment of pay 6d. per day from 21/6/15 to Mrs. M. Oliver. (Mother.)	

Payment by Worcs. Terr. Association, commencing 9.5.16.

Mother's address :-

Mrs. M. Oliver.
No. 1. Weston Terrace.
Paignton.
Devon.
England.

26th May 1916.

Reg No.	Rank.	Name.	Corps.	Remarks.	Date.
3888.	Dr.	Viner. J. W. H.	A/241 Battery.	To Hospital	20/5/16
3402.	Gnr.	Priest. C. W.	do.	" "	21/5/16
2441.	Dr.	Edwards. F. J.	do.	" "	21/5/16.
2031.	"	Rouse. E. W.	do.	" "	24/5/16.
1095.	"	Langley. B.	do.	" "	24/5/16.
799.	Gnr.	Maullin. W.	B/241 Battery.	" "	21/5/16.
2693.	"	Powell. J.	do.	" "	22/5/16.
347.	Bdr.	Allen. W.	do.	" "	24/5/16.
2275.	"	Rogers. W.	do.	" "	25/5/16.
3016.	a/Bdr.	Harper. A. E.	C/241. Battery.	" "	22/5/16.
144.	"	Wolley. P. J.	D/241. Battery	" "	20/5/16
1124.	Gnr.	Desborough. J.	do.	" "	20/5/16
199.	Dr.	Redmayne. C. B.	do.	" "	21/5/16.
2930.	Dr.	Farley. B.	A/241. Battery.	From Hospital.	20/5/16.
3402.	"	Priest. C. W.	do.	" "	22/5/16.
3900.	"	Cooper. A.	C/241 Battery.	" "	21/5/16.
2053.	"	Long. V.	do.	" "	22/5/16
2271.	"	Yoxall. H.	do.	" "	25/5/16.
3090	Gnr.	Fox. C. D.	do.	" "	26/5/16
68.	Dr.	Kinsley. P. (D.A.C. attd to)	do.	" "	20/5/16.
2006.	Bdr.	Gwilliam. H.	C/241 Bty.	Returned from Highland C.C.S. taken on strength again.	24/5/16.
2580.	Dr.	Jones. E.			
1124.	Gnr.	Desborough. J.	D/241/ Bty.	To No 4. C.C.S. struck off strength.	24/5/16.

— CONFIDENTIAL —

WAR DIARY

of.

241st (S.M.) BDE. R.F.A.

(VOLUME XX)

from 1/6/16   to 30/6/16

Army Form C. 2118.

WAR DIARY
or
INTELLIGENCE SUMMARY.
(Erase heading not required.)

Instructions regarding War Diaries and Intelligence Summaries are contained in F.S. Regs., Part II. and the Staff Manual respectively. Title pages will be prepared in manuscript.

Hour, Date, Place	Summary of Events and Information	Remarks and references to Appendices
CO UIR.		
1/6/16	Surveying Positions in 29th Divn area about Q. 15b. (57D. SE 20,000) "B" & "C" Batteries. Preparing Positions in "E Divn" area about Q.H.a.	W.F.b.
2/6/16	Surveying Batteries as above. Surveying	W.F.b.
3/6/16	" " " " " Batteries	W.F.b.
4/6/16	" " " " "	W.F.b.
5/6/16	" " " " "	W.F.b.
6/6/16	" " " " "	W.F.b.
7/6/16	" " " " "	W.F.b.
8/6/16	Evening. D. Bty (How) went to positions S.W. of HEBUTERNE.	W.F.b.
9/6/16	Surveying Batteries still on above work. 242nd Bde were in positions on our	W.F.b.

Army Form C. 2118.

WAR DIARY
or
INTELLIGENCE SUMMARY.
(Erase heading not required.)

Instructions regarding War Diaries and Intelligence Summaries are contained in F. S. Regs., Part II. and the Staff Manual respectively. Title pages will be prepared in manuscript.

Hour, Date, Place	Summary of Events and Information	Remarks and references to Appendices
C.D.U.I.V		
10/6/16	Uneventful. Batteries carrying on with improvements. D Bty registering	W.B.
11/6/16	C.O. on leave. Major S.J. Thompson Commanding. Being also Uneventful.	W.B.
12/6/16	" " Batteries no action	W.B.
13/6/16	" " "	W.B.
14/6/16	" " "	W.B.
15/6/16	C.O. returned from leave. Batteries	W.B.
16/6/16	Uneventful. " " no action	W.B.
17/6/16	" " "	W.B.
18/6/16	" " "	W.B.
19/6/16	A.T.S. & C. Bty. were to have this position this evening but relieved W.B.	

(73989) W4141—463. 400,000. 9/14. H.&J.Ltd. Forms/C. 2118/10.

Army Form C. 2118.

WAR DIARY
or
INTELLIGENCE SUMMARY.
(Erase heading not required.)

Instructions regarding War Diaries and Intelligence Summaries are contained in F.S. Regs., Part II. and the Staff Manual respectively. Title pages will be prepared in manuscript.

Hour, Date, Place	Summary of Events and Information	Remarks and references to Appendices
COUIN. 20/9/16	Manœuvrique A.B.&C. Batys continuing with digging also submerging with heavy amounts of ammunition. Batteries as above.	WSL WSL WSL
21/9/16		
22/9/16		
23/9/16 evening. A.B. &C. Batys moved into position at places mentioned above. (1st Day of Bombardment)		WSL
24/9/16	A /Bty in billets in ENGLEBELMER. B & C Batys in trenches near BEAUSSART. D Bty retired from 5 a.m. first HEo NTs during day. To no. St night. Patricio & howzers.	
25/9/16		WSL
26/9/16	D Bty fired 25/9/16 about wounding 3 men	WSL
27/9/16	" " " "	WSL WSL

(73989) W4141—463. 400,000. 9/14. H.&J.Ltd. Forms/C. 2118/10.

Army Form C. 2118.

WAR DIARY
or
INTELLIGENCE SUMMARY.
(Erase heading not required.)

Instructions regarding War Diaries and Intelligence Summaries are contained in F.S. Regs., Part II and the Staff Manual respectively. Title pages will be prepared in manuscript.

Hour, Date, Place	Summary of Events and Information	Remarks and references to Appendices
27/6/16	Bon Porte Gun Horse, Gun Groups — all A/Bdy.	
28/6/16	died from wounds. A big detachment moved up to Mouton-Regnatines — Reserve for 2/7/16 BOIS d'HOLLANDE BEAUCOURT. CHATEAU tenn and PULISIEUX trench.	WPb
29/6/16	B.C. ship detachments to positions. Ranging.	WPb
30/6/16	2 days postponed from stille butter returning front	WPb WPb

G. Nelson
LIEUT. COLONEL,
COMMG. 241 SOUTH MIDLAND FIELD ARTILLERY BRIGADE

16-6-1916

Reg No.	Rank.	Name.	Corps.	Remarks.	Date.
1060.	Sgt.	Roberts. W.	A/241. Bty.	Rejoined from course of Gunnery.	10.6.16.
1095.	Dr.	Langley. B.	ditto.	To. No. 29. C.C.S. struck off strength.	9.6.16.
69,555.	"	Cox. F.	ditto.	Joined from D.A.C. taken on strength.	9.6.16.
2085.	"	Rimmer. C. J.	B/241. Bty.	To. No. 4. C.C.S. struck off strength.	12.6.16.
3029.	Gnr.	Rivers, J.	ditto.	Granted Proficiency Pay Class II. from	19.1.15.
3816	Ftr.	Humphries. J. A.	C/241. Bty.	Returns from BEAUQUESNE, with "D" Gun.	14.6.16.
2939	Gnr.	Seabright. F.	ditto.		
239.	Gnr.	Long. V.	D/241. Bty.	Temporary attached to 242nd. Bde. R.F.A.	11.6.16.
101.	Sgt.	Gibbons. H.	ditto.	Temporary attached to Divl. Salvage Corps	12.6.16.
	2/Lieut.	Spencer. F.W.	ditto.	Rejoined from Course of Gunnery. HAVERNAS.	
35.	Dvr.	Lamb. W. (servant)	ditto.		10.6.16.

16/6/1916.

Reg No.	Rank.	Name.	Corps.	Remarks. Date.
66.	Dvr.	Turner. W.	D/241. Battery.	Joined from D.A.C. taken on strength 13·6·16
2209	"	Bennett. G.	C/241. "	Re-engaged. Completed AF.W.3126. Papers to RECORDS. 14·6·16
	Lieut.	Cross. H. F.	B/241. "	Struck off strength, from 1·6·16 Authority. WAR OFFICE. AG.4a.
	2/Lieut.	Smith. D. C.	Joined from 3/2nd. S.M.F.A Bde. 15·6·16. taken on strength. (Date of commission. August 16/1915.)	
	2/Lieut.	Lowe. A. J.	Attached to D/241. Battery.	Returned to 243rd. Bde. R.F.A. from attachment. 14·6·1916
	Lieut.	W. A. Woods.	B/241. Battery.	
2729	Gunner.	Ragbourne. W. G.	A/241. "	
2097	"	Whatmore. L.	B/241. "	
1679.	Pte	Angell. F. (R.A.M.C)	Attached to C/241. Bty.	Granted leave from 11-6-16. to 17-6-16.
17	Q.M.S	Painter. P. C.	D/241. Bty.	
72429.	Gnr.	Herring. J	Hd Qrs.	
2970.	Dvr.	Barnett. F. J	A/241. Bty.	Granted leave from 16·6·16 to 22·6·16.

16/6/1916.

Reg No.	Rank.	Name.	Corps.	Remarks.	Date.
3848.	Gnr.	Burman. A.E.	A/241. Bty.	To Hospital	10.6.16
2681	Dvr.	Price. A.S.	ditto.	" "	10.6.16
3138.	"	Ayris. H.J.	ditto.	" "	10.6.16
2930	"	Farley. B.	ditto.	" "	12.6.16
3176	Gnr.	Brace. W.	ditto.	" "	14.6.16
3324	Whlr.	Watts. A.	B/241. Bty.	" "	9.6.16
867	Sgt.	Nixon. C.G.	ditto.	" "	15.6.16
2243	Bdr.	Hicks. E.	C/241 Bty.	" "	10.6.16
3504	Gnr.	Swift. E.M.	ditto.	" "	11.6.16
323	Sgt.	Pulley. G.	ditto.	" "	15.6.16
3218	Dvr.	Jones. G.H.	ditto.	" "	16.6.16
733	Gunner	Hawkins. C.	D/241. Bty.	" "	15.6.16
	Lieut.	Hayes. M.S.	ditto.	" "	11.6.16
	Lieut.	Hayes. M.S.	D/241. Bty.	From Hospital	13.6.16
2802	Dvr.	Turner. W.F.	A/241 Bty.	" "	9.6.16
2175	"	Smith. H.G.	ditto.	" "	10.6.16.
3848	Gnr.	Burman. A.E.	ditto.	" "	13.6.16
3329	Dvr.	Hales. W.	B/241. Bty.	" "	13.6.16
3324	Whlr.	Watts. A.	ditto.	" "	13.6.16.
3016.	Gnr.	Harper. A.E.	C/241. Bty.	" "	12.6.16.
196.	"	Forrester. J.	D/241. Bty.	" "	10.6.16.
182	Dvr.	Wood. J.F.	ditto.	" "	12.6.16.

23/6/1916.

Reg No.	Rank.	Name.	Corps.	Remarks.	Date.
181.	Sgt.	Manton. H. H. (AVC)	Attached to B/241. Bty.	Transferred to No.4. Section, 48th. D.A.C, for duty	8.6.16.

23rd June. 1916

Reg. No.	Rank	Name	Corps	Remarks	Date
733	Gunner	Hawkins. C.	D/2/41. Bty.	To. No.4. C.C.S. struck off strength.	20.6.16
589	Dvr.	Birkett. H.	D/2/41. Bty.	Joined from 48. D.A.C. Reinforcements taken on strength.	18.6.16
483	"	Haydon. C. G.			
1038	Gnr.	Carpenter. J.			
101	Sgt.	Gibbons. H.	D/2/41. Bty.	Rejoined from attachment to Divn. Salvage Corps.	18.6.16
239	Gnr.	Long. V.	D/2/41. Bty.	Rejoined from attachment to 242. Brigade.	20.6.16
60	Dr.	Joyce. T. J.	D/2/41. Bty.	Attached to 242nd. Bde. temporary.	20.6.1916
2299	Pte.	Merriman. F.	R.A.M.C. 2nd. Field Amb. S.M. Division.	Joined for attachment. Private. Merriman A/2/41. Bty. " Sands. D/2/41. Bty.	20.6.1916
2103	"	Sands. S. J.			
—	Captain.	C. G. Hearn. (A.V.C.) attached to Hd. Qrs.		Granted leave from 18.6.16 to. 24.6.16	
	2/Lieut.	C. T. Jones.		Joined from 3/2nd. S.M. Bde. R.F.A. 21.6.16 Date of Commission. 28.9.1914.	

23rd June 1916.

Reg No.	Rank.	Name.	Corps.	Remarks.	Date.
2645.	Gunner	Mason. W. J.	Hd Qrs	To Hospital.	22.6.16
2641.	"	Moore. T.	B/241. Bty.	" "	18.6.16
3061.	Dvr.	Barnett. H.	ditto	" "	21.6.16
3887.	"	Husson. B. G.	C/241. Bty.	" "	18.6.16
62.	"	Bradley. H.	D/241	" "	17.6.16
696.	Sgt.	Hoyle. T. M.	A/241.	" { To Base Hospital	} 21/6/16.
194.	Tptr.	Shelley. F.	D/241	" { for dental treatment	
2031.	Dvr.	Rouse. E. W.	A/241.	" From Hospital.	16.6.16.
2930	"	Farley. B.	ditto.	" "	17.6.16.
3176.	Gnr.	Brace. W.	ditto.	" "	17.6.16.
2113.	Cpl.	Brettell. G.	ditto.	" "	18.6.16.
3135	Dvr.	Ayris. H. J.	ditto.	" "	19.6.16.
2641.	Gnr.	Moore. T.	B/241 Bty.	" "	19.6.16.
62.	Dvr.	Bradley. H.	D/241. Bty.	" "	19.6.16.
2929.	Driver	Tongue. C.	attached to A/241	From 2nd Section D.A.C.	} 19.6.16.
2681.	Dvr.	Price. A. S.	A/241. Bty.	{ To No. 29. C.C.S. struck off strength.	20.6.16
3004	Gunner	Vale. J. F.	C/241. Bty.	{ Returns from Signalling Course.	19.6.16.
3504	Gunner	Swift. E. M.	C/241. Bty.	{ To No. 4. C.C.S. struck off strength.	} 15.6.16.

30/6/1916

Reg No.	Rank	Name	Corps.	Remarks.	Date
	Lieut.	W. A. Woods.	B/241. Bty.	Returned from leave	26.6.16.
3833.	Gunner	Beeson. F.	C/241. "	Rejoined from Y/48. T.M.Bty.	24.6.16.
	Captain.	Saunders. C. K.	A/241 "	To Hospital.	22.6.16.
	Lieut Colonel.	J. R. Colville. D.S.O.	Hd Qrs.	Granted leave from 8.6.16. to 14.6.16	
356.	Bdr.	Ridby. A.	48th. D.A.C.	attached to A/241. Bty. as Mounted Orderly.	26.6.16.
1439.	Bdr.	Phelps. J. W.	" " "	attached to B/241. Bty as Mounted Orderly.	26.6.16.
1640.	Bdr.	Merrix. A.	" " "	attached to C/241. Bty as Mounted Orderly.	26.6.16.

June 30th/1916.

Reg No.	Rank	Name.	Corps.	Remarks	Date.
2056.	Dr.	Penry. A.C.	A/241. Bty.	To Hospital.	25.6.16
981.	A/Bdr.	Potter. J.L.	" "	" "	27.6.16
2764.	Gunner	Sharpe. C.	" "	" "	27.6.16
2503	"	Hale. A.	" "	" "	27.6.16
		suffering from wounds by Artillery fire.			
2642.	Gunner	Mayall. F.H.	B/241. Bty.	To Hospital.	19.6.16
2341.	"	Buckley. A.C.	" "	" "	25.6.16
198.	Cpl.	Hipwell. G.H.	D/241. Bty.	To Hospital.	24.6.16
56	Bdr.	Smith. D.	" "	" "	24.6.16
154.	Gunner	Seaton. H.	" "	" "	24.6.16
197.	"	Packwood. H.	" "	" "	26.6.16
		Wounded through premature.			
3887.	Dr.	Husson. B.G.	C/241. Bty.	From Hospital.	28.6.16
3061.	"	Barnett. H.	B/241.	" "	24.6.16
2645.	Gnr.	Mason. W.J.	Hd Qrs.	To No 29. CCS struck off strength.	24.6.16
3436.	Cpl	Hill. J.J.	A/241. Bty.	Transferred to ENGLAND to take up Commission, struck off strength.	27/6/16
2503.	Gunner	Hale. A.	A/241. Bty.	Died from wounds caused by enemy Artillery fire struck off strength.	28.6.16
	Captain	Kellar. J.B.	A/241. Bty.	Joined from 242nd Bde taken on strength.	24/6/16
408	Dvr.	Hawkins. J.			

2nd June 1916

Reg. No.	Rank.	name.	Corps.	Remarks	Date.
	Captain.	Smith. H. (R.A.M.C.) attached to Hd Qrs.			
2498.	Gnr.	Hall G. H.	Hd Qrs.		
2332.	Dr.	Battersea. K.	A/241. Bty.		
2383.	"	Clarke. W.			
2965.	"	Cook. W.	B/241. Bty.	Granted leave	
2090.	"	Watkins. S.		from —	28.5.16.
764.	Sgt Whlr	Gittins. S.	C/241 Bty.	to —	4. 6.16
195.	Gnr.	Asher. J. W.	D/241. Bty.		
123.	Dr.	Agnes. W.			
337	Gnr.	Baskerville. P. J.	C/241. Bty.	allotment of pay. 6d per day to Mother from	16. 5. 15.
				Paid by Woolwich up to —	7. 8. 16.
				Paid by Worcs. Terr.l Association commencing	8. 8. 16.

Mother's name and address.

Mrs. Bessie Baskerville,

36. Foregate Street.

Worcester.

2nd June 1916.

Reg No.	Rank.	Name.	Corps.	Remarks.	Date.
466	Bdr.	Severn. J.W.	D.A.C. attached to A/241 Battery.	While attached, performed duties of Pay Clerk for 4th S.M. Bde. from 1.4.16, to 15.5.16.	
466.	Bdr.	Severn. J.W.	D.A.C. attached to A/241. Battery	Appointed Battery Pay Clerk, vice 696. Sgt Hoyle, returned to duty with effect from 22.5.1916.	
	2/Lieut.	Thacker. W.J.	C/241. Battery. (Authority 48th. Divn. 26.5.16.)	Struck off strength from	28.3.16.
1066.	Sgt.	Roberts. W.	A/241 Bty.	Proceeded on Course of Gunnery.	28.5.16.
2386.	Gnr.	Crumpv. W.J.	A/241. Bty.	Rejoined from attachment to 48th. D.A.C.	31.5.16.
2761.	"	Saunders. W.			
	Lieut.	Pridmore. R.G.	D/241. Bty.	Returned from Course of Gunnery. HAVERNAS.	27.5.16.
153.	Gnr.	Nelson. L.A.			
	2/Lieut.	Spencer. F.W.	D/241. Bty.	Proceeded on Course of Gunnery. HAVERNAS.	28.5.16.
35.	Dr.	Lamb. W. (servant)			

2nd June 1916.

Reg No.	Rank.	Name.	Corps.	Remarks.	Date.
29	B.S.M.	Hopwell. G.	D/241. Battery.	From Hospital.	26.5.16
199	Dr.	Redmayne. C.B.	do.	" "	26.5.16
152	Gnr.	Hannett. A.	do.	" "	28.5.16
2386	Gnr.	Crump. W.J.	A/241 Bty.	Posted to Hd Qrs.	31/5/16.
2206.	Dr.	Morris. H.	Hd Qrs.	Posted to A/241. Bty.	
347	Bdr.	Allen. W.	B/241. Battery.	struck off strength To 29. C.C.S.	28/5/16.
115.	Dr.	Packwood. C.W.	D/241. Battery.	Re-engaged. Papers to Records. Completed. A.F. W. 3126.	27.5.16.
110.	Sgt.	Heath. W.	" "		
116.	Dr.	Groudle. A.G.	" "		
2242.	Dr.	Wedgbury. A.H.	C/241. Bty.	Re-engaged. Papers to Records. Completed. A.F. W. 3126.	29.5.16.
2309.	Sdlr.	Annis. W.H.	C/241. Bty.	Allotment to Mother transferred to Wife. 6d a day from	22.5.16.

<u>Wife's address.</u>

Mrs. Minnie Louisa Georgina Annis.
6. Bromsgrove Street.
Worcester.

2nd June 1916.

Reg No.	Rank.	Name.	Corps.	Remarks.		Date.
3135.	Dr.	Ayris. H. J.	A/241. Battery.	To Hospital.		26.5.16
2930.	"	Farley. B.	do.	"	"	28.5.16
2802.	"	Turner. W. J.	do.	"	"	28.5.16
2934.	Gnr.	Davis. E. J.	do.	"	"	28.5.16
1085	"	Reynolds. W.	do.	"	"	30.5.16
782.	Bdr.	Burston. J.	B/241. Battery.	"	"	27.5.16
2329.	Dr.	Hale. W.	do.	"	"	28.5.16
861.	Cpl.	Bowcott. J.	do.	"	"	28.5.16
952.	Dr.	Beard. G.	do.	"	"	1.6.16
2356.	a/Bdr.	Bantam. W.	C/241. Battery.	"	"	29.5.16
427.	Gnr.	Hayter. W. H.	do.	"	"	31.5.16
3396.	Dr.	Baddeley. E. H.	do.	"	"	31.5.16
3887.	"	Husson. B. G.	do.	"	"	1.6.16
2054.	"	Bould. J.	do.	"	"	1.6.16
152.	Gnr.	Hamnett. A.	D/241. Battery.	"	"	26.5.16
196.	"	Forrester. J.	do.	"	"	1.6.16
	Lieut.	W. A. Woods.	B/241. Battery.	"	"	28.5.16
3888.	Dr.	Viner. J. W. H.	A/241. Bty.	From Hospital.		29.5.16
2441.	"	Edwards. F. J.	do.	"	"	31.5.16
799.	Gnr.	Maullin. W.	B/241. Bty.	"	"	27.5.16
2278.	Bdr.	Rogers. W.	do.	"	"	30.5.16
861.	Cpl.	Bowcott. J.	do.	"	"	31.5.16
2693.	Dr.	Powell. J.	do.	"	"	1.6.16
3887.	"	Husson. B. G.	C/241. Bty.	"	"	27.5.16
427.	Gnr.	Hayter. W. H.	do.	"	"	1.6.16
3396.	Dr.	Baddeley. E. H.	do.	"	"	1.6.16

9/6/1916

Reg No.	Rank.	Name.	Corps.	Remarks.	Date.
3068.	Dr.	Maggs. W.	Hd Qr.		
2385.	"	Crompton. R.	A/241. Bty.		
69,555.	"	Cox. F. (attached from DAC.)	"		
2094.	"	Oliver. T. P.	B/241.		
756.	Sgt.	Duggins. A.	C/241.	Granted leave from 4.6.16. to 11.6.16.	
2947.	Bdr.	Jones. A.	"		
94	Dr.	Coles. G.	D/241		
329.	"	Furness. P.	"		
333	Staff. Far. Sgt.	Sheward. A.	B/241. Bty.	Completed A.F. W. 3126. Granted leave from 4.6.16. to 3.7.16	
2730.	Dr.	Risburn. W.H.	A/241. Bty.	Granted leave from 6.6.16. to 13.6.16.	

9/6/1916.

Reg No.	Rank.	Name.	Corps.	Remarks.	Date.
2644	Dr.	Morris. A.E	Hd Qrs.	Allotment of Pay to Mother transferred to Wife from 18.5.16, date of marriage.	
				Wife's name and address.	
				Mrs. Louisa Morris.	
				37, Wood Street.	
				Kidderminster.	
395	Dr.	Judge. A.	D/241. Bty.	Re-engaged. Completed. A.F.W.3126. Papers to Records	6.6.16.
114	Cpl	Shepherd. F.	ditto.	Re-engaged. Completed. A.F.W.3126. Papers to Records.	7.6.16.
193	a/Bdr.	Ainsley. H.R.	ditto.	Promoted to Bdr, vice Bdr. Hipwell promoted Cpl.	11.4.16.
542	Dr.	Lorriman. A.E.	ditto.	Appointed a/Bdr 11.4.16, vice a/Bdr Ainsley promoted Bdr.	
46	Gnr.	Smith. S.G	ditto.	Appointed a/Bdr 4.5.16, vice a/Bdr. Cox. E. Killed in action	
3816	Ftr.	Humphries. J.A.	C/241. Bty.	Proceeded to BEAUQUESNE with Guns for Repairs. 4.6.16. (Temp.)	
2939	Gnr.	Seabright. F.	ditto.		
2744	Dr.	Reynolds. R.	C/241 Bty.	Proceeded to R.E. STORES COIGNEUX to assist in making camouflages. 8.6.16. (Temp.)	

9/6/16.

Reg No.	Rank	Name	Corps.	Remarks	Date
2175.	Dr.	Smith. H. G.	A/241. Bty.	To Hospital.	2.6.16.
3113.	Cpl.	Brettell. G.	do.	" "	5.6.16.
3085.	Dr.	Rimmer. C. J.	B/241. Bty.	" "	7.6.16.
2414.	Bdr	Coombs. J. R.	C/241. "	" "	4.6.16.
182.	Dr.	Wood. J. F.	D/241 "	" "	7.6.16.
	Lieut.	W. A. Woods.	B/241. Bty.	From Hospital.	4.6.16.
1085.	Gr.	Reynolds. W.	A/241. Bty.	From Hospital.	2.6.16.
2934		Davis. E. J.	" "	" "	2.6.16.
2930.	Dr.	Farley. B.	" "	" "	2.6.16.
3135.	"	Ayris. H. J.	" "	" "	3.6.16.
3825.	Gnr.	Jeffrey. H.	B/241. "	" "	4.6.16.
952.	Dr.	Beard. G.	" "	" "	6.6.16.
782.	Bdr	Burston. J.	" "	" "	7.6.16.
3887.	Dr.	Husson. B. G.	C/241 "	" "	7.6.16.
144.	a/Bdr.	Wolley. R. J.	D/241 "	" "	7.6.16.
3965	Dr.	Windsor. A. H.	A/241. "	{ From Hospital. To Base. Struck off strength.	9.5.16.
1013.	Gnr.	Cotterill. J.	D/241. Bty.	{ Joined from D.A.C. taken on strength	6.6.16.
	2/Lieut.	A. J. Lowe.	243rd. Bde.	Attached to D/241. Battery. (Temp.)	8.6.16.

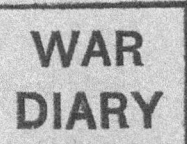

Headquarters,

241st BRIGADE, R.F.A.

(48th Division)

J U L Y

1 9 1 6

Attached:

Appendices.

Army Form C. 2118.

WAR DIARY
or
INTELLIGENCE SUMMARY.
(Erase heading not required.)

Instructions regarding War Diaries and Intelligence Summaries are contained in F.S. Regs., Part II. and the Staff Manual respectively. Title pages will be prepared in manuscript.

Hour, Date, Place	Summary of Events and Information	Remarks and references to Appendices
1/7/16	"Z" day. C.O. performing liaison duty with G.O.C. 87 Inf. Bde. the evening (5.30 pm) previous. Dis. on MAILLY— A Bty. opened fire 6.25 am on BEAUCOURT CHATEAU.	
7.30 am	enclosed fire (Trench) Assaulting heads up reached enemy wire (lower target cleared) wounded returned to zero line.	233 Gnr. BOSWORTH.F.R. "D" Bty awarded military medal for good work in maintaining telephone wires during these operations.
11.0 am	Closed firing about 12.30 pm. Awaited orders that enemy (Gen. Watson's) were counter attacking & B & C Btys opened fire. No counter attack ever materialised.	
3.0 pm		
9.30 am	opened fire.	
10.30 "	ceased fire.	
9.30 "	Bns ordered to be in readiness to move by 11.45 am.	

Army Form C. 2118.

WAR DIARY
or
INTELLIGENCE SUMMARY.
(Erase heading not required.)

Instructions regarding War Diaries and Intelligence Summaries are contained in F.S. Regs., Part II. and the Staff Manual respectively. Title pages will be prepared in manuscript.

Hour, Date, Place	Summary of Events and Information	Remarks and references to Appendices
1/7/16 (Cont.)	D Bty firing continuously	
2/7/16 2.45 AM	A Bty shelled from line BEAUCOURT CHATEAU – trench line been intermittently all day.	WFB
11.45 pm	Orders received that 144th & 145th Inf Bde moves orders on . 3.30 am cancelled	
2.0 am	B+C Bty Brig. Came into action on BEAUSSART.	
	D Bty Continuous firing	
3/7/16 5.0 pm	A Bty shelled on 2/7/16 orders received by A Bty to come out of action at night own rejoin remainder of Bde in COIN.	WFB
HQrs Cannon HQ; B & C Bty.		
4/7/16 4:30 am	A Bty arrived in COIN having been heavily shelled while evacuating position	WFB

(73989) W4141—463. 400,000. 9/14. H.&J.Ltd. Forms/C. 2118/10.

Army Form C. 2118.

WAR DIARY
or
INTELLIGENCE SUMMARY.
(Erase heading not required.)

Instructions regarding War Diaries and Intelligence Summaries are contained in F.S. Regs., Part II. and the Staff Manual respectively. Title pages will be prepared in manuscript.

Hour, Date, Place	Summary of Events and Information	Remarks and references to Appendices
5/7/16 noon	Bn relieved 169 Bde in action in front of COLINCAMPS.	O.R.W.
4 pm	[illegible] Bournemouth	
11 pm	Bournemouth	
6/7/16 2 am	Bn were carried out [illegible] during heavy rain.	w.s.k.
7/7/16 11 pm 6.2 am	[illegible] front line	w.s.k.
	after first attack by infantry.	
8/7/16	Great activity on both sides in COURCELLES	w.s.k.
9/7/16	Great activity in enemy trenches by day	w.s.k.
10/7/16	" " " "	w.s.k.
11/7/16	" " " "	w.s.k.
12/7/16	" " " "	w.s.k.
13/7/16	Some artillery by day & very active in trenches	w.s.k.
14/7/16	Quiet by day, activity by night	w.s.k.

Army Form C. 2118.

WAR DIARY
or
INTELLIGENCE SUMMARY.
(Erase heading not required.)

Instructions regarding War Diaries and Intelligence Summaries are contained in F.S. Regs., Part II. and the Staff Manual respectively. Title pages will be prepared in manuscript.

Hour, Date, Place	Summary of Events and Information	Remarks and references to Appendices
COURCELLES.		
15/7/16	Activity enemy by night. Gusen Travere Telephonic communications	
16/7/16	note at Bq H.Q.P. activity " above "	wire
17/7/16	activity " "	wire
18/7/16	C.O., Orderly Officer, Bgn Commander, Signallers etc. proceeded to HQ of 5th Bde to take over positions round AVELUY WOOD. Wires were examined.	wire
19/7/16	Bn Relieved by 120th Bde. R.F.A.	wire
20/7/16	Proceeded to Morgan near COUIN	wire
21/7/16	Brigade observed A & C & Hq Group Battalion observed "B" to the Centre Group 49th Divn in HEDAUVILLE. Bgn position A = W.10.a.3.6	wire

Army Form C. 2118.

WAR DIARY
or
INTELLIGENCE SUMMARY.
(Erase heading not required.)

Hour, Date, Place	Summary of Events and Information	Remarks and references to Appendices
22/7/16	Activity at night on communications "B" W.3.b.2.7 "C" W.9.d.9.5	wtk wtk
23/7/16	" " " "	wtk
24/7/16	" " " "	wtk
25/7/16	" " " "	wtk
26/7/16	" " " "	wtk
27/7/16	" " " "	wtk
28/7/16	48th Divs: Positions at X 13.b.61. Bde remained in wagon lines. "D" Bty on move. Retired to Divs: D Bty remained to 49th	wtk
29/7/16	"D" Bty continued journey to ST. OUEN. Other Btys active on moves to ST OUEN	wtk
30/7/16		wtk
31/7/16	communication at night	wtk wtk

J R Coben
LIEUT. COLONEL,
2nd SOUTH MIDLAND FIELD ARTILLERY BRIGADE

A P P E N D I C E S.

July 7th/1916.

Reg No.	Rank	Name	Corps.	Remarks.	Date.
323.	Sgt.	Pulley. G.	C/241. Bty.	Transferred to ENGLAND. (sick.) struck off strength	21-6-16.
2744.	Dvr.	Reynolds. R.	C/241. "	Returns from R.E's. after assisting in making camoflage. (permanent)	1-7-16.
994.	Dvr.	Read. A.	C/241 "	Performed the duty of Rough Rider from — to —	31.3.16 1.7.16.
132796. 988.	Dr. "	Whiston. Bonsfield.	D/241 "	Reinforcements joined from 48th. D.A.C. taken on strength.	29/6/16.
533.	Gnr.	Hartley.	D.A.C.	Attached to D/241. Battery. Mounted Orderly.	2.7.16.

July 7th/1916

Reg No.	Rank.	Name.	Corps.	Remarks.	Date.
3030	Gunner	Walters. H.	A/241. Battery.	To Hospital. Bullet wound in right forearm	1.7.16
1022	Bdr.	Raby. W. A.	" "	To Hospital.	1.7.16
3131	Gnr.	Canty. J.	" "	" "	1.7.16
994	Dvr.	Read. A.	C/241. "	" "	2.7.16
3043	Gnr.	Partridge. C.	" "	" "	2.7.16
	Captain.	A. F. Penny.	A/241. "	" "	6.7.16
	"	J. B. Kellar.	" "	" "	6.7.16
2056	Gnr.	Penny. A. C.	A/241 "	From Hospital	1.7.16
867	Sgt.	Nixon. C. G.	B/241 "	" "	5.6.16
3181	Gnr.	Glazzard. S.	} A/241 "	Reinforcements joined from 48th D.A.C. taken on strength.	} 29.6.16
3119	"	Shuter. F.			
3359	"	Holland. W. J.			
2091	Gnr.	Hill. J.	A/241 "	Transferred sick to ENGLAND struck off strength.	16.3.16
2341	Gnr.	Buckley. A. E.	B/241 "	To C.C.S. 26.6.16. struck off strength.	
892	Cpl Ftr.	Cotterill. A. F.	B/241 "	Retained in ENGLAND for Home Service, from 4.7.16 struck off strength. Authority A.G's. Office. THE BASE. No. 2996.	

14th July 1916.

Reg No.	Rank.	Name.	Corps.	Remarks.	Date.
		Promotions.			
893.	a/Bdr.	Haughton. G.	B/241. Battery.	To be Bdr, vice Bdr. Allen evacuated.	4.6.16.
2166.	Gnr.	Adams. W.	ditto.	To be a/Bdr, vice a/Bdr Haughton promoted.	4.6.16.
803.	Cpl	Vale. E.	C/241. Battery.	To be Sergt vice 323 Sergt Pulley. G. evacuated.	21.6.16.
3147.	Gnr.	Dale. E. S.	B/241. Bty.	Proceeded on Signalling Course at 48th Divl Arty Hd Qrs. (Temp.)	9-7-16.

14th July 1916.

Reg No.	Rank	Name	Corps	Remarks	Date
3078	Dvr	Lewis. G.	A/241. Battery	To Hospital.	8.7.16
2206	"	Morris. H.	ditto	" "	10.7.16
3833	Gnr.	Beeson. F.	C/241. Battery	" "	11.7.16
3131	Gnr.	Canty. J.	A/241. Battery	From Hospital.	12.7.16
2356	a/Bdr.	Bantom. W.	C/241 do.	" "	10.7.16
2002	Cpl	Newey. W. G.	Hd Qrs.	Posted to A/241 Bty. from 14-7-16 (Permanent)	
808	Cpl	Higgs. W.	48th. D.A.C.	Posted to Hd Qrs Staff, from 14-7-16. (Permanent) taken on strength.	
2642	Gnr.	Mayall. F. H.	B/241. Battery	Transferred sick to ENGLAND. struck off strength.	30-6-16
2095	Dvr.	Davis. J.	B/241. Battery	Joined from 48th. D.A.C. taken on strength	12-7-16
640	Gnr.	Bullivant. H.	D/241. Battery	Rejoined Unit from attachment to 242nd Brigade. Permanent	9-7-16
1068	Sgt.	Johnson. S. J.	A/241. Battery	Proceeded on Anti-Gas Course 11-7-16.	
962	Cpl	Ashwin. R.	B/241 "		
2975	Bdr.	Spencer. F.	C/241 "	time of Course from	12-7-16
214	a/Bdr.	Eaton. R.	D/241 "	to	15-7-16

21-7-1916.

Reg No.	Rank.	Name.	Corps.	Remarks	Date.
3001	Dvr.	Powell. C. F.	A/241. Battery.	To Hospital.	17.7.16.
2429.	"	Dovey. E. A.	—"—	" "	17.7.16.
3078.	"	Lewis. G.	—"—	" "	19.7.16.
2730.	"	Risburn. W. H.	—"—	" "	19.7.16.
893.	Bdr	Haughton. G.	B/241 Battery.	" "	19.7.16.
3962	Dvr.	Mitchell. F.	—"—	" "	20.7.16.
3154.	Gnr.	Wilde. G.	—"—	" "	20.7.16.
194.	a/Bdr.	Wolley. R. J.	D/241. Battery.	" "	19.7.16.
237	Bdr.	Rixon. F. {Wounded in head by German Shell.}	—"—	" "	20.7.16.
3078.	Dvr.	Lewis. G.	A/241. Bty.	From Hospital.	14.7.16
2206.	Gnr.	Morris. H.	—"—	" "	15.7.16
1022.	Bdr.	Raby. W. A.	A/241. Bty.	Transferred to ENGLAND sick} struck off strength 5.7.16}	
3030.	Gnr.	Walters. H.	A/241. Bty.	To. C.C.S. 17.7.16} struck off strength.}	
3822.	Gnr.	Billing. O. G.	A/241. Bty.	Killed in action. 20.7.16} struck off strength.}	
3833	Gnr.	Beeson. F.	C/241. Bty.	To. No. 29. C.C.S. 14.7.16} struck off strength.}	

21.7.1916.

Reg No.	Rank.	Name.	Corps.	Remarks.	Date.
2243.	Bdr.	Hicks. E.	C/241. Battery.	From Hospital. To Base. 26.6.16. struck off strength.	
3874.	Dvr.	Loder. A. C.	C/241. Battery.	Proceeded to Military Prison (2 years) struck off strength. 19.7.16.	
2861.	S.S.	Westwood. T.	C/241. Battery.	Joined from B/243. Bty. (Perm.) taken on strength 16.7.16.	
198.	Cpl.	Hipwell. G. H.	D/241. Battery.	Wounded, transferred to ENGLAND struck off strength.	28.6.16.
56.	Bdr.	Smith. D.	—"—		28.6.16.
154.	Gnr.	Seaton. H.	—"—		2.7.16.
197.	"	Packwood. H. M.	—"—		8.7.16.
425.	Gnr.	Carpenter. J. W.	C/241. Bty, attached to X.18. T.M.Bty, or 92. T.M. Bty.	Transferred sick to ENGLAND — 19.6.16. struck off strength.	
1068.	Sgt.	Johnson. S. J.	A/241. Battery.	Rejoined from Anti-Gas Course. (Perm.)	15.7.16.
962.	Cpl.	Ashwin. R.	B/241. "		
2975.	Bdr.	Spencer. F.	C/241. "		
214.	a/Bdr.	Eaton. R.	D/241. "		

21.7.1916.

Reg No.	Rank.	Name.	Corps.	Remarks.	Date.
379	Dvr.	Ford. Wm. A.	H.Q. No.4. Coy Train. A.S.C.	Rejoined from attachment. (Temp)	19.7.16.
	Captain.	A. L. Chandler.	A/241. Battery.	Joined from B/243. Bty. 21.7.16 taken on strength.	
	Captain. Captain.	A. F. Penny. J. B. Kellar.	A/241. Battery.	Transferred sick to ENGLAND struck off strength 13.7.16.	
	Captain.	E. M. J. O'Farrell.	(R.AMC) Atd 2xs.	Joined from 11th Field Amb. taken on strength. 12.7.16.	
	Captain.	H. Smith.	(RAMC) Atd 2xs.	Transferred to 48th D.A.C. struck off strength. 12.7.16.	

21.7.1916.

Reg No.	Rank.	Name.	Corps.	Remarks.	Date.
		Inserted	for the information of the R.A. Section. 3rd. Echelon. Base.		
	2/Lieut.	A.B. Edwards.	B/241. Battery.	Posted on —	25.2.16.
	2/Lieut.	A.C. Williams.	A/241	" "	6.3.16.
2963	Gnr.	Allard. F. }	Date of Attachment to 48th. D.A.C.		
3829.	"	Oliver. C.N. }	(as reinforcements) for T.M.Bty. 22.4.16.		
2569.	"	James. J.	Joined 48th. Div Arty for attachment on 4.8.1915.		As per A. Form. B. 213. d/30.6.16.
306	Bdr.	Rigby. A. }			
1439.	"	Phelps. W. }	D.A.C.	Joined this Bde for attachment. 26.6.16.	
1640	"	Merrix. H. }			
2591.	Gnr.	Keyte. C.C.	Hd Qrs. }	Rejoined from	4.9.15.
3426	"	Drew. F.G.	A/241. Bty. }	48th Div Arty.	19.2.16.
3924.	Dvr.	Walker. L.J.	Posted to	A/241. Bty.	2.4.16.
164.	Sgt.	Wendon. F.J.	A.V.C.	Joined from 243rd Bde for attachment.	18.5.16.
2299	Pte.	Merriman. F. }	R.A.M.C.	Joined for attachment. 20.6.16	
2103	"	Sands. S.J. }			
1910.	"	Chatterton. A.	— " —	Transferred with B.A.C. to 48th. D.A.C. 15.5.16	
2186	"	Church. W.J	— " —	Transferred with (old) D/Bty to 243rd. Bde. 18.5.16	
1504	Cpl	Pearce. W.	— " —	Proceeded on 1 months leave from 10.4.16 to 9.5.16 Retained in ENGLAND by 3rd line, and struck off strength from that date.	

July 21st/1916.

Reg No.	Rank	Name	Corps	Remarks	Date
2287	Gnr.	Baylis. A. J.	Amm Column	Transferred to C.C.S. on struck off strength.	5.3.16.
2416	Dvr.	Cole. G.	—"—	Transferred to Divl Salvage Corps struck off strength. Authority G.R.O. 1408 d/15.2.16	23.2.16.
2491	Gnr.	Hill. J.	A/241. Bty.	Transferred sick to ENGLAND. 16.3.16. struck off strength, as per A.F.B.213. d/7/7/16.	

28/7/1916.

Reg No.	Rank.	Name.	Corps.	Remarks.	Date.
1034.	Bdr.	Bramwich. A. W.	A/241. Battery.	To Hospital.	21.7.16.
2839.	Gnr.	Wilson. E.	" "	" "	23.7.16
2332	Dvr.	Battersea. K.	" "	" "	23.7.16
3133.	Bdr.	Best. H.	" "	" "	24.7.16.
3817.	Gnr.	Morris. D. C.	" "	" "	24.7.16.
2441.	Dr.	Edwards. F. J.	" "	" "	24.7.16.
1076	"	Bright. A. C.	" "	" "	26.7.16.
1007	"	Haynes. C.	" "	" "	26.7.16.
2930	"	Farley. B.	" "	" "	26.7.16
789.	Gnr.	Maullin. W.	B/241	" "	21.7.16.
819.	Sgt.	Boulton. G.	"	" "	22.7.16.
321.	Dvr.	Frost. E.	D/241	" "	26.7.16.
	Captain.	A. C. W. Hobson.	C/241	" "	24.7.16.
2839.	Gnr.	Wilson. E.	A/241. Bty.	From Hospital.	25.7.16.
3078.	Dvr.	Lewis. G.	" "	" "	26.7.16.
3051.	Gnr.	Powell. C. F.	" "	" "	26.7.16.
3962	Dvr.	Mitchell. J.	B/241	" "	27.7.16
144.	a/Bdr.	Wolley. R. J.	D/241	" "	26.7.16.
	Captain.	A. C. W. Hobson.	C/241 Bty.	To C.C.S. (Temp;)	25.7.16.

28/7/1916.

Reg No.	Rank.	Name.	Corps.	Remarks.	Date.
959.	Gnr.	Bodenham. J.	Ad 2n.	Posted to A/241.(Perm)	24.7.16.
1691.	"	Mutter G.	A/241. Battery.	" Ad 2n.(Perm)	24.7.16.
465.	Gnr.	Collett. A. E.	A/241. Battery.	Joined from B/243 Battery.	
73901.	Dvr.	Bloomfield. A.		taken on strength.	21.7.16
1034.	Bdr.	Bramwich. A. W.	A/241. Battery.	To No. 35. C.C.S. struck off strength.	22.7.16
981.	a/Bdr.	Potter. J. L.	A/241. Battery.	Transferred to ENGLAND struck off strength.	5.7.16
466.	Bdr.	Severn. J. W.	48th. D.A.C.	Posted to A/241. Bty.	
2029.	Gnr.	Greaves. J. H.		taken on strength.	27.7.16
3147.	Gnr.	Dale. E.	B/241. Battery.	Rejoined from Signalling Course. (Perm)	22.7.16
123.	Cpl Ftr.	Holmes. E.	B/241. Battery.	Joined from Base taken on strength.	26.7.16.
2688.	Fitter.	Parker. W. R.	C/241. Battery.	Joined from 48th DAC. taken on strength.	24.7.16.
2619.	Gnr.	Law. W. H.	C/241. Battery.	Evacuated to C.C.S. by 11th Field Amb. struck off strength.	20.7.16.

July 28th/1916.

Reg No.	Rank.	Name.	Corps.	Remarks	Date.
3043.	Gnr.	Partridge. E.	C/241. Bty.	Transferred to ENGLAND struck off strength.	4·7·16
260.	Gnr.	Sutton. J.	D/241. Bty. attached to T.M.Bty. H.Q.	Transferred to 48th. D.A.C. struck off strength.	24·7·16
919	Gnr.	Grubb. T.	C/241. Bty.	Allotment of Pay 6d per day to wife from 9·5·16. Married 9·5·16. <u>Wife's address.</u> Mrs. E. Grubb. New End. Ashwood Bank. REDDITCH	
994	Dvr.	Read. A.	C/241. Bty.	Performs duty of Rough Rider from to	1·7·16 31·7·16
239.	Gnr.	Long. V.	D/241. Bty.	Attached to 242. Bde. Hd Qrs. (Temp)	21·7·16

48th Divisional Artillery.

9------------

241st (South Midland) BRIGADE

ROYAL FIELD ARTILLERY

AUGUST 1 9 1 6 ::::::

Army Form C. 2118.

WAR DIARY
or
INTELLIGENCE SUMMARY.
(Erase heading not required.)

Instructions regarding War Diaries and Intelligence Summaries are contained in F.S. Regs., Part II. and the Staff Manual respectively. Title pages will be prepared in manuscript.

Hour, Date, Place	Summary of Events and Information	Remarks and references to Appendices
In the field		all map references to Sheet 57d S.E. 1/20,000.
1/8/16	Uneventful. Bde HQ in HEDAUVILLE. D/Bty resting at ST. OUEN, A,B,C Bties in action as before.	
2/8/16	As above.	w/e
6.30 pm	Orders received for HQ & relieve HQ Right Group TFA. 4 9th Div on 5/8/16	w/e
3/8/16	Lieut Col & Adj J.C. Riley proceeded to HQ Rt. Group RA. 49th Div to learn charge-over at W.n.a.5. to learn front parc to relief.	w/e
4/8/16	Partial relief by deployment of this HQS. still being carried out	w/e
5/8/16	" " " "	w/e
6/8/16	" " " "	w/e
7/8/16	" " " "	w/e
8/8/16 12 noon	Bde HQ assumed command of Rt. Group RA 49th Div comprising the	w/e

WAR DIARY
or
INTELLIGENCE SUMMARY.

(Erase heading not required.)

Army Form C. 2118.

Hour, Date, Place	Summary of Events and Information	Remarks and references to Appendices
	following matters	
	A/ ⎫ B/ ⎬ 2+5. A/ ⎫ C/ ⎭ C/ ⎬ 2+1 C/2+8. D/ ⎭	
9/8/16.	On the whole quiet. Bombardment in night. especially heavy to LEIPSIC SALIENT noted.	w.e.e.
10/8/16. 11/8/16.	Normal day with night bombardments w.e.e. D/Bty went up to OUEN to relieve action.	w.e.e.
12/8/16. 13/8/16.	as above. D/Bty on roads. — D/Bty moved to wagon lines by ALBERT.	w.e.e. w.e.e. w.e.e.
14/8/16.	D/Bty went into action night 13/14 for remainder as above.	w.e.e.

Army Form C. 2118.

WAR DIARY
or
INTELLIGENCE SUMMARY.
(Erase heading not required.)

Instructions regarding War Diaries and Intelligence Summaries are contained in F. S. Regs., Part II and the Staff Manual respectively. Title pages will be prepared in manuscript.

Hour, Date, Place	Summary of Events and Information	Remarks and references to Appendices
In the field 15/8/16.	Average day. Throughout this period BGtys continuously engaged in assisting the attacks of ANZAC Division and 12th Div in the neighbourhood of MOUQUET FARM.	W.S.C.
16/8/16	Average day with fleeting targets by night.	W.S.C
17/8/16	As above.	W.S.C.
18/8/16 5 pm	Batteries assisted attack of K.R. Division on trenches in X.2.a & c. when hour by hour reached capture.	W.S.C.
19/8/16	Average day. Barrage maintained to prevent counter-attack on ground gained the previous day. Capt. T.C. Bury admitted to hospital.	W.S.C.
20/8/16	Average day. During [?] definite objectives assumed temporary [?]	

WAR DIARY
or
INTELLIGENCE SUMMARY.

(Erase heading not required.)

Army Form C. 2118.

Instructions regarding War Diaries and Intelligence Summaries are contained in F.S. Regs., Part II. and the Staff Manual respectively. Title pages will be prepared in manuscript.

Hour, Date, Place	Summary of Events and Information	Remarks and references to Appendices
21/8/16 5 pm	By 2Lt. W.G. CLEMENTS. Attack by 4th & 25th Divisions on trenches to South of LEIPSIC SALIENT. — Trenches re-opened. Batteries in Ra Group now covering 7th Inf. Bde.	WTC.
22/8/16	Day quiet except for some heavy shelling on enemy lines trenches.	WTC.
23/8/16	Day quiet — no (or for 22/8/16	WTC.
24/8/16	Attack by 1st + 3rd Divisions on HINDENBURG TRENCH N.E. of LEIPSIC SALIENT. Batteries covered this and 3/7th (from Centre Group 49th Division) less 1 Ra Group for the attack	WTC.
25/8/16	Heavy shelling of enemy front ground	WTC.

WAR DIARY
or
INTELLIGENCE SUMMARY.

(Erase heading not required.)

Army Form C. 2118.

Instructions regarding War Diaries and Intelligence Summaries are contained in F. S. Regs., Part II. and the Staff Manual respectively. Title pages will be prepared in manuscript.

Hour, Date, Place	Summary of Events and Information	Remarks and references to Appendices
26/8/16.	Oct 25/8/16. 45th Infy. Bde. now covered by R. Group.	W.S.G.
27/8/16.	Reorganisation. R. Group 49th Div Army lent to 25th Divartrig, & with it HQ 241 Bde & A & C/241 Btys. D/241 left position in main having attempt to relieve German in front line German nineteenth HQ of LEIPSIC SALIENT tried D/241 Bty in position in AVELUY WOOD on W.4.a.7.4. C/241 retire to wagon line preparatory to reinforcements to R. group.	W.S.G.
28/8/16.		
29/8/16.	Day average. Some heavy shelling by Germans.	W.S.G. W.S.G.

Army Form C. 2118.

WAR DIARY
or
INTELLIGENCE SUMMARY.

(Erase heading not required.)

Instructions regarding War Diaries and Intelligence Summaries are contained in F. S. Regs., Part II. and the Staff Manual respectively. Title pages will be prepared in manuscript.

Hour, Date, Place	Summary of Events and Information	Remarks and references to Appendices
30/8/16	Day quiet, quiet nights firing	1/16
31/8/16	as above.	1/16

J.M.C.
LIEUT. COLONEL,
SOUTH MIDLAND FIELD ARTILLERY BRIGADE

(73989) W4141—463. 400,000. 9/14. H.&J.Ltd. Forms/C. 2118/10.

48th. DIVISIONAL ARTILLERY

241st. BRIGADE R.F.A.

SEPTEMBER 1916.

Army Form C. 2118.

WAR DIARY
or
INTELLIGENCE SUMMARY.
(Erase heading not required.)

241st BDE, R.F.A.

Hour, Date, Place	Summary of Events and Information	Remarks and references to Appendices
In the field.		All map references to 57D SE 1/20,000
1/9/16	Quiet.	w/k.
2/9/16	"	w/k.
3/9/16	"	
5.10 am	Preparation for attack on 3rd inst.	
	Attack by 75th Bde on Turk Trench R31A9.1 to R31D4.8. Unable to hold this. All batteries engaged. A & B/241 covering 75th Bde attack and C & D/241 covering 49th Div attack N. of THIEPVAL.	
4/9/16	Uneventful. Gunmen artillery active on back areas.	w/k.
5/9/16	Uneventful.	w/k.
6/9/16 2.45 am	Germans fired gas & harassing shell into ANCRE Valley & round group H 9 W.h. a .7.7. 32nd Bde took over from 15th Bde. Group now A/241 & B/241 15th Bde HQ now under...	w/k.

Army Form C. 2118.

WAR DIARY
or
INTELLIGENCE SUMMARY.
(Erase heading not required.)

Instructions regarding War Diaries and Intelligence Summaries are contained in F. S. Regs., Part II. and the Staff Manual respectively. Title pages will be prepared in manuscript.

Hour, Date, Place	Summary of Events and Information	Remarks and references to Appendices
7/9/16	Tactical command of 11th Div. Arty. in our area. German artillery action on work area.	w.r.b.
8/9/16	D/241 out of action at wagon line. C/241 relieves C/246 near MESNIL.	w.r.b.
9/9/16	Uneventful.	w.r.b.
10/9/16	" "	w.r.b.
11/9/16	German artillery active on work areas. Registration for attack on 14/9/16 and preparations.	w.r.b.
12/9/16	Continues preparations.	w.r.b.
13/9/16	" "	w.r.b.
14/9/16 6.30.	Attack by 30 one on R31 B 03 - 23 - 32 - 51 - 60 - R31 D 79. Bde HQ and A/241 and D/241 engaged. Operations successful	w.r.b.

WAR DIARY
or
INTELLIGENCE SUMMARY.
(Erase heading not required.)

Army Form C. 2118.

Instructions regarding War Diaries and Intelligence Summaries are contained in F.S. Regs., Part II. and the Staff Manual respectively. Title pages will be prepared in manuscript.

Hour, Date, Place	Summary of Events and Information	Remarks and references to Appendices
15/9/16.	Quiet. 147th Inf. Bde. relieved 32nd Inf.Bde.	W.R.6.
16/9/16 6.30 pm	attacks on trenches still held by Germans in R.31.c. by 147th Bde. unsuccessful. Quiet.	W.R.6.
17/9/16		W.R.6.
18/9/16	Bde. H.Q. relieved by 24st Bde.H.Q. Returned to HEDAUVILLE. Batteries (18 pdr.) still in action. B/241 preparing position on Railway W. of OZIERES.	W.R.6.
19/9/16	unsuccessful.	W.R.6.
20/9/16	Bde. H.Q. moved to BOUZINCOURT.	W.R.6.
21/9/16	unsuccessful. A/241 preparing position about W.6 D 4.5. and B/241 at Q 35 T u.7.	W.R.6.
22/9/16.	unsuccessful.	W.R.6.

Army Form C. 2118.

WAR DIARY
or
INTELLIGENCE SUMMARY.
(Erase heading not required.)

Instructions regarding War Diaries and Intelligence Summaries are contained in F. S. Regs., Part II. and the Staff Manual respectively. Title pages will be prepared in manuscript.

Place	Date	Hour	Summary of Events and Information	Remarks and references to Appendices
July/Aug	23/9/16		Uneventful.	W.P.6
	24/9/16		D/241 went into position about X 4 a 4.8. A/241 & B/241 into positions mentioned above.	W.P.6
	25/9/16		Uneventful	W.P.6
	26/9/16	12.30	Attack on THIEPVAL in which all batteries cooperated.	W.P.6
	27/9/16		Gun No. 2 of B/241 hit causing 5 casualties. Lt Col Colville left to command half group of 4th Div owing to Lt Col WEST having been killed on Stuff Redoubt	W.P.6
	28/9/16		German counterattack batteries very active. German counterattack on SCHWABEN REDOUBT.	W.P.6
	29/9/16		Batteries very active. Shell hit gun pits at C/241 position at Q 2 & a 4.3 causing 7 casualties	W.P.6
	30/9/16		on night of 29/30 Sept one section of each battery was relieved. A, B & C by Battery of 18th Div. arty. D/241 by battery of 25th Div. arty.	W.P.6

Army Form C. 2118.

WAR DIARY
or
INTELLIGENCE SUMMARY.
(Erase heading not required.)

Place	Date	Hour	Summary of Events and Information	Remarks and references to Appendices
			On night 30 Sept/1 Oct relief completed. During the month 1 Military Cross (Lt PRIDMORE D/241) and 5 Military Medals awarded to the Brigade.	n.t.o.

Signed,
R. CURFA
Comdg. 241 Bde R.F.A.

Vol 20

CONFIDENTIAL.

WAR DIARY.

of.

2 Her. (S.M.) Bde. R.F.A.

from 1-10-16.   to 31-10-16.

Volume X XIV

Army Form C. 2118.

WAR DIARY
or
INTELLIGENCE SUMMARY.
(Erase heading not required.)

Instructions regarding War Diaries and Intelligence Summaries are contained in F. S. Regs., Part II. and the Staff Manual respectively. Title pages will be prepared in manuscript.

Place	Date	Hour	Summary of Events and Information	Remarks and references to Appendices
In the field.	1/10/16		Evening - Batteries emptied relief of Batteries of 1st D.A. from 49th D.A. D from 18th D.A.	W.D.6
	2/10/16		A + B from 18th D.A. C from 49th D.A. Brigade moved to WARLINCOURT. HEDAUVILLE at 7.15 am. vice ACHEUX, LOUVENCOURT. - AUTHIE - PAS. (51D NE 1/20000) arrived WARLINCOURT midday.	
	3/10/16		At WARLINCOURT. C.O. and B.C.s reconnoitring positions on SAILLY THE BUTERNE Plain.	W.D.
	4/10/16		Wagon lines moved to GAUDIEMPRE. C.O. + B.C.s continued reconnaissance.	W.D.6
	5/10/16		Evening Bde moved into positions as under (51D NE 1/20000)	W.D.6
			H.Q. SAILLY. J 18 B 17 A/241 E 26 A + 5. 20. B/241 K 2 A 6 3 C/241 K 2 B 6 3.	

Army Form C. 2118.

WAR DIARY
or
INTELLIGENCE SUMMARY.
(Erase heading not required.)

Instructions regarding War Diaries and Intelligence Summaries are contained in F. S. Regs., Part II. and the Staff Manual respectively. Title pages will be prepared in manuscript.

Place	Date	Hour	Summary of Events and Information	Remarks and references to Appendices
In the field	6/9/16		D/741 J C B 86 (In How group)	
	7/9/16		Batty reconnoitres Right group	wire
	8/9/16		A/741 B/741 C/741 A/140 B/140 were manoeuvring & wire-registration.	wire
	9/9/16		B/140 left group. A/143 joins. Registration	wire
	10/9/16		manoeuvring and wire cutting	wire
	11/9/16		" " " "	wire
	12/9/16		" " " "	wire
	13/9/16		" " " "	wire
			Capt. A.C.W. Hobson rejoins and assumes duties of Adjutant	
	14/9/16		manoeuvring & wire. as above	wire
	15/9/16		" " " "	wire
	16/9/16		Night 741. two separate sections took up positions temporarily near BENVILLERS. on reconnaissance	wire

2353 Wt. W2544/1454 700,000 5/15 D. D. & L. A.D.S.S./Forms/C. 2118.

WAR DIARY
INTELLIGENCE SUMMARY

Army Form C. 2118.

Place	Date	Hour	Summary of Events and Information	Remarks and references to Appendices
	17/10/16		of groups due to sudden erosion of concentration and movement of 17th & 9th Divisions	WSL
	18/10/16		Reorganisation of Bde and Groups. Since Six gun 18pdr Batteries became by merger of sections as under — A division B/241 and C/241	WSL
			A/241 received B/241 " C/241 " A division B/243 and C division C/243 B C " B/243 " D " C/243 B D divisions. Of Brigade and Group comprises as under. A/241 at K.14 c 2.5.15. B/241 " K.2 A 6.3. C/241 " K.2 B 6.3. D/241 " J 6 B 8.6. and a composite battery of centre sections of B & C Batteries at K.14 c 15.30	WSL

Army Form C. 2118.

WAR DIARY
or
INTELLIGENCE SUMMARY.
(Erase heading not required.)

Instructions regarding War Diaries and Intelligence Summaries are contained in F. S. Regs., Part II. and the Staff Manual respectively. Title pages will be prepared in manuscript.

Place	Date	Hour	Summary of Events and Information	Remarks and references to Appendices
In the field	19/10/16		Quiet - Completion of reorganisation - some wire cutting near SUNKEN ROAD	W/e
	20/10/16		Quiet - Some wire cutting near SUNKEN ROAD. Enemy Trench Mortar Battery demolished a section of our Trench opposite Battalion	W/e
	21/10/16		Unsuccessful Box and Strip raid run on Pin and Arrangements deep. E.2 & c.5.5. and K.11.A.3.H.	W/e
	22/10/16		Quiet.	W/e
		4.40	Heavy German Bombardment	
		5.15	S.O.S. received - German attempts to raid HEBUTERNE Trenches	
	23/10/16		Quiet. Wire cutting	W/e
	24/10/16		" " "	W/e
	25/10/16		" " "	W/e
	26/10/16		" " " D/n slightly shelled	W/e
	27/10/16		" " "	W/e

Army Form C. 2118.

WAR DIARY
or
INTELLIGENCE SUMMARY.
(Erase heading not required.)

Instructions regarding War Diaries and Intelligence Summaries are contained in F. S. Regs., Part II. and the Staff Manual respectively. Title pages will be prepared in manuscript.

Place	Date	Hour	Summary of Events and Information	Remarks and references to Appendices
In the field	28/10/16		Uneventful. Wire cutting.	W.R.6.
	29/10/16		Wire cutting. (A/Bty retaliating on enemy aircraft).	W.R.6.
	30/10/16		Wire cutting. (A/Bty cutting in front of C/Bty).	W.R.6.
	31/10/16		Weather improves. Wire cutting as above.	W.R.6.

J N Colvin
Lieut. Colonel,
Comdg. 241st. South Midland F.A. Bde.

Vol 21

– CONFIDENTIAL –

WAR DIARY.

of

241st (S.M.) Bde. R.F.A.

(Volume ~~XXV~~)

From 1/11/16   to 30/11/16

Army Form C. 2118.

WAR DIARY
or
INTELLIGENCE SUMMARY.
(Erase heading not required.)

Instructions regarding War Diaries and Intelligence Summaries are contained in F. S. Regs., Part II. and the Staff Manual respectively. Title pages will be prepared in manuscript.

Place	Date	Hour	Summary of Events and Information	Remarks and references to Appendices
In the field	1.11.16		Period uneventful. A/241 B5y night firing	All references to Sheet 57-D N.E. 1/20.000.
	2.11.16		Brigade formed "blue pocket" during night to assist 31st Division, who carried out three raids on the right. One party was unsuccessful.	
	3.11.16		Period uneventful. A/241 B/241 B5y wire cutting - weather bad.	
	4.11.16		Period uneventful. Weather keeping bad. Wire cutting continued	
	5.11.16		Period uneventful. Wire cutting continued.	
	6.11.16		Brigade formed intense barrage during night to assist a raid by 31st Division. B/240 & D/240 now under command of Lieut. Col. COLVILLE D.S.O. for this operation. Night firing by A/241 B5y.	
	7.11.16		Wire cutting A & B/241 B5y. Same Batteries night firing	
	8.11.16		Period uneventful. Weather bad. A/241 & B/241 Batteries night firing.	
	9.11.16		Period uneventful. Night firing & wire cutting by A/241 B5y.	
	10.11.16		Period uneventful. A/241 B5y night firing	
	11.11.16		Wire cutting by A/241 B5y.	
	12.11.16		B/241 were placed at disposal of O.C. 240 Bde to cut wire in preparation for a raid N.W. of GOMMECOURT. A/241 B5y & B/241 B5y night firing	

2353 Wt. W2544/1454 700,000 5/15 D. D. & L. A.D.S.S./Forms/C. 2118.

WAR DIARY or INTELLIGENCE SUMMARY

Army Form C. 2118.

Place	Date	Hour	Summary of Events and Information	Remarks and references to Appendices
In the field	13/11/16		The Brigade formed a flank barrage for an attack by 5th Army. Attack successful. BEAUMONT HAMEL taken. Our Brigade front kept quiet. Slow gun fire kept up all day.	AAWTH
	14/11/16		Very misty. A/241 Bty & B/241 Bty night firing.	AAWTH
	15/11/16		Very misty early. D/241 Bty fired 500 rounds special smoke shell & formed a screen about 500 yds long. A/241 Bty fired throughout the day in bursts under the D.D.V.S. Third Army inspected horses of the Brigade. At 3.p.m. the Brigade came under the orders of C.R.A. 31st Division for tactical purposes.	AAWTH
	16/11/16		Period uneventful. A/241 Bty & B/241 Bty night firing.	AAWTH
	17/11/16		Brigade again formed false "pocket" to assist raid by 31st Division. Raid successful.	AAWTH
	18/11/16		Intense Barrage put up by Brigade at dawn in connection with operations by II & III Corps.	AAWTH
			All remained quiet on Brigade front.	
	19/11/16		Period uneventful. A/241 & B/241 did night firing. One HE D.C.1516 B C/241 Bty burst rounding the axis. On enquiry held under 100 5th Army it was found that an HE shell had burst in gun & blown breach & part of breech ring away, but no flame attacked anyone in the Battery.	AAWTH
	20/11/16		The Brigade formed barrage for raid by 147th Infty. Bde. Raid very successful. The	

WAR DIARY
or
INTELLIGENCE SUMMARY.
(Erase heading not required.)

Army Form C. 2118.

Place	Date	Hour	Summary of Events and Information	Remarks and references to Appendices
In the field	8/11/16 – 22/11/16		was found to be well cut – all wire cutting for this raid done by B/241 Bde. A/241, B/241 & D/241 fired bursts of fire all night in view of suspected enemy activity. A/241 Bty fired bursts of fire all day as it was very misty. A/241, B/241 & D/241 again fired all night. The Brigade Front was shortened on the 20th Inf. Bde. 40 D. Div. being relieved by 93rd Inf. Bde. Front went from K.11.b.1.2 to K.3.D.7.7.	
	23/11/16		C/241 Bty ranged on by German aeroplane then written with 5.9 How. after this horse lines were withdrawn to a flank. Position shelled all day. One gun received direct hit & was completely destroyed. Gun pit set on fire but was put out after 15 mins. This position was at K.2.b.60.15. During night C/241 Bty moved to camouflaged position at K.14.c.15-30.	
	24/11/16		C/241 Bty registered from new position. Period uneventful.	
	25/11/16		Period uneventful	
	26/11/16		One section of A/241, B/241 & D/241 each relieved by 165 Bde.R.F.A. sections. Rest of A/241, B/241 & D/241 Btys relieved C/241 Bty withdrawn. Brigade Hdqrs. handed over control to O.C. 165 Bde. R.F.A. On completion of relief Brigade stayed night at P.A.S. 93rd Inf. Bde. sent letter to 31st Div. Arty. thanking the Brigade for their support.	

Army Form C. 2118.

WAR DIARY
or
INTELLIGENCE SUMMARY.
(Erase heading not required.)

Place	Date	Hour	Summary of Events and Information	Remarks and references to Appendices
In the field	28/11/16		Brigade remained at PAS preparing to march.	
	29/11/16		Brigade marched from PAS through THIEVRES, ORVILLE, DOULLENS to MEZEROLLES. Brigade marched past G.O.C. in PAS who expressed satisfaction with the general turn out. The march was well carried out with no straggling.	
	30/11/16		Brigade rested at MEZEROLLES.	

A.W.Hobson
Capt & Adjt
241st (S.M.) Bde R.F.A.
for O.C.

- CONFIDENTIAL -

WAR DIARY.

of.

241st (S.M) Bde. R.F.A.

from 1/12/16   to 31/12/16

Volume ~~XXVI~~

Army Form C. 2118.

WAR DIARY
or
INTELLIGENCE SUMMARY.
(Erase heading not required.)

Instructions regarding War Diaries and Intelligence Summaries are contained in F.S. Regs., Part II and the Staff Manual respectively. Title pages will be prepared in manuscript.

XXVI

Place	Date	Hour	Summary of Events and Information	Remarks and references to Appendices
Field	1/12/16		Brigade moved via CANDAS - TALMAS - GVILLERS-BOCAGE	WD6
	2/12/16		" to MOLLIENS AU-BOIS.	WD6
	3/12/16		2IC Bde went up to see positions occupied by 104 Bde RFA	WD6
	4/12/16		Bdes went to reconnoitre positions	WD6
	5/12/16		1 section per bty went into action relieving 104 Bde RFA	WD6
	6/12/16		Remaining sections in action.	
			Bde in action HQ. X5 D36 (near POZIÈRES)	
			A/241 M31 B8.5	
			B/241 M31 B4.5 } near MARTIN PUICH	
			C/241 S2 B9.5	
			D/241 M32 B7.3. C.O on leave.	
	7/12/16		uneventful weather misty	WD6
	8/12/16		" "	WD6
	9/12/16		" "	WD6
	10/12/16		" "	WD6
	11/12/16		" Autunge an aeroplane reconnaissance	WD6

2353 Wt W2544/1454 700,000 5/15 D.D.&L. A.D.S.S./Forms/C. 2118.

Army Form C. 2118.

WAR DIARY
or
INTELLIGENCE SUMMARY.
(Erase heading not required.)

Instructions regarding War Diaries and Intelligence Summaries are contained in F. S. Regs., Part II and the Staff Manual respectively. Title pages will be prepared in manuscript.

Place	Date	Hour	Summary of Events and Information	Remarks and references to Appendices
	12/12/16		Fairly quiet & near	WD
	13/12/16		Uneventful. More attempts of artillery in air moves to dugouts near Bn HQ	WD
	14/12/16		CONTALMAISON VILLA. Uneventful - still misty	WD
	15/12/16		1 section per battery relieved by corresponding Bty of 242 Bn. (Stepn & Bty) & relieve sections in dugouts to rest. Bns BEHENCOURT.	WD
	16/12/16		Remaining sections (except CBty) relieves & moves to BEHENCOURT.	WD
	17/12/16		Uneventful. In rear since cleaning up.	WD
	18/12/16		"	WD
	19/12/16		"	WD
	20/12/16		Battery staffs & signallers relieved by 1 section A/70. Training of gun Processes & nest	WD

WAR DIARY or INTELLIGENCE SUMMARY

Army Form C. 2118.

Place	Date	Hour	Summary of Events and Information	Remarks and references to Appendices
Huts in BEHENCOURT	21/12/16		Remainder of C/241 relieved & proceeded to BEHENCOURT	W&G
	22/12/16		Musketry. Horse exercise	W&G
	23/12/16		" "	W&G
	24/12/16		" "	W&G
	25/12/16		Christmas Day. Musketry	W&G
	26/12/16		Musketry	W&G
	27/12/16		"	W&G
	28/12/16		"	W&G
	29/12/16		C.O. & Adjutant went up to 240 Bde & new positions prior to relief. 1 NCO & one by 241 Bde	W&G
	30/12/16		Half the gunners with the B.C. and a Subaltern from each Battery went up the motor lorries to relieve half each Battery of 240 Bde. The remainder of the Bde continued training.	ACJH
	31/12/16		The rest of the gunners went up by motor lorry. When they arrived the Battery Commander took over from 240 Bde as follows:—	ACJH

2353 Wt. W2544/1454 700,000 5/15 D.D.&L. A.D.S.S./Forms/C. 2118.

Army Form C. 2118.

WAR DIARY
or
INTELLIGENCE SUMMARY.
(Erase heading not required.)

Instructions regarding War Diaries and Intelligence Summaries are contained in F. S. Regs., Part II. and the Staff Manual respectively. Title pages will be prepared in manuscript.

Place	Date	Hour	Summary of Events and Information	Remarks and references to Appendices
			A/241 relieved C/240 at a position at S3A1.3.	
			B/241 " B/240 " " " S1D 18.99.	
			C/241 " A/240 " " " S3A29.28.	
			D/241 " D/240 " " " M3LD2.4.	
			At 12 noon the C.O. took over the front from O.C. 240 Bde. He established his Headquarters at BAZENTIN-LE-PETIT CEMETERY at S8D8.9. The Battery Positions were very bad and flooded. Ammunition Supply was by railway from BAZENTIN in the case of A, B, & C Batteries and from PEAKE WOOD in the case of D/241 Battery.	
			The same day the wagon lines moved up to relieve the 240 Bde wagon lines. These were at the following points:-	
			Headquarters Staff at E3A1.4.	
			A/241 B⁵ W7C9.6. ⎫ at ALBERT	
			C/241 B⁵ E3D7.7. ⎬	
			B/241 B⁵ X16A1.2. ⎫ at CONTALMAISON	
			D/241 B⁵ X16D1.3. ⎬	aawtt

Army Form C. 2118.

WAR DIARY
or
INTELLIGENCE SUMMARY.
(Erase heading not required.)

Instructions regarding War Diaries and Intelligence Summaries are contained in F. S. Regs., Part II. and the Staff Manual respectively. Title pages will be prepared in manuscript.

Place	Date	Hour	Summary of Events and Information	Remarks and references to Appendices
			The whole Relief was carried out very smoothly and everything was quiet on the front from the time of taking over until the end of the year.	A/W.T.H.
	1/1/17			
			A.W.T Hobson	
			Capt. & f/Adjt.	
			A.O.C. 241 Bde. R.F.A.	

Army Form C. 2118.

WAR DIARY
or
INTELLIGENCE SUMMARY.
(Erase heading not required.)

Instructions regarding War Diaries and Intelligence Summaries are contained in F. S. Regs., Part II. and the Staff Manual respectively. Title pages will be prepared in manuscript.

Place	Date	Hour	Summary of Events and Information	Remarks and references to Appendices
	1.1.17		The O.C. Brigade was made Brevet Lieutenant Colonel, and Major J.S. THOMPSON received the D.S.O. in the New Years List. The Batteries commenced work on their new positions. A certain amount of registration was carried out but without much success owing to mist. Firing on German trenches and approaches by night.	AWH
	2.1.17		Registration continued. A quiet day. Fired on German trenches day & night.	AWH
	3.1.17		Uneventful. Fired on German trenches & approaches all day and night.	AWH
	4.1.17		C. Battery was heavily shelled by 8 inch Hows from 10 a.m. to 3.30 p.m. The men were temporarily withdrawn from the position. No casualties. A quiet day for the other Batteries. Fired on German trenches all day & night.	AWH
	5.1.17		Uneventful. Firing at intervals all day and night on German trenches and approaches in neighbourhood of WARLINCOURT continued.	AWH
	6.1.17		Uneventful. Firing all day & night continued.	AWH
	7.1.17		A Battery heavily shelled all day. The men were withdrawn & no casualties suffered. One gun was completely destroyed with its carriage by a 5.9" How shell. Unaventful for rest of the Brigade. Firing all day & night continued.	AWH

Army Form C. 2118.

WAR DIARY
or
INTELLIGENCE SUMMARY.
(Erase heading not required.)

Place	Date	Hour	Summary of Events and Information	Remarks and references to Appendices
	8.1.17		Uneventful. Firing day and night continued	AWJH.
	9.1.17		Uneventful. Firing day and night continued	AWJH.
	10.1.17		Registration of G.IRD TRENCH just behind BUTTE DE WARLINCOURT carried out by aeroplane. Very successful in the case of C and B. Batteries. Aeroplane unable to see A Battery owing to banks of mist. Day and night firing continued. Period marked by great increase in hostile Artillery. Rounds were fired round A.C. and D. Batteries at intervals without doing any damage.	AWJH
	11.1.17		German Artillery again very active, many rounds falling round A.C. and D. Battery positions. No damage done. Firing day and night continued.	AWJH
	12.1.17		Uneventful. Misty. Firing day & night continued	AWJH
	13.1.17		Uneventful. Firing day & night continued	AWJH
	14.1.17		The Wagon Lines relieved one another as follows within the Brigade:— C. Battery moved from DOLLS FARM E19D.7.7. to N27.C.9.6. A Battery moved forward to CONTALMAISON about X.16.D.1.2.	

Army Form C. 2118.

WAR DIARY
or
INTELLIGENCE SUMMARY.
(Erase heading not required.)

Place	Date	Hour	Summary of Events and Information	Remarks and references to Appendices
In the Field	27/7/17		Uneventful. During the night 27th Bg moved one section forward to M 29 a 7 & for wire cutting. C/172 Bty joined the group arriving mid-section at H 11 d & 5.	
	28/7/17		Uneventful	Reconnaissances for Br. Cne. CRG 241 Bombarda

CONFIDENTIAL

WAR DIARY

of

241or (S.M.) Bde RFA

from 1/1/17 to 31/1/17

(VOLUME XXVII)

Army Form C. 2118.

WAR DIARY
or
INTELLIGENCE SUMMARY.
(Erase heading not required.)

Instructions regarding War Diaries and Intelligence Summaries are contained in F. S. Regs., Part II. and the Staff Manual respectively. Title pages will be prepared in manuscript.

Place	Date	Hour	Summary of Events and Information	Remarks and references to Appendices
	5/2/17		The command passed from the French at 8 a.m. Registration carried out.	AWDH
	6/2/17		Brigade Headquarters moved to CAPPY on the Divisional Artillery being formed into two groups. The Batteries of the Brigade came under command of Lt. Col. Lord Wynford at 12 noon. O/C under A of Corps.	AWDH AWDH
	7/2/17		Uneventful.	AWDH
	8/2/17		Uneventful.	AWDH
	9/2/17		"	WDH
	10/2/17		"	WDH
	11/2/17		"	WDH
	12/2/17		"	WDH
	13/2/17		" Aveugre lines moved to Bois D'HAPPE, CAPPY	WDH
	14/2/17	9.50 am	B/241 Bty position shelled by 10.5 cm where damage to material slight, 15 prisoners D & L Uneventful	WDH
	15/2/17		" B/241 moves forward position to H29D7&8	WDH
	16/2/17		"	WDH
	17/2/17		"	WDH

2353 Wt. W2544/1454 700,000 5/15 D. D. & L. A.D.S.S./Forms/C. 2118.

Army Form C. 2118.

WAR DIARY
or
INTELLIGENCE SUMMARY.
(Erase heading not required.)

Instructions regarding War Diaries and Intelligence Summaries are contained in F. S. Regs., Part II. and the Staff Manual respectively. Title pages will be prepared in manuscript.

Place	Date	Hour	Summary of Events and Information	Remarks and references to Appendices
In the Field	18/2/17		In use cutting manoeuvre	W36
	19/2/17		"	W36
	20/2/17		"	W36
	21/2/17		Coy Commdr returned to commence tour	
	22/2/17		"	W36
	23/2/17		Bn HQ Approved to issue instr action to commence reorganisation of Battn into three Groups Conference	W36
	24/2/17		manoeuvre	W36
	25/2/17		Bn HQ issued instrs with action on H.2 & 8.6 to commence reorgp. Lewis gun group & Rifle grenade grp Rifle and grenade sections (A, B & D) Coys under command of their Coy Commdrs	8/1/17 W36
	26/2/17		Coy in Groups manoeuvre	W36

Vol 24

CONFIDENTIAL

WAR DIARY.

of

241 or (S.M.) Bde R.F.A.

(VOLUME XXVIII)

1-2-17   28-2-17.

WAR DIARY
or
INTELLIGENCE SUMMARY.

(Erase heading not required.)

Army Form C. 2118.

Place	Date	Hour	Summary of Events and Information	Remarks and references to Appendices
	14.1.17 (contd)		B. Battery moved back to DOLLS FARM E.3.D.7.7.	
	15.1.17		The firing in the German trenches was very much increased & simulated an attack on the BUTTE, but the Germans remained very quiet. Behind COLVILLE was an away all day visiting the French opposite PERONNE and reconnoitring positions as the Brigade was to be relieved in the MARTINPUICH area and go down opposite PERONNE to take over from the French. Firing all day and night to normal extent. Uneventful. ALLTH RCCIST RCIST	
	16.1.17		Uneventful. Warning orders for relief received	
	17.1.17		Uneventful. Day and night firing increased	
	18.1.17		Uneventful. B. Battery withdrew a section. These were put on a light railway & taken to BAZENTIN. Stores by road to the wagon line. Day and night firing continued. B Battery received another section at wagon lines. RCIST	
	19.1.17		Uneventful. B. Battery withdrew another section as before. Day and night firing continued	
	20.1.17		Uneventful. B. Battery withdrew the remaining section. The Brigade covered the same front as before, but with only two 18 pr guns 18 Pr. RCIST	

Army Form C. 2118.

WAR DIARY
or
INTELLIGENCE SUMMARY.
(Erase heading not required.)

Instructions regarding War Diaries and Intelligence Summaries are contained in F. S. Regs., Part II. and the Staff Manual respectively. Title pages will be prepared in manuscript.

Place	Date	Hour	Summary of Events and Information	Remarks and references to Appendices
	21/1/17	12 noon	Batteries and one 4 gun Howitzer Battery, it having been decided in view of the relief to have the third section of D/241 at the wagon line. 1 Section of A/241 relieved by one Section of B/172 at gun position. 1 Section of B/241 relieved by one Section of C/172 at gun position. 1 Section of D/241 relieved by one section of D/172 at gun position	AHR
		10.30 pm	The remaining sections relieved as follows :— A/241 relieved by B/172 at gun position. B/241 relieved by C/172 at gun position. 1 section D/241 relieved by 1 section D/172 at gun position. One section from each wagon line marched back to PIERREPOT and were relieved at the wagon lines as under :— A/241 by B/172 B/241 by A/172 C/241 by C/172 D/241 by 72nd Bde. D.A.C. The Command remained with Colonel COLVILLE. Day and night	

Army Form C. 2118.

WAR DIARY
or
INTELLIGENCE SUMMARY.
(Erase heading not required.)

Instructions regarding War Diaries and Intelligence Summaries are contained in F.S. Regs., Part II. and the Staff Manual respectively. Title pages will be prepared in manuscript.

Place	Date	Hour	Summary of Events and Information	Remarks and references to Appendices
	22.1.17		firing continued. Rest of Brigade Wagon lines moved down to PIERREGOT. 2nd i/c in command was handed over to Colonel STIRLING, & Lt.Col. 7th Bde. and Colonel ODEVILLE with his Headquarters proceeded by motor lorry to PIERREGOT.	
	23.1.17		The Brigade rested at PIERREGOT and commenced cleaning up after being in the mud at the forward area.	
	24.1.17		Uneventful.	
	25.1.17		Colonel COLVILLE accompanied the Adjutant and Battery Commanders by motor bus to HERSE COURT and thoroughly reconnoitred the positions which the Brigade were to take over.	
	26.1.17		The Brigade marched to HAMELET.	
	27.1.17		Uneventful	
	28.1.17		Uneventful	
	29.1.17		Working Parties under an officer from each Battery went up by motor bus to HERSE COURT to work on the new positions and to	

Army Form C. 2118.

WAR DIARY
or
INTELLIGENCE SUMMARY.
(Erase heading not required.)

Place	Date	Hour	Summary of Events and Information	Remarks and references to Appendices
	30-1-17		laying out communications. Colonel COLVILLE accompanied by his Adjutant and Signal Officer reconnoitred to O.P.s opposite PERONNE and HALLE. Very fine points to view were found but the exact location was not decided upon. The O.P.s should be the best for observation since the Brigade left FLANDERS.	
	31-1-17		Further working parties were sent to the forward area round HERBECOURT Unsuccessful Bus Driver tried hard to get the front line but MRL	

W.R. Edwards
for LIEUT. COLONEL,
COMMG. 141 SOUTH MIDLAND FIELD ARTILLERY BRIGADE

WAR DIARY
or
INTELLIGENCE SUMMARY.
(Erase heading not required.)

Army Form C. 2118.

Place	Date	Hour	Summary of Events and Information	Remarks and references to Appendices
In the field			Two machine guns being captured. Artillery fire was reported to be very accurate. 4.92. 143rd Infantry Res. put German dead seen at 19. The S.O.S. Group had the assistance of the following Batteries for this raid A/742. B/740, A/742, C/742. A/W.H.	
	9/3/17		Uneventful. Short organised bombardment of BIACHES at 11 pm. A/WH.	
	10/3/17		Uneventful. A/W.H.	
	11/3/17		Registration carried out for a proposed small raid by 8th R. Warwick Regt. in the evening. Raid was postponed owing to other operations not affecting the Group. A/W.H.	
	12/3/17		Registration for raid continued. Raid cancelled in the evening. A/W.H.	
	13/3/17		Uneventful. 92 Brigade recognized reserve positions with Battery Commanders. A/W.H.	
	14/3/17		Wire cutting recommenced by A/241. Uneventful A/W.H.	
	15/3/17		A/241 wire cutting with detached Section B/742 also cut wire. The enemy D.Ps. in the neighbourhood of PERONNE and HALLE were bombarded by D/241 and A/241. Registration in addition to foregoing was carried out by	

Vol 25

CONFIDENTIAL

WAR DIARY

of

241 av (S.M.) Bde RFA

VOLUME XXIX

from 1/3/17   to 31/3/17

WAR DIARY or INTELLIGENCE SUMMARY

Army Form C. 2118

Place	Date	Hour	Summary of Events and Information	Remarks and references to Appendices
In the field	1/3/17		Wirecutting throughout the day by all 18 Pr. Batteries. Destructive fire on various points by D/241.	Ref. Map. Sheet 62d 1/40000
"	2/3/17		Wirecutting continued. Period uncventful. AWTH.	
"	3/3/17	2.30 am	The Sub Group assisted by A/26, A/240 and C/241 covered an attempted raid by 143rd Infantry Brigade. The raid was unsuccessful, the Infantry being unable to approach the enemy wire. The enemy made no attempt to reply to our Barrage. AWTH.	
"	4/3/17		Wirecutting continued. Registration of trench junctions and points of tactical importance carried out by 18 Pr. Batteries in conjunction with aeroplane. Uneventful. AWTH.	
"	5/3/17		Wirecutting and registration for a raid in the evening. Raid cancelled, weather bad. AWTH.	
"	6/3/17		Uneventful. AWTH.	
"	7/3/17		Uneventful. AWTH.	
"	8/3/17		Registration for raid by 6th Battn. R. Devonshire Regt. Raid took place at 9 pm. The German trenches at RICHES being entered. Three prisoners and	

WAR DIARY
or
INTELLIGENCE SUMMARY.

(Erase heading not required.)

Army Form C. 2118.

Place	Date	Hour	Summary of Events and Information	Remarks and references to Appendices
XXIII	1/2/17		The Brigade rested at HAMELET. aaaTH.	
	2/2/17		The Brigade marched to CAPPY with half of each Battery. The other half of each Battery remained at HAMELET. aaaTH. Major Chandler M.C. assumed command of the Brigade or H. of Colville temporarily, acting O.R.H. aaaTH. Remainder of Brigade marched to CAPPY. One half of each Battery moved up to the forward area between HERBECOURT, FLAUCOURT and the River SOMME.	
	3/2/17		A/241 moved into an empty position at about H23 A 4.4 D/241 " " " " " H13 B 2.3 (3gun) " " " " " H34 D 8 0.5.5 (1 ") B/241 relieved a Battery of the French 1st Division at H28 A 7.5.0.6 C/241 " " " " " H23 & D 8.4 Headquarters moved into dug outs at H23 A 8.6. The commenced received in the hands of the French. All wagon lines were together on the CAPPY-ECLUSIER road. The Brigade registered. On arrival the remainder of the Battery went into position. D/241 front in a detached section by C/241 at H34 D 8.0.5.5. The French retained command. aaaTH	

WAR DIARY
or
INTELLIGENCE SUMMARY.

(Erase heading not required.)

Army Form C. 2118.

Place	Date	Hour	Summary of Events and Information	Remarks and references to Appendices
In the field	16/3/17		All Batteries in the Group A.L.U.7.	
	17/3/17		The Group was registering all day for raids. A 241 cut wire all day with a detached section. Brigade received warning to be ready to move at short notice as it was expected that the enemy intended to withdraw. The Raid to be covered by the Group was cancelled, it having been ascertained that the enemy had withdrawn. Uneventful for the Group. A.L.U.7.	
	18/3/17		O.C. Brigade and Battery Commanders reconnoitred to positions in, and SOUTH of, BIACHES and in the BARLEUX area. Officers also were out reconnoitring for O.P's. Uneventful period as there was no enemy within range. A.L.U.7.	
	19/3/17	1am	C/241 moved a section of guns over the SOMME RIVER and CANAL crossing at BAZINCOURT FARM in pontoons. The section proceeded via HALLE into action at I 26 A 4.9. and covered from THREE TUBS WOOD to DOINGT.	
			Positions were reconnoitred in LA CHAPELETTE and I 21 A and I 28 A.	
		10pm	D/241 detached Section moved via FLAUCOURT, BARLEUX and	

Army Form C. 2118.

WAR DIARY
or
INTELLIGENCE SUMMARY.
(Erase heading not required.)

Instructions regarding War Diaries and Intelligence Summaries are contained in F. S. Regs., Part II. and the Staff Manual respectively. Title pages will be prepared in manuscript.

Place	Date	Hour	Summary of Events and Information	Remarks and references to Appendices
In the field	20.3.17	10 pm	Came into action at I.33.C.9.4. in CHAPPELETTE. Sent THREE TURKS WOOD to DOINGT to cover our advanced posts, though no enemy were reported within range.	
	21.3.17		Remainder of C/241 moved over river into action at I.26.A.4.9. Uneventful sleep. Positions reconnoitered in I.24.C and I.35.A Uneventful. HQrs moved to railway trucks at LA CHAPPELETTE (09.B.3.8.) Remainder of D/241 moved to I.33.C.9.4. A/241 came into action in ETERPIGNY at D/A K.85. and B/241 at 015.C.35.20. All wagon lines moved forward close to Battery Positions. Major C.R. Nickalls assumed command of the Brigade while Lieut.Col. Colvill completed 48 firing day's battery. Left Sections of D, Lt Half Batteries A/241 HQrs Wagon line established itself on Station Road, LA CHAPPELETTE. A/241 and B/241 in ETERPIGNY, C/241 at the Aerodrome PERONNE and D/241 in the Station Yard, LA CHAPPELETTE.	
	22.3.17		C/241 moved Battery position forward to I.27.D.50.25 aeu7th Further forward Battery positions and O.Ps. reconnoitered. Uneventful. No sign of presence of the enemy discovered. Uneventful ae.u.7h	
	23.3.17		Further reconnoitering. Uneventful ae.u.7h.	

WAR DIARY
or
INTELLIGENCE SUMMARY.

Army Form C. 2118.

Place	Date	Hour	Summary of Events and Information	Remarks and references to Appendices
Sheffield	24.3.17		B/241 moved a section to I.29.B.1.4. Further reconnoitring. Unsuccessful.	
	25.3.17		Remainder of B/241 moved into action at I.29.B.1.4. A/241 moved and same into action in DOINGT with wagon lines by guns. D/241 moved to I.29.B.1.0. and went into action. B/241 wagon lines were in PERONNE.	
	26.3.17		HQrs moved to BUSSU via PERONNE. A/241 and B/241 moved into action in TINCOURT and came under command of Lt.Col. Lord Wynford. A/241 and B/240 came under Lieut Col Colville's orders and went into action at J.3.D.8.7 and J.3.D.6.8. respectively. Unsuccessful.	
	27.3.17	6.30am	D/241 moved into action in TEMPLEUX LA FOSSE with wagon lines at ASSECOURT LE HAUT. The Battery supported the Infantry (141st Inf. Bde.) in a successful action against the high ground in E.20. successful.	
	28.3.17		D/241 moved a section forward to LONGAVESNES. B/241 moved into Reserve at BUIRE. A/241 moved into action at J.5.D.6.8. A/240 and B/240 left the Brigade. C/241 moved into action at LONGAVESNES. successful.	
	29.3.17		Remainder of D/241 moved to LONGAVESNES into action. A/241, C/241 and D/241 wagon lines moved to TINCOURT. A/241 moved forward into action at	

Army Form C. 2118.

WAR DIARY
or
INTELLIGENCE SUMMARY.
(Erase heading not required.)

Place	Date	Hour	Summary of Events and Information	Remarks and references to Appendices
In the field	30.3.17		E16A4.1. C/241 moved to E16D04. B/241 moved into action at E15 B0.4 and D/241 at E15 B12. Alsott	
	31/3/17	5pm	Registration by all Batteries for attack on E.P.E.H.Y. Barrage fixed in front of E.P.E.H.Y while Infantry Patrols went out. Unsuccessful. Further registration of barrage. Unsuccessful assault.	

A.W.Turton
Capt & Adjt
For O.C. 241 South African [illegible]

Vol 26

— CONFIDENTIAL —

WAR DIARY

of

241st (S.m.) Bde R.F.A.

1-4-17   30-4-17

Volume XXX

WAR DIARY or INTELLIGENCE SUMMARY

Army Form C. 2118.

Place	Date	Hour	Summary of Events and Information	Remarks and references to Appendices
	1/4/17	6.30 a.m.	The Brigade fired a barrage to cover the 143rd Infantry Brigade into conjunction with the 144th Infantry Brigade attacked EPEHY. The attack was completely successful, and a gun and 18 prisoners were taken. Close watch was kept all day for counter attack and O.P.'s were found forward of EPEHY. The remainder of the day was, however, uneventful. ACWH	
	2/4/17		Uneventful. Forward positions reconnoitred.	
		6 p.m. to 6.30 p.m.	C/241 fired a barrage on LEMPIRE for half an hour before patrols of the 144th Infantry Brigade attempted to occupy the village. The patrols came under M.G. fire and withdrew. ACWH	
	3/4/17	5.30 a.m.	A section of B/242 moved forward and came into action at E 11 B 1.1. Uneventful. Lieut F.H. ADSHEAD of C/241 was wounded while reconnoitring for an O.P. in EPEHY. ACWH	
	4/4/17		The remainder of B/242 moved forward to the detached section at E 11 B 1.1. before dawn. C/241 before dawn moved four guns into action at E.10 B.0.2. and a detached section into action at F.1.C.9.5. ACWH	

WAR DIARY
or
INTELLIGENCE SUMMARY.

(Erase heading not required.)

Army Form C. 2118.

Place	Date	Hour	Summary of Events and Information	Remarks and references to Appendices
	5/4/17		B/141 and C/141 were placed temporarily under command of O.C. 240 Brigade to assist in an attack on L'EMPIRE. The attack was unsuccessful. A/141 and D/141 were in observation, but were not required. AdWH.	
	6/4/17		C/141 detached section was withdrawn and put into action with the remainder of the Battery. D/141 moved a section forward into action at E6 B5-7. and A/141 moved a section forward into action at W30 C90. 057. A horse in EPEHY used by B/141 as an O.P. was hit and one man was badly wounded. AdWH.	
	7/4/17		Uneventful. AdWH.	
	8/4/17		Brigade Hdqrs. moved from TEMPLEUX LAFOSSE and Hdqrs. Wagon Lines moved from BUSSU to VILLERS FAUCON. B/141 was shelled and two telephonists were wounded, one afterwards dying of his wounds. A/141 moved four guns to CHAUFOURS WOOD south.	
	9/4/17		O.C. 211 Brigade R.F.A. came to Brigade Hdqrs. and C/211 and D/211 were sent up for attachment to this Brigade. C/211 moved into action at	

WAR DIARY
or
INTELLIGENCE SUMMARY.
(Erase heading not required.)

Army Form C. 2118.

Place	Date	Hour	Summary of Events and Information	Remarks and references to Appendices
	10/4/17		E.5.C.7.6. and D/241 moved into action at the quarry at E.18.D.07. A&WTH.	
	11/4/17		The attached Batteries registered Unevertful. A&WTH.	
			Uneventful. A&WTH.	
	12/4/17	2.30 p.m.	The 125th Infantry Brigade pushed forward posts to P20.12.Copse. The 2/1 Brigade and D/241 covered the advance. The Copse was occupied successfully with little resistance. Owing to the 7th Devons hid Brigade arriving late to take telephone or other means of communication it was not until 3 a.m. that any news got back from the advancing infantry to the Battalion Headquarters. This resulted in a large expenditure of ammunition needlessly. A&WTH.	
	13/4/17		Registration. At dusk the remainder of A/241 moved in by the Advanced Section at W.30.c.8.1. and the remainder of D/241 moved up to the position at E.6.D.6.3. B/241 wagon lines moved forward to a Quarry at E.27.D.0.4. A&WTH.	
	14/4/17		Uneventful. A&WTH.	
	15/4/17		Uneventful. A&WTH.	
	16/4/17	5 am	B/241 moved forward and came into position at F.8.C.4.6 and D/241 moved forward to a position at F.7.B.6.8. All Batteries registered GATELET	

WAR DIARY
or
INTELLIGENCE SUMMARY.
(Erase heading not required.)

Army Form C. 2118.

Place	Date	Hour	Summary of Events and Information	Remarks and references to Appendices
	16.4.17	10 pm	COPSE, PETIT PRIEL FARM and other strong points during the day in readiness to cover an attack by the 143rd Infantry Brigade in the evening.	
			The Brigade covered the attack by 143rd Infantry Brigade. The Infantry got held up at CATELET COPSE. The 6th Btn. R. Warwicks progressed on the left. The 5/2 R. Warwicks were unable to make progress. Casualties among the Infantry heavy by a minor operation. AWJH	
	17.4.17		Uneventful. The Infantry occupied without opposition the points unsuccessfully attacked last night. AWJH	
	18.4.17		Uneventful. AWJH	
	19.4.17		B/241 and D/211 were placed under orders of OC. 240 Bde. to assist in an operation. Uneventful. AWJH	
	20.4.17		Uneventful. AWJH	
	21.4.17		C/241 moved one gun forward to F.8.C.50.25. Uneventful. AWJH	
	22.4.17		Registration of high ground in F.12.A in preparation for an attack on St. Quiet and uneventful. AWJH	
	23.4.17		C/211 was moved forward to a position about F.8.A.2.6. Registration	

WAR DIARY
or
INTELLIGENCE SUMMARY.

(Erase heading not required.)

Army Form C. 2118.

Date	Hour	Summary of Events and Information	Remarks and references to Appendices
24.4.17		continued. ACWTH	
		The Brigade less A/241 and D/241 units C/241 and B/240 covered the 6.P. Gloucesters in an attack on the Knoll in F.12.A. The attack was unsuccessful, the enemy holding the trench on top in considerable strength. ACWTH.	
25.4.17		The Brigade as above covered a further attack on the Knoll in F.6.A, the 14th Infantry Brigade advancing under our barrage. The attack was only partly successful, our Infantry only getting established on the slopes of the Knoll and not on the top. The Batteries stood by all day as the situation was very obscure, but the time was quiet. ACWTH	
26.4.17		Unsuccessful. The situation remained obscure and there was very little firing on either side. ACWTH.	
27.4.17		The situation was no more clear. Unsuccessful ACWTH.	
28.4.17		Unsuccessful ACWTH	
29.4.17		B/241 and C/241 were shelled from 7.30 am to 11am. The personnel were withdrawn to a flank and little damage was done. One D.R. was slightly wounded. Orders that the 211 Brigade would relieve the Brigade were	

Army Form C. 2118.

WAR DIARY
or
INTELLIGENCE SUMMARY.
(Erase heading not required.)

Instructions regarding War Diaries and Intelligence Summaries are contained in F.S. Regs., Part II. and the Staff Manual respectively. Title pages will be prepared in manuscript.

Place	Date	Hour	Summary of Events and Information	Remarks and references to Appendices
	30-4-17		received. O.C. C/241 reconnoitred a position in 59th Divisional area at L.15.D.6.0. occupied by B/210 Battery and O.C. D/241 reconnoitred a position in the same area at L.2.B.5.2. occupied by D/210 Battery. At dusk B/241 withdrew a section of guns to its wagon lines. C/241 moved a section from its position to a position at L.15.D.6.0. where it came into action — the wagon lines of this section went to BOUCLY. A section of A/211 came into action with C/241 in place of the section of the latter moved to the other position. allott. A section of B/211 moved into position alongside A/241. Meanwhile, C/241 withdrew a second section at dusk it being replaced by a second section of A/211. The command passed from Lt. C/241 to O.C. A/211. B/241 withdrew another section to its wagon lines. A/241 withdrew a section to its wagon lines at TINCOURT, it being replaced by another section of B/211. D/241 moved a section into action at L.2.B.5.2., the wagon lines of	

WAR DIARY
or
INTELLIGENCE SUMMARY.
(Erase heading not required.)

Army Form C. 2118.

This section being at HAMLET. A&45H.

Honours and Awards during the month:-

Lieut F. H. ADSHEAD C/241 M.C. - Immediate reward.

No 83159 Gunner JAMES A.W. B/241 M.M.

A&45H

A.W.Thomson
Capt & Adjt
p OC 241 Brigade R.F.A.

11/5/17

Vol 27

CONFIDENTIAL.

WAR DIARY.

of

241st. (S.m.) Bde. R.F.A.

(Volume ~~XXXI~~)

From 1/5/17. To 31/5/17

Army Form C. 2118.

WAR DIARY
or
INTELLIGENCE SUMMARY.
(Erase heading not required.)

Place	Date	Hour	Summary of Events and Information	Remarks and references to Appendices
	1/5/17		Uneventful. At dusk the remaining guns of A/241 and B/241 moved out to TINCOURT. D/241 moved into action at L.21.B.3.3. and came under the command of the C.R.A. 59th Div. Arty. C/241 moved into action at L.21.B.3.7. and came under the C.R.A. 59th Div. Arty. also.	62ème
	2/5/17	10am	Brigade Hdqrs. moved to TINCOURT- command passing to T.P. 210 Bde. R.F.A. A.a.J.H.	4
	3/5/17 to 9/5/17		A/241 and B/241 at TINCOURT training. C/241 and D/241 in action under 59th D.A. spent a very uneventful time during this period. On 3/5/17 D/241 wagon lines moved into HAMELET and C/241 wagon lines moved into BOUCLY PARK. a.a.J.H.	4
	10/5/17		A/241 and B/241 were placed under command B 59th Div Arty for a proposed attack, and moved into action at L.21.B.4.2. and L.21.B.4.0. respectively. a.a.J.H.	
	11/5/17		Batteries commenced registration but were stopped at 11 a.m., it being understood that the attack would not take place. a.a.J.H.	
	12/5/17		C/241 and D/241 were withdrawn. C/241 moved to its wagon lines	5

WAR DIARY
or
INTELLIGENCE SUMMARY.

Army Form C. 2118.

Place	Date	Hour	Summary of Events and Information	Remarks and references to Appendices
	13/5/17		in BOUCLY PARK. D/241 and wagon lines moved to TINCOURT. B/241 wagon lines moved from TINCOURT to HAMELET. Uneventful. ALWH.	62cNE
	14/5/17		A/241 and B/241 were withdrawn from action. A/241 moved to its wagon lines at TINCOURT, B/241 moved to its wagon lines at HAMELET. ALWH	
	15/5/17		B/241 moved to TINCOURT. The Brigade prepared to march early on the following day. The O.C. Brigade and the Adjutant visited the 1st Australian F.A. Batteries in the neighbourhood of BEAUMETZ to make arrangements for the Brigade to relieve the 1st Aus. F.A. Bde. ALWH	57eNE
	16/5/17		The Brigade marched to BEAULENCOURT via TEMPLEUX LA FOSSE - MOISLAINS - MANANCOURT - MESNIL - ROCQUIGNY - LE TRANSLOY. At BEAULENCOURT the Brigade were billetted in a standing camp for the first time since landing in France. The march was uneventful, weather cold and a few showers. ALWH	57C
	17/5/17		Battery Commanders visited the 1st Aust. F.A. Batteries which they were relieving. The Brigade rested in camp. ALWH	

WAR DIARY
or
INTELLIGENCE SUMMARY.

Army Form C. 2118.

57 CNE

Place	Date	Hour	Summary of Events and Information	Remarks and references to Appendices

	18/8/17		Batteries moved to wagon line positions along the WEST side of the road from J.31.C.7.4. to P.1.A.7.8. At dusk four guns each of B/241, C/241 and D/241 relieved four guns of the 2nd, 3rd and 101st Aust. F.A. Brigade respectively, and three guns of A/241 relieved three guns of 1st Aust F.A. Battery. The Battery Positions were as follows:-
			
			 A/241 1 Section J.21.B.05.95.
			         1 Section J.15.B.8.4.
			         1 Section J.9.C.8.7
			
			 B/241 J.16.C.1.6.
			 C/241 J.15.A.1.4.
			 D/241 J.10.C.1.0.	

	19/8/17		Hdqrs moved to wagon lines at VELU WOOD. Lieut. Col. Hodgson relieved 1st Aust. F.A. Bde. at J.14.C.7.2. Command passed to Col Colville at 6 p.m. At dusk the remainder of Batteries relieved the remainder of the	

Army Form C. 2118.

WAR DIARY
or
INTELLIGENCE SUMMARY.
(Erase heading not required.)

Place	Date	Hour	Summary of Events and Information	Remarks and references to Appendices
	20/5/17		1st Aust 7. A. Batteries. The whole relief was completed quite smoothly.	(appx H)
	21/5/17			
	22/5/17		Uneventful a.a.17H.	
	23/5/17			
	24/5/17		A/24¹ was withdrawn to their wagon lines at dusk to be in Reserve. They had orders to reconnoitre positions to cover the whole of the Divisional front, and to have a Section harnessed up from one hour before dawn daily until the "All clear" was received from every Battalion in the line.	
	25/4/17			
	26/4/17		Uneventful a.a.17H.	
	27/4/17			
	28/4/17			
	29/4/17		Brigade H.Qrs shelled with 5.9s from 5.32 p.m. to 9.4 p.m. about 30 rounds in all. B/241 heavily shelled but no damage was done. C/241 heavily shelled from 5.30 to 9 p.m. 4 gun pits hit. Two guns put out of	

Army Form C. 2118.

WAR DIARY
or
INTELLIGENCE SUMMARY.
(Erase heading not required.)

Place	Date	Hour	Summary of Events and Information	Remarks and references to Appendices
	30/5/17		action. At dusk B/241 moved a section to the position at J.15 B.8.4. vacated by A/241 on 24/5/17. Quiet. Uneventful. At dusk C/241 moved a section to J.9.C.8.7. It was decided not to move the Batteries notwithstanding the fact that they had been shelled, as no suitable positions could be found. South Uneventful south	
	31/5/17		Honours and Awards during the month. Mentioned in Despatches - Major E. Musker B/241 Capt & Adjt. R.W.Hobson Lieut. F.H. Bulstead. M.C. C/241 Bar to Military Medal 840058 Bombr F.A.BOSWORTH D/241 17.5.17 Military Medal 840142 Bombr H.R.AINSLIE D/241 17.5.17 Casualties during the month. Wounded 831608 Gr. TWINBERROW P.A. A/241	

Army Form C. 2118.

WAR DIARY
or
INTELLIGENCE SUMMARY.
(Erase heading not required.)

Place	Date	Hour	Summary of Events and Information	Remarks and references to Appendices
	31/5/17		Wounded 442 Corpl S.S. STEVENSON G. A/241 Wounded 825,509 Gunner MUTTER G. Hdqrs/241 Bde R.F.A. Wounded 831047 Corpl. TRAHEARN P.A. Hdqrs/241 Bde R.F.A. A.W.T.Hobson	

Vol 28

CONFIDENTIAL.

WAR DIARY.

of

241er (S.M.) Bde. R.F.A.

(Volume XXXII)

from 1/6/17   to 30/6/17

Army Form C. 2118.

WAR DIARY
or
INTELLIGENCE SUMMARY.
(Erase heading not required.)

Place	Date	Hour	Summary of Events and Information	Remarks and references to Appendices
In the Field	1/6/17		Uneventful. Weather fine. ACWTH	
	2/6/17	12 noon	The 49th, 50th and 113th Australian Btys were placed under command of Group COLVILLE. The Group became the Left Group 42 Div. Arty with a Zone from S.W. of PRONVILLE to just S. of the BAPAUME-CAMBRAI road at K.30.9. Uneventful. ACWTH	
	3/6/17		Uneventful. ACWTH	
	4/6/17	5 pm	Enemy shelled C/741. Personnel were withdrawn and no casualties resulted. After fire had ceased it was found that two gun pits had been hit and two guns were knocked out and withdrawn. ACWTH	
		9 pm	A dummy position was built at J.9.D.8.7. Uneventful. ACWTH	
	5/6/17		50th Australian Bty heavily shelled.	
	6/6/17	2 pm.	For 35 minutes the cross roads and area round in D.15.B were bombarded by the Group. C/741 put a gun into a gun pit constructed to make it look like a shell hole. This gun was afterwards photographed from the air, and both on the ground and on the air photograph it was most difficult	

Army Form C. 2118.

WAR DIARY
or
INTELLIGENCE SUMMARY.
(Erase heading not required.)

Place	Date	Hour	Summary of Events and Information	Remarks and references to Appendices
	7.6.17		to distinguish them.	
			B/241 were heavily shelled by all calibres up to 8 inch hows. The personnel were withdrawn and no casualties were suffered.	
			D/241 moved a howitzer into position in BOURSIS at T.6.C.1.3. and A/241 moved a gun into position at T.5.D.25.15. These guns were put forward for sniping purposes. Adut.	
			A severe thunderstorm destroyed all the Enemy's telephone communications	
			A/241 flooded out of their gun pits and horse lines.	
	8.6.17		During the night of 8/9m the BAPAUME-CAMBRAI road and MOEVRES were bombarded.	
			In consequence of the hostile shelling on Battery positions it was decided to keep a position for each Battery as a Defence position and to put a section of guns in each. These guns were only to be used in an emergency. The remaining guns of each Battery were to be put in other positions.	
			At dusk sections of B try were moved in accordance with above	

and at 12 midnight the following were the Group dispositions.

A/241 1 gun J.5.D.25.15. Remainder in reserve at VEU.

B/241
J.15.B.8.4. (2 guns) Defence position
J.21.B.05.95. (ditto)
J.16.C.1.6. "

C/241
J.15.C.2.6. (2 guns) Defence position
J.15-A.1.4. "
J.9.C.B.7. "

D/241
J.16.C.1.0. (5 hours)
J.6.C.1.3. (1 hour)

49º Aust.Bty. I.6.B.65.50 (2 guns) Defence position
J.13.2.5. (4 guns)

50º Aust.Bty. I.12.B.87.05. (2 guns) Defence position
J.7.A.4.9. (4 guns)

113 How Aus.Bty. J.14.A.2.9. 2 hours
J.7.C.4.3. 2 hours.

Army Form C. 2118.

WAR DIARY
or
INTELLIGENCE SUMMARY.
(Erase heading not required.)

Instructions regarding War Diaries and Intelligence Summaries are contained in F. S. Regs., Part II and the Staff Manual respectively. Title pages will be prepared in manuscript.

Place	Date	Hour	Summary of Events and Information	Remarks and references to Appendices
	9.6.17		All the moves were safely carried out. AEWJH	
	10.6.17		Uneventful. AEWJH	
	11.6.17		Uneventful. At 10.15 pm Command Posts in D.11.C. and D.11.C. were bombarded	
	12.6.17		D/241 fired lethal shell. AEWJH	
	13.6.17		Uneventful. AEWJH	
			Registration. Uneventful. AEWJH	
	14.6.17	1.30 am	B/241, C/241 and D/241 covered a raiding party of B/tn 4th & 5th Gloucesters who were attacking the post at K.2.a.0.7. The raid was unsuccessful as our party ran into a strong German patrol in "99s" Grand Rand. 4.9" B5 at J.18.2.6. heavily shelled. AEWJH	
	15.6.17	2.55 am	The Group barraged the trenches in front of PRONVILLE in support of an operation further South. B/241 were heavily shelled during the evening. AEWJH	
	16.6.17		Uneventful. AEWJH	
	17.6.17		Registration. The O.C. Brigade registered D/241 and B/241 on to the	

WAR DIARY
or
INTELLIGENCE SUMMARY.

Army Form C. 2118.

Place	Date	Hour	Summary of Events and Information	Remarks and references to Appendices
	18.6.17		enemy post at K.1.B.8.7. from a captive balloon	AAA7H
			Further registration.	AAA7H
	19.6.17	1am	The Group with two sections of 240 Bde placed under Lt Col Colville's Command covered the 6th R. Warwicks who carried out a raid on the enemy post at K.1.B.8.7. A V shaped box was formed with a creeping barrage up the centre. The raid was quite successful & we took an officer and eight other ranks prisoners. Remainder of the day uneventful	AAA7H
	20.6.17		Registration in front of PRONVILLE. B/741 heavily shelled.	AAA7H
	21.6.17		Further registration. Orders were received that the 241 Bde would be relieved by the 1st Australian F.A. Bde. to be completed by 24th inst. The 1st Aust Bde. arrived at our wagon lines at VELU and "double-banked".	
	22.6.17	1am	The Brigade covered a raid by the 8th R. Warwicks on the copse at and the dug outs at . The raid was unsuccessful and 2 prisoners were taken & many of the enemy were killed. It was alleged	

WAR DIARY
or
INTELLIGENCE SUMMARY.
(Erase heading not required.)

Place	Date	Hour	Summary of Events and Information	Remarks and references to Appendices
	23.6.17		that four of our shells fell short, causing casualties to our troops. The O.C. Bde. made exhaustive enquiries and demonstrated that the shell in question were enemy shell, thus triumphantly vindicating the character of the Brigade. At dusk four guns of B/241 and C/241 were relieved by four guns of 2nd Aust B.G. and 3rd Aust B.G. D/241's horse in BOURSIS was relieved by a horn of 101st Aust B.G. while 3 more horse in the DOIGNES position were also relieved.	
	24/6/17		At dusk remaining guns of 241 Bde were relieved by remaining guns of 1st Aust. Bde. Commanding horse to 1st Aust. Bde on completion Relief W/6 Bde marched to BENDIGO CAMP - 52.1.3 (Map ornmng sheet ALBERT 1/40,000).	W/6 W/6 W/6
	25/6/17		Bde in rear.	
	26/6/17		" " "	
	27/6/17		Art. Overall to Wear to PARIS. Major	

Army Form C. 2118.

WAR DIARY
or
INTELLIGENCE SUMMARY.
(Erase heading not required.)

Place	Date	Hour	Summary of Events and Information	Remarks and references to Appendices
	28/6/17		E. Marches in command	WSG
	29/6/17		Bde in rear	WSG
	30/6/17		Col Colvill re-assumes command	WSG
			Bde in rear	WSG

W. Curran Rice
Lieut. Colonel,
for Comdg. 241 South Midland F.A. Bde.

CONFIDENTIAL.

WAR DIARY.

of.

241st (S.M.) Bde. R.F.A.

Volume XXXIX

from 1/10/17   to 31/10/17

Army Form C. 2118.

WAR DIARY
or
INTELLIGENCE SUMMARY.
(Erase heading not required.)

Instructions regarding War Diaries and Intelligence Summaries are contained in F. S. Regs., Part II. and the Staff Manual respectively. Title pages will be prepared in manuscript.

Place	Date	Hour	Summary of Events and Information	Remarks and references to Appendices
Intifices	1/10/17	—	Uneventful. Bde in rear at MOORDPEERE.	wfc
	2/10/17	—	" "	wfc
	3/10/17	—	" "	wfc
	4/10/17	12.30 am	Orders received to move to WATOU area on 5th inst. Bde in rest.	wfc
	5/10/17	8.15 am	Bde marching via WAEMBERS - CAPPEL - HARDIFOOT - WINNIBEELE to WATOU (together 57A)	wfc
	6/10/17	noon	Bde relieves 5th Bde in line. Modern sub area, Div Arty	wfc
			HQ I & D 18.	
			A/741 C 30 c 5.7	
			B/741 C 30 c 5.5	
			C/741 C 30 c 7.9	Belgium sheet 28.
			D/741 C 30 c 4.5	
			Bde organised in a group with Sub Area. Wagon lines moved to H 15 d (sheet 28)	
	7/10/17		Attempt to get horses towards ammunition continues. Gunner activity in our sector. Continued counter-preparing. Preparing for advance.	wfc
	8/10/17			wfc

Army Form C. 2118.

WAR DIARY
or
INTELLIGENCE SUMMARY.
(Erase heading not required.)

Instructions regarding War Diaries and Intelligence Summaries are contained in F. S. Regs., Part II. and the Staff Manual respectively. Title pages will be prepared in manuscript.

Place	Date	Hour	Summary of Events and Information	Remarks and references to Appendices
In the field	10/10/17	5.20 am	Attack launched. left Div Inf. in front of Group. was slow in coming through. F.O.O. working forwards further the morning moving forward owing to adverse weather conditions.	
	10/10/17		Bad weather	
	11/10/17		Bad weather. F.O.O. working gun front of Difficulty firing. B.M. 182nd and 183rd Bdes	
			10 guns 4 hows. the ZONNEBEEK Ry.	
	12/10/17		Y R.E. S-POLDERS Railway	
		3.25am	3rd Australian Division attacks	
	13/10/17		Relieved by 144 Bde R.F.A. (72 Div)	
	14/10/17		Bde marches to ESQUELBECQ area	
	15/10/17			
	16/10/17		Bde marches to ANNEZIN	
	17/10/17		PIBLANC NAZAIRE — to relieve 72nd gun lines	

Army Form C. 2118.

WAR DIARY
or
INTELLIGENCE SUMMARY.
(Erase heading not required.)

Instructions regarding War Diaries and Intelligence Summaries are contained in F. S. Regs., Part II. and the Staff Manual respectively. Title pages will be prepared in manuscript.

Place	Date	Hour	Summary of Events and Information	Remarks and references to Appendices
	18/10/17		Battery commenced to withdraw Guns. Brought from CBF A 19 into action two sections R. Bty. Men taking one section being completed.	(3)
	9/10		Relief completed. Positions as under:—	
			H.Q. S.23.A.4.3	
			A Bty. in both	
			B Bty. T.13.b.58.78 from No 16 CFA Bde	(1)(2)
			C Bty. T.13.b.44 + 23 CFA	
			D Bty. in batteries	
	20/10/17		In batteries as before T.13.b.4.3 S.24.c.1.5	
	21/10/17		J/Spr [illegible]	
	22/10/17		Nothing to report	
	23/10/17		Orders received to send A to S.25.A then N.W. to HQ 8 CFA Bde + 5 Bty.	(3)(4)(5)
			Received orders to take over (tunnels) from the 8 CFA Bde who were taking they	
	24/10/17		8 CFA Bdes were in action [illegible]	

WAR DIARY
or
INTELLIGENCE SUMMARY.

(Erase heading not required.)

Army Form C. 2118.

Place	Date	Hour	Summary of Events and Information	Remarks and references to Appendices
	25/10/17		Owing to heavy rain, Divisional Artillery relieved by 3rd C.A.F.A. Bde. 9 Mega Bty. remained. 1st Bde. C.F.A. Brigade moving to [illeg]	(80)
	26/10/17			(81)
	27/10/17			
	28/10/17		Lt. Col. J.R. Colville D.S.O. appointed. Major R. Macleod M.C. [illeg]	(82)
	29/10/17		on the mountain front in Rawalpindi manoeuvring	(83)
	30/10/17			(84)
	31/10/17		W.C. Williams Captain A/G to be 2nd Bn. [illeg]	

www.ingramcontent.com/pod-product-compliance
Lightning Source LLC
Chambersburg PA
CBHW080852010526
44117CB00014B/2239